CONFRONTING EQUITY AND INCLUSION INCIDENTS ON CAMPUS

This timely book unpacks critical incidents occurring on college and university campuses across the nation. Featuring the voices of faculty, staff, and students, this edited volume offers an interdisciplinary exploration of contemporary diversity, equity, and inclusion (DEI) challenges at the intersections of race, class, gender, and socioeconomic status, while illuminating lessons learned and promising practices. The narratives in this book articulate contemporary challenges, unpack real events, and explore both failed and successful responses, ultimately shining a spotlight on emerging solutions and opportunities for change.

Marrying theory and practice, *Confronting Equity and Inclusion Incidents on Campus* provides a framework for building more inclusive campuses that embody equity and the values of community. A key resource for professionals, students, and scholars of higher education, this volume provides understanding for fostering educational spaces that cultivate belonging among all members of higher education communities, including those historically underrepresented and marginalized.

Hannah Oliha-Donaldson is an Assistant Teaching Professor in the Department of Communication Studies at the University of Kansas, USA.

CONFRONTING EQUITY AND INCLUSION INCIDENTS ON CAMPUS

LESSONS LEARNED AND EMERGING PRACTICES

Edited by
Hannah Oliha-Donaldson

NEW YORK AND LONDON

First published 2021
by Routledge
52 Vanderbilt Avenue, New York, NY 10017

and by Routledge
2 Park Square, Milton Park, Abingdon, Oxon, OX14 4RN

Routledge is an imprint of the Taylor & Francis Group, an informa business

© 2021 Taylor & Francis

The right of Hannah Oliha-Donaldson to be identified as the author of the editorial material, and of the authors for their individual chapters, has been asserted in accordance with sections 77 and 78 of the Copyright, Designs and Patents Act 1988.

All rights reserved. No part of this book may be reprinted or reproduced or utilized in any form or by any electronic, mechanical, or other means, now known or hereafter invented, including photocopying and recording, or in any information storage or retrieval system, without permission in writing from the publishers.

Trademark notice: Product or corporate names may be trademarks or registered trademarks, and are used only for identification and explanation without intent to infringe.

Library of Congress Cataloging-in-Publication Data
Names: Oliha-Donaldson, Hannah, editor.
Title: Confronting equity and inclusion incidents on campus : lessons learned and emerging practices / edited by Hannah Oliha-Donaldson.
Identifiers: LCCN 2020025042 (print) | LCCN 2020025043 (ebook) | ISBN 9780367210120 (hardback) | ISBN 9780367210144 (paperback) | ISBN 9780429264825 (ebook)
Subjects: LCSH: College environment–United States. | Minority college students–United States. | Minority college teachers–United States. | Discrimination in higher education–United States. | Educational equalization–United Staets.
Classification: LCC LB2324 .C658 2021 (print) | LCC LB2324 (ebook) | DDC 378.1/982–dc23
LC record available at https://lccn.loc.gov/2020025042
LC ebook record available at https://lccn.loc.gov/2020025043

ISBN: 978-0-367-21012-0 (hbk)
ISBN: 978-0-367-21014-4 (pbk)
ISBN: 978-0-429-26482-5 (ebk)

Typeset in New Baskerville
by SPi Global, India

Contents

Preface   viii
Hannah Oliha-Donaldson

Part I: Introduction   1

1   Contesting Marginality and Traditions of Silence: Resisting
Diversity's Failures and Assumed Centers, and Setting the Course
for Change   3
Hannah Oliha-Donaldson

2   A Genealogy of "Diversity": From the 1960s to Problematic
Diversity Agendas and Contemporary Activism   15
Hannah Oliha-Donaldson

3   Dismantling the Trifecta of Diversity, Equity, and Inclusion:
The Illusion of Heterogeneity   34
Tina M. Harris

Part II: Interpersonal Context: Critical Conversations   57

4   Scholar-Mothers Navigating Maternal Microaggressions
in the Academy: "You Should Be Home Snuggling Your Baby"   59
Lisa S. Kaler, Leah N. Fulton, Zer Vang, and Michael J. Stebleton

vi CONTENTS

5 Managing the Classroom as a Military Veteran and Graduate
Instructor: "Please Don't Call Me By My First Name"   79
Dianna N. Watkins-Dickerson

**Part III: Organizational Context: Pedagogical Limitations and
Opportunities**   95

6 Pedagogical Failures: Challenging Assumed Centers and Engendering
Community Through Personal and Pedagogical Reflexivity   97
Meggie Mapes

7 Envisioning Equity and Inclusion Through Art   108
Audra Buck-Coleman and Rashawn Ray

**Part IV: Organizational Context: Becoming a Diversity Worker,
Planning for Change, and Crafting Pathways Forward**   125

8 Muslim Students Combatting Institutional Inertia with
Participatory-Action Research   127
Saugher Nojan

9 BIPOC Students Using Polyvocal Narratives, Co-Witnessing,
and Spectral Engagement: "Seen" But Not Heard   141
Meshell Sturgis, Brian J. Evans, Anjuli Brekke,
Andrea Delgado, and Erin Lee

10 Becoming Professors of Equity at San Diego State University:
Reflecting on Professional Seminars on Implicit Biases and
Microaggressions   159
Yea-Wen Chen, Feion Villodas, Felicia Black, Sureshi Jayawardene,
Roberto Hernandez, Daniel L. Reinholz, and Thierry Devos

**Part V: Organizational Context: Dealing with Organizational
Culture and Climate**   171

11 Experiencing Symbolic and Linguistic Violence at Predominately
White Institutions as Student and Professor   173
Angela N. Gist-Mackey

CONTENTS vii

12 Accented Others, Women, and Immigrants: A Conversation
about Institutional Stalling and Dismissal 188
Anne C. Dotter and Cécile Accilien

**Part VI: Community and Structural Challenges: Managing the
Effects of Social Tensions** 201

13 'The Blackface Incident': Diversity, Equity, and Inclusion
under Fire at a Southern Women's College 203
Jade C. Huell and Crystal U. Davis

14 The Ripple Effect of Bias, Hate, and Activism: A Nation
in Crisis, a Campus in Turmoil, and Pathways Forward 219
Cherese F. Fine, Kendra D. Stewart-Tillman,
DeOnte T. Brown, and Jerad E. Green

Part VII: Conclusion 239

15 Dealing with the Past and Preparing for "Diversity's" Future:
"Wicked" Problems and Multilevel Solutions for Higher Education 241
Hannah Oliha-Donaldson

Editor 258
Contributors 259
Index 265

Preface

Hannah Oliha-Donaldson

I remember the day the idea for this book was conceived. It had been emerging at the periphery of my mind for years, but I never quite took hold of it. I knew I was confused about the state of diversity, equity, and inclusion (DEI) issues in higher education and by ongoing challenges in a supposedly "post-racial" and gender-affirming epoch. I was struck, over and over again, by a peculiar dialectical tension: passion for DEI exhibited by some, and a deep-seated apathy so evident in others. It seemed there were two universes in academia. There was the universe where we claimed to be critically inclined, democratically oriented, and socially engaged, marching to the beat of equity in all its forms. Then there was the universe that was actually real, where success was still determined by race, ethnicity, gender, socioeconomic status, religion, national geographic origin, and language, among others. There was clearly an invisible and unspoken, yet ever-present assumed center around which those on the periphery pivoted and maneuvered. All of these things were pictures in my mind that I looked at over and over again for clues to answer the fundamental DEI question: how do we move forward? How do we become the institutions we claim we are on our websites and in mission and diversity statements? How do we move from word, which we are very good at speaking and writing, into deed, an area in which many, if not most, institutions struggle (Adserias, 2017)?

My questions became a whirlwind when a ricochet of events began to take over national news, campus-wide forums, and personal dialogues in 2015. One after another, stories of prejudice on campuses across the nation began to emerge, launching a national dialogue on diversity, equity, and inclusion in American higher education. The tipping point came when, as I watched the news, a video was shown of a fraternity singing a racist song at the University of Oklahoma (McLaughlin, 2015). As a singer myself, I know that one is often told to sing with gusto, as a demonstration of passion. These young men sang with an abundance of gusto and conviction, "There will never be a n___ at SAE...You can hang him from a tree, but he'll never sign with me. There will never be a n___ at SAE." They sang this to the tune of the innocent nursery rhyme, "If you're happy and you know it clap your hands."

The image stopped me in my tracks. It wasn't just the song they sang and the emotions it rendered; it was the vision of "all-American," ascriptively white young men, in formal attire, doing the thing that students that looked just like them assured me and others was reprehensible, prejudiced, and beyond the scope of the twenty-first century. Every semester I heard this in my classes from a new crop of students. Yet there I was, seeing a thing I could not unsee. As the year progressed and incident after incident took place, the idea at the edges of my mind took hold, and this volume was birthed.

In a season where debates over the "forgotten" or "left behind" white American vie for air time alongside footage of and debates about police brutality on black bodies (see Neville et al., 2016), the detainment of brown bodies (young and old) on the U.S.–Mexico border, the ravages of misogyny and its performance through sexual violence directed at women, and travel restrictions into the U.S. placed on Islamic nations, the debates are spilling over into higher education.

Between the fall of 2016 to 2017, the Anti-Defamation League found that white supremacist propaganda on campuses increased by 258% (Kerr, 2018). Further, there was an uptick in identity-based hate crimes across the board. The U.S. Department of Education also found the number of reported hate crimes on campuses across the nation increased by 25% from 2015 to 2016 (Bauman, 2018). More than ever before, diversity policies and practices are under scrutiny, and campuses are being forced to give an account of how they are answering the call for social justice in this pivotal moment.

THE VISION FOR THIS VOLUME

Without a doubt, institutions are in a season of crisis that calls for focused attention on DEI issues. By visiting websites and reviewing media, one sees that campuses have perfected the art of rhetorically mobilizing inclusive language, but the ruptures over the last few years illuminate the need for answers and solutions for creating inclusive and equitable campuses, both in *word* and *deed*. In response to this need, this text presents a collection of narratives reflecting lived experiences in higher education. It features failed diversity moments, the lessons they offer, and possibilities for engendering change.

x PREFACE

Oftentimes, institutions, departments, and faculty members are reticent to dialogue about diversity issues, or they are simply immobilized by the challenges of change-making in such complex bureaucratic networks that are higher-education institutions. As such, students and scholars of higher education, faculty, staff, and administrators are invited to use this text as a launchpad to spur the critical dialogues necessary for defining, clarifying, and actualizing inclusive practices. It may be used to review interpersonal, organizational, community, and sociocultural barriers to inclusion, belonging, and just outcomes. Importantly, it may be used to review emerging trends and challenges in higher education and implications for practice, while offering resources and ideas for improving the recruitment and retention of the historically underrepresented. It is my hope that by sharing the lived experiences of higher-education professionals (faculty, administrators, and staff) and that of students with different identities and roles, this volume will create space for students and scholars of higher education and academic and administrative units to see diversity issues from multiple angles, to engage in critical conversations, and to continue and/or begin identifying potential practices for change.

This volume mobilizes narratives of lived experience to illuminate critical fissures in engendering the full engagement of underrepresented and minoritized groups. These narratives articulate contemporary challenges at the intersections of race, gender, religion, national origin, and other intersecting identities, while creating room for dialogue about pathways forward, both personally and institutionally. For those beginning the foray into unpacking DEI issues, these cases may be used as a primer for understanding pressing challenges facing institutions.

OVERVIEW

This text advances a systems perspective by demonstrating how DEI challenges at interpersonal, organizational, community, and structural levels impact individual and organizational experiences and outcomes, respectively (see Oetzel et al., 2007).

To set the stage, the first three chapters articulate the aims and scope of this volume. Chapter 1 illustrates the tensions necessitating this volume by overviewing critical incidents and introducing the multilevel framework anchoring this text (see Bronfenbrenner, 1977). Further, this chapter answers the critical question: "how did we get here?", with "here" being defined as the proliferation of diversity talk, even in the midst of unremitting disparities and persistent identity-based hate crimes and bias-motivated incidents targeting historically marginalized groups.

Chapter 2 charts the development of the diversity framework. It traces the roots of equity and inclusion efforts from the 1940s to today, presenting critical moments impacting contemporary DEI practices and contributing to ongoing challenges. By illuminating limitations of DEI frameworks, this chapter depicts the backdrop of contemporary failed DEI moments. Chapter 3, by Tina M. Harris, provides definitional clarity for DEI while addressing problematic cleavages between the three. She closes by presenting promising practices for actively addressing inequities and disparities impacting historically marginalized groups through comprehensive DEI practices.

The second section features critical incidents manifesting at the interpersonal level. The first chapter in this section (Chapter 4) features the voices of three students from diverse backgrounds that have faced "maternal microaggressions" while obtaining doctoral degrees. Kaler, Fulton, and Vang share critical incidents, the impact, and intersecting identity, academic, and role challenges faced by scholar-mothers. Stebleton, a faculty ally, joins the conversation by offering strategies for supporting marginalized students.

Chapter 5 features interpersonal challenges faced by a black graduate student, detailing her resistance of microaggressions and the deficit framing of her institutional membership. Watkins-Dickerson closes by offering strategies for supporting historically underrepresented teaching assistants that may face challenges to their credibility in their classrooms and from faculty in their program. Both chapters offer critical insights on key challenges facing underrepresented students while presenting strategies for addressing institutional barriers to their success.

Organizational structures and their impact on experience and outcomes are evaluated, beginning in section three. These chapters address challenges manifesting in the classroom and in formal and informal institutional spaces. In Chapter 6, Mapes begins by offering tools for destabilizing privilege and the power of assumed centers in the classroom. By presenting her own personal failure, Mapes illustrates that although we do not always succeed, we must remain reflexive as practitioners while constantly seeking to create space in our classrooms for student growth.

In Chapter 7, Buck-Coleman and Ray present the results of an art-based intergroup dialogue project geared at increasing students' understanding of diversity. The authors expected to see increased appreciation for diverse others by the 2016 cohort of students experiencing this practice, but the local, organizational, and national context interceded. Instead, this cohort's undergraduate careers were negatively shaped by campus and community identity-based hate and bias incidents.

This section also features experiences shared by faculty, student affairs practitioners, and graduate students illustrating problematic formal and informal organizational norms, policies, and practices and their impact on

xii PREFACE

organizational membership. Chapter 8 presents participant-action research (PAR) as a form of student activism used to secure a prayer space for Muslim students. Nojan walks readers through every step of the process by presenting practical strategies for using PAR to spur institutional change. Nojan also presents how such efforts may be co-opted by institutions for reinforcing their diversity programs.

In Chapter 9, five students with various identities reflect on their experiences and the challenges of being "diversity workers" (Ahmed, 2012) in an organizational space that privileges talk over transformation. For these students, the challenge is embedded in the ensuing tension that arises while doing the "work," but feeling unheard. Sturgis et al. address possibilities and challenges when one is called on (by personal and/or institutional mission) to become a diversity worker.

In the next chapter (Chapter 10), Chen et al. present promising practices for conducting bias trainings. They present principles for practice and self-care when faced with the very biases one is attempting to redress in training contexts. The review of this training program developed by this interdisciplinary group of faculty offers an opportunity to explore critical identity challenges with leading bias trainings, while practiced strategies for negotiating difficult conversations among higher education practitioners are offered.

Chapter 11 offers a snapshot of one person's embodiment of failed diversity moments as both a student and faculty member. Gist-Mackey charts her course from student to faculty, illustrates how two institutions negotiated incidents of bias in profoundly different ways, and unpacks how her identity was implicated in both cases. Her narrative is used to reflect on DEI institutional crisis-management strategies and the hidden labor of underrepresented faculty.

Finally, in Chapter 12, Dotter and Accilien reflect on their experiences as foreign nationals at a large Midwestern university. Presenting instances of linguistic, racial, and gender-based bias, they reflect on the ensuing interpersonal challenges, which later revealed institutional failures in addressing and remedying DEI issues. These faculty close with promising practices for dealing with marginalization and organizational reticence.

Both community factors and social structures are evaluated in the next section. This section features narratives that particularly illuminate the larger social context within which DEI issues manifest in higher education. These chapters offer perspective into how incidents in local communities and at the national level impact organizational behavior, norms, practices, and experiences. Chapter 13 addresses the impact of a blackface incident that resulted in student protests. Huell and Davis illustrate how similar incidents occurring in other organizations and contexts may have a ripple effect. Huell and Davis also show how mismanaging such challenges may result in the departure of faculty and students. In closing, Huell and Davis present strategies for responding promptly and effectively to diversity failures while minimizing collateral damage.

In Chapter 14, a group of higher education professionals, many of whom work in diversity and multicultural affairs departments, reflect on how national dialogues about police brutality spilled onto a campus, leading to a swell of student, faculty, and staff activism. From sit-ins and walkouts to the evaluation of institutional racial legacies, Fine et al. capture how issues at the national level can impact a campus community and lead to organizational change.

Finally, the book concludes by presenting a perspectival framework for understanding the intricacies of DEI incidents, notably Rittel and Webber's (1973) "wicked problems" framework. Further, this chapter presents the possibilities and applications of social ecology as a multilevel approach to comprehensively and effectively frame and address DEI issues. Finally, promising practices weaving together critical claims from each chapter are presented.

This edited volume is designed to offer an interdisciplinary survey of contemporary DEI challenges. It features the voices of faculty and students in communication, education, ethnic studies, art, and sociology. Further, insight is offered by multicultural affairs administrators, departmental chairs, and others who offer in-depth examinations of pressing DEI challenges such as microaggressions, invisible labor, maternal microaggressions, religious identity performance, racial trauma, organizational resistance to change, and much more. Contributors share from a diverse body of literature to provide theoretically and experientially grounded solutions for framing and addressing DEI challenges and the clash between groups.

DISTINCTIVE FEATURES

A distinctive feature of this volume is the marriage of both theory and practice. Chapters present narratives featuring failed DEI moments or a useful practice, reflect on impact, review lessons learned, and offer promising practices. The promising practices section, in particular, emphasizes practical strategies and models for actualizing change, both at interpersonal and organizational levels. It illuminates moves that other practitioners have employed, along with institutional practices that are impacting organizational cultures and climates across the nation. This area will be particularly useful for those seeking take-aways and transferable knowledge that may positively impact their personal practice and institutional spaces. Finally, in the spirit of encouraging dialogue and critical conversations, each chapter

xiv PREFACE

will close with discussion questions that may be used to interrogate pressing equity and inclusion concerns and pathways forward. It is my hope that this volume will become a valuable companion for centering, unpacking, challenging, and coaching on DEI issues. Importantly, this book features experiences that carefully articulate the historical and contemporary national context in which colleges and universities are functioning, and the impact of this context on the framing of diversity issues.

CONCLUSION

The middle of the 1960s, the height of the civil rights movement and a number of other liberation movements, brought a tidal wave of open access to higher education for groups historically left out. From that point onward, intense tensions over access, equity versus equality, and the operationalization of inclusion have been a part of the landscape. Burgeoning DEI conflicts suggest that 60 years later, there is still work to be done. Further, they magnify the need for ongoing dialogue around strategies for engendering social justice in higher education.

We hope the narratives presented in this volume will encourage practitioners to review the many sides of ongoing DEI challenges and engage in transformational, troubleshooting, and problem-solving dialogues. This volume offers an invitation to further explore the vision of making institutions safe spaces for all, such that anybody (regardless of how these bodies are constituted biologically, historically, politically, and socially) can achieve their fullest potential without being hindered by institutional norms, policies, and practices that may be perceived as alienating, delimiting, or unjust.

REFERENCES

Adserias, R. P., Charleston, L. J., & Jackson, J. F. L. (2017). What style of leadership is best suited to direct organizational change to fuel institutional diversity in higher education? *Race Ethnicity and Education*, 20(3), 315–331. DOI: 10.1080/13613324.2016.1260233

Ahmed, S. (2012). *On being included: Racism and diversity in institutional life.* Durham, NC: Duke University Press.

Bauman, D. (2018). After 2016 election, campus hate crimes seemed to jump. Here's what the data tell us. *The Chronicle of Higher Education.* https://www.chronicle.com/article/Hate-Crimes-on-Campuses-Are/245093

Bronfenbrenner, U. (1977). Toward an experimental ecology of human development. *American Psychologist*, 32, 513–531.

Kerr, E. (2018, February). White supremacists are targeting college campuses like never before. *Chronicle of Higher Education.* https://www.chronicle.com/article/White-Supremacists-Are/242403

McLaughlin, E. (2015, March). Sigma Alpha Epsilon is no stranger to scandal and sanctions. CNN. https://www.cnn.com/2015/03/09/us/sigma-alpha-epsilon-fraternity/index.html

Neville, H. A., Gallardo, M. E., & Sue, D. W. (Eds.). (2016). *The myth of racial color blindness: Manifestations, dynamics, and impact.* Washington, DC, US: American Psychological Association.

Oetzel, J., Dahr, S., & Kirschbaum, K. (2007). Intercultural conflict from a multi-level perspective: Trends, possibilities, and future directions. *Journal of Intercultural Communication Research*, 36, 183–204.

Rittel, H. W. J., & Webber, M. M. (1973). Dilemmas in a general theory of planning. *Policy Sciences*, 4, 155–169.

PART I

INTRODUCTION

Chapter 1

Contesting Marginality and Traditions of Silence: Resisting Diversity's Failures and Assumed Centers, and Setting the Course for Change

Hannah Oliha-Donaldson

> *I will no longer be made to feel ashamed of existing. I will have my voice: Indian, Spanish, white. I will have my serpent's tongue - my woman's voice.... I will overcome the tradition of silence.*
>
> —Gloria Anzaldúa

Writing from a jail cell in Birmingham, Alabama, Martin Luther King, Jr. (1963), the civil rights activist, and arguably, one of the architects and forerunners of twentieth-century social movements, penned the words, "I am in Birmingham because injustice is here.... Anyone who lives inside the United States can never be considered an outsider anywhere within its bounds" (para. 3). Praised for his compelling vision of American community and possibility, he spoke powerfully and wrote soberly about a place where all are welcome, where all can succeed, where the only limits are those we place on ourselves. His vision and that of others like him sparked and sustained over a half-century of activism and change-making that have transformed the world in which we live.

His notion that anyone living in the "United States can never be considered an outsider anywhere within its bounds" remains aspirational and an unfulfilled dream for some. It remains the possibility and the opportunity, the hope and the long-awaited desire. For others, it is a fear, the outcome of letting go and losing it all; the result of becoming ordinary, truly one among many. It is the nightmare to which one must never succumb: the loss of control of the essential, identity, and all its attendant privileges (Ahmed, 2012; Mohanty, 1984).

4 HANNAH OLIHA-DONALDSON

So, on the outskirts of King's American community remains an in-between place; a borderland in which those defined as "other" reside (see Anzaldúa, 1987). It is a place of struggle, fear, and hope. A place where the rights of full citizenship are just a few paces away, yet feel otherworldly and unattainable.

Living in the in-between place is the experience of not being quite "outside" or quite "inside." It reflects and perpetuates an in/out duality. This in/out duality marks the tension that will be the refining and defining force of the twenty-first century in the U.S. This duality and its attendant tensions is one of the reasons for contemporary social, political, and institutional ruptures. It has fostered an identity crisis, a nation with two faces: on the one side, equality holds court, promising opportunity to all, easy access, and open doors. On the other side, inequities reign, disciplining and punishing through boundaries, exclusion, and unequal standards. We are a nation that, hundreds of years after the ratification of the constitution in 1788, is still under construction.

As this work goes on, we continue to grapple with how to negotiate, manage, and, for some, undo this duality, both in its historical and contemporary formations. Indeed, the current historical moment is rife with tensions because of the manifestation of this duality through persistent racial and gender formations: the #BlackLivesMatter and #MeToo movements reflect these tensions. Importantly, the manifestation of contemporary social challenges suggest that the past continues to play a far-reaching formative role in institutions, human interactions, and in determining the limits and boundaries of access, agency, and equity. These social problems speak to ongoing struggles to manage this in/out duality.

Over the years, this duality has been embraced by some and rejected by others, but always reaffirmed. It is reaffirmed in and through class inequality. Racism, sexism, xenophobia, homophobia; these are the vehicles of its passage through social and institutional life (see Neville et al., 2016; U.S. Department of Justice, 2019). As a fundamental institution, higher education has emerged as a battleground in the ongoing acceptance by some, and rejection by others, of this duality. Over the last few years, we have seen evidence of this struggle through protests and counter-protests, the suspension and firing of officials deemed "tone deaf," legal pushback against affirmative action in college admissions (Kramer, 2019), fierce conflict over institutional symbols and landmarks deemed offensive (fnsnews, 2016; Brown, 2019), and equity demands presented by students to institutions deemed unsafe, unwelcoming (Editor, 2016), and oppositional to their success. More than ever before, these tensions are spilling onto university campuses in the U.S., which already have unique diversity, equity, and inclusion challenges (DEI). With the goal of advancing community, illuminating the impact of the in/out duality and its operationalization in

CONTESTING MARGINALITY AND TRADITIONS OF SILENCE

contemporary higher education, and reaffirming through lived experience, the necessity of fostering educational spaces that cultivate true inclusion and belonging for all, this volume is presented as a sober reflection of where we are, and an invitation to explore the infinite possibilities of community.

TENSIONS RISING

In the following section, I illuminate the general backdrop warranting this volume. The Midwest experienced a contentious fall in 2015, when a series of universities were forced to grapple with tensions over diversity issues. At the University of Missouri-Columbia, students responded to ongoing acts of racial marginalization and prejudice as one voice: Concerned Student 1950. This coincides with the date the university admitted its first African American student (Latham, 2016). Concerned Student 1950 presented a list of demands, chief among them was the resignation of Tim Wolfe, University of Missouri System President. Over a two- to three-month period, students used social media to agitate for change, initiated a hunger strike, and the football team announced its intent to abstain from its official duties. The result was Wolfe's forced resignation (Latham, 2016).

In the midst of unfolding ruptures at the University of Missouri-Columbia, a number of campuses in Kansas were also forced to initiate community dialogues to address racial prejudice and discrimination. Community forums, protests about the negative experiences that some historically marginalized group (HMG) members had faced, and a report by an advisory committee illuminating DEI issues led the University of Kansas to openly acknowledge these tensions and respond through multiple channels. In one response, then-Provost Neeli Bendapudi asserted:

> Similarly, I felt upset, defensive, and protective when I realized that my personal idyllic, storybook experience of KU was not shared by all. There is significant self-work I must do to be more awake to the realities of all individuals on our campus. We cannot rely solely on problematic deficit-based approaches that suggest that diverse students, staff, and faculty must do even more to realize equal levels of success as their majority peers. We are all a part of the problem and have the potential to be a part of the solution. (Neeli Bendapudi, as cited in Shorman, 2016)

This note and the events preceding it attended to the differences in experience along racial and ethnic lines at this university.

Across the country at Claremont McKenna College in Los Angeles, students succeeded in agitating for the resignation of a key administrator in November of 2015 (University Business, 2016). The activating situation was

6 HANNAH OLIHA-DONALDSON

a student publishing her experiences with discrimination at this institution. Tensions over diversity issues also led to two hunger strikes initiated to seek the resignation of Mary Spellman, Assistant Vice President and Dean of Students, who was viewed as racially insensitive by some, following her assertion that the campus must "better serve students, especially those who don't fit our [Claremont McKenna] mold" (University Business, 2016). Arguably, unbeknownst to this official, this terminology mobilized notions of an "in" and "out" group, of a normalized student and an "other," setting off a firestorm.

One hundred faculty signed a petition in support of the students seeking Spellman's resignation, yet an open letter signed by another 300 students was circulated in support of the dean. Amidst the rising tensions, Spellman resigned, and the president of Claremont McKenna College created two new positions to address diversity issues.

These tensions later spilled into 2017. At the same institution, students protested against the appearance of a Black Lives Matter critic, Heather Mac Donald, that year. Students later demanded an apology from the president of a sister institution belonging to the same consortium of institutions, Pomona College, for a "patronizing" email he sent on academic freedom and free speech in response to the Mac Donald protest. Students demanded that a revised email be sent to the university community:

> Apologizing for the previous patronizing statement, enforcing that Pomona College does not tolerate hate speech and speech that projects violence onto the bodies of its marginalized students and oppressed peoples, especially Black students who straddle the intersection of marginalized identities, and explaining the steps the institution will take and the resources it will allocate to protect the aforementioned students. (Denson et al., 2017).

In February of that year, the University of California at Berkeley (UC-Berkeley) cancelled an engagement because of concerns over the inflammatory views of the speaker, Milo Yiannopoulos, Breitbart editor and conservative speaker. Protests resulted in fires and reports of violence. Indeed, prior to reaching UC-Berkeley, several stops on Yiannopoulos' tour were cancelled, there were a string of protests against his invitation at several campuses, and one person was shot during a protest at the University of Washington. In August of that year, a white supremacist rally began at the University of Virginia and later turned deadly in Charlottesville, Virginia.

Similar tensions continued to unfold in 2019. A professor, claiming academic freedom, mobilized the n____ word while teaching from James Baldwin's *The Fire Next Time* (Flaherty, 2019). In an op-ed, other faculty pushed back, claiming academic freedom was not an excuse to use language that harms students, turning "the very principle that makes true learning possible into a mechanism for enforcing institutional racism" (Flaherty, 2019, para. 18). They further noted the urgency of faculty becoming "more self-critical in their positions of power and racial (as well as gender and other forms of) privilege" (Flaherty, 2019, para. 19; see also Jenkins, 2009).

Finally, in 2019, the South Carolina system presidential finalist list met opposition: out of 11 semi-finalists, no female candidates were selected. Amid backlash, system trustees did not choose from among four finalists and reopened the search (see also Brown, 2019; Mangan, 2019). It is evident that calls for inclusion, greater accountability, and critical reflection about decision-making, and the effects on campus climate are reverberating like never before. Yet there remains a critical question: how did we get here?

HOW DID WE GET HERE?

Beyond an exploration of current ruptures, it is critical to briefly examine "how we got here," to this place of protests and counter-protests, equality demands, terminated contracts, and academic freedom wars. There are a number of catalysts, but a noteworthy antecedent must be addressed, as it is the backdrop hidden in each narrative and failed DEI moment addressed in this volume. The many incidents of the last few years reveal the two universes that exist in higher education: the projected image institutions portray (which typically centers diversity ideals and social justice), and the real world, organized around assumed margins and centers. Specifically, recurring identity-based incidents reveal that HMGs are only conditionally included in higher education, and parity is lacking (Yant, 2017). They further reveal that race remains a central faultline—a chronic battleground. Critically, the diversity failures of the last few years exposed the reality that many institutions hide: behind well-crafted diversity statements and carefully appointed diversity figureheads, there remains a normalized "we" and an accepted "center" around which those deemed "diverse" and "other" must pivot (Bell & Hartmann, 2007, p. 909). Challenges to this order is willfulness (Ahmed, 2012) that is disciplined by being labeled "difficult," "a poor fit," or "angry," and may result in isolation or exclusion. This center is normalized through the framing of "others" as those who "are welcomed, learned from, or accepted at a table, in a fabric, or in a pot that would otherwise be bland, plain, and basically colorless" (Bell & Hartmann, 2007, p. 909).

In her critique of "western feminism," Mohanty (1984) claims that "it is possible to trace a coherence of effects resulting from the implicit

8 HANNAH OLIHA-DONALDSON

assumption of 'the West' (in all its complexities and contradictions) as the primary referent in theory and praxis" (p. 334). Similarly, in U.S. higher education, there are effects resulting from the implicit positioning of white and male bodies as primary referents in institutional life. One of these effects is the proliferation of apathy and "disconsciousness" (Oliha-Donaldson & Montgomery, 2019). Those with majority identities, because of this privileged standpoint that frames their experiences as normative, become disconscious over time; that is to say, their standpoint allows them to overlook or ignore inequity, fostering a lack of awareness about, or an apathetic stance towards injustice (Oliha-Donaldson & Montgomery, 2019). This is buttressed by a deeply held, privilege-oriented notion that only those most impacted should care about and advocate for change. The result is the proliferation of socialized apathy, and the delusion of the center that its privileges are earned and justified, and that its social and organizational framing as "center" is both natural and neutral.

Because of this socialized apathy, those with majority identities are conditioned to miss injustice. They are able to move through life relatively untouched by institutionalized forms of prejudice (McIntosh, 1989), political and legal harassment (Neville et al., 2016), and systemic oppression. Consequently, those framed as "center" can work in the same space as historically marginalized racial, gender, and religious minorities, among others, and never truly "see" injustice. Describing her own experiences with white privilege, Peggy McIntosh (1989), an anti-racism activist and feminist, illustrates how apathy and disconsciousness become conditioned responses:

> I think whites are carefully taught not to recognize white privilege, as males are taught not to recognize male privilege… I have come to see white privilege as an invisible package of unearned assets that I can count on cashing in each day, but about which I was "meant" to remain oblivious. (McIntosh, 1989, p. 10)

The result, according to McIntosh, is being "conditioned into oblivion" about the existence of personally and structurally held privileges (McIntosh, 1989, p. 10) and the impact on others.

In short, ongoing equity and inclusion challenges can be traced to the failures of the diversity agenda and institutionally sanctioned assumed centers around which higher education spaces are ordered. This has led to differences in sensemaking about what diversity is and what it should do, failure to "see" disparities and respond appropriately, perceived illegitimacy of claims that higher education is raced and gendered, and enduring tensions along identity lines (see Oliha-Donaldson, 2017).

Chapters in this volume illustrate these challenges by documenting the fragmentation caused by how different bodies are experiencing higher education spaces. Importantly, they also detail how HMGs are pushing back against social and cultural exclusion, the delegitimization of their experiences, and a normalized, apathetic stance born of privilege.

THE INVITATION: PATHWAYS FORWARD

The critical incidents presented in this introduction illustrate the tensions taking over the discursive terrain and sociocultural landscape at institutions across the nation. Their presentation is not to problematize colleagues and campuses mentioned, but to offer exemplars and illustrate the challenges facing higher education professionals and institutions. It is estimated that by December of 2015, students had "presented lists of race-equality demands to at least 78" campuses (Latham, 2016, para. 3). Students are calling for every space on college and university campuses to reflect their unique needs and histories, and for leadership to acknowledge the multidimensional nature of their identities (Pappano, 2017). Critically, these shifts reflect pushback against an assumed center and the in/out duality on which it stands.

The effects of current tensions around diversity are far-reaching; chief among them is the ousting of officials deemed problematic. Latham (2016) notes:

> Concerned Student 1950 targeted President Wolfe at the homecoming parade because he did not respond to its request for a dialog(sic). He publicly responded only after the student started his hunger strike and only one day before the financially and powerful alumni-influential football team declared support for the cause. President Wolfe aptly remarked, 'Had I gotten out of the car to acknowledge the students and talk with them, perhaps we wouldn't be where we are today.' (para. 5)

Failure to respond with the vigor and compassion students are calling for will greatly impact university and college professionals ill-prepared to negotiate emerging social and demographic shifts in their classrooms and units. Kelderman (2019) notes that "equity and inclusion, in particular for racial minorities, women, and LGBTQ students have become rallying cries on campuses across the country" (para. 4). From forced apologies and suspensions to resignations, the costs of ignoring the needs of historically marginalized and underrepresented stakeholders are grave, both personally and institutionally.

As will be discussed in Chapter 2, the social movements of the 1960s and 1970s were a pivotal point in higher education in the U.S.; we are in the midst of another such moment. Tensions are spilling over, students are searching for new and productive language to discuss their differences,

10 HANNAH OLIHA-DONALDSON

faculty are looking for meaningful ways to address these challenges pedagogically and pragmatically, and higher education professionals are searching for productive ways to guide dialogue and policy towards positive institutional change. Campuses can choose not to respond and risk losing students to higher education spaces deemed *more welcoming* and *inclusive*, or they can view these emerging tensions for what they are: an invitation to embrace growth and possibility.

The chapters in this volume elucidate the fact that while we've perfected the art of diversity talk (Ahmed, 2012), there is still work to be done in operationalizing equity and inclusion. Despite the many programs, plans, diversity statements, and "diversity czars" hired to solve DEI issues (Newkirk, 2019), institutions are still struggling to make the leaps that will lead to second-order change, which moves beyond band-aids and superficial "quick-fix" remedies to transformational change—a fundamental change in an organizations core (Adserias, 2017; see also Kezar, 2008). In upcoming chapters, I and contributors of this volume will argue that this twenty-first century moment demands that we "see" DEI issues multidimensionally and respond with efficacious tools emerging from both theory and practice. It is my hope that the narratives and promising practices offered in this text will offer both *perspective* and *strategy*.

To facilitate the development of both perspective and strategy, this text advances a multilevel praxis and draws specifically from Bronfenbrenner's (1977) social ecological framework (see also Klein et al., 1999; Oetzel et al., 2006). Multilevel frameworks engage principles of systems thinking by interrogating how various elements of a system are interlocked in a web of causation (Bronfenbrenner, 1977); systems thinking posits that when something happens at one level, it will invariably impact other levels.

A social ecological perspective is a particularly useful tool as it demonstrates that we cannot understand human behavior and social systems without understanding how they are systematically ordered and constructed through interlocking micro (intra- and interpersonal), meso (organizational), exo (community), and macro (policy and cultural) interactions and processes (Oetzel et al., 2007). In short, "an ecological perspective implies reciprocal causation between" an individual and their environment (McLeroy et al., 1988, p. 354). From an organizational perspective, rather than exploring individual actions, interpersonal behaviors, and organizational policies and practices in isolation, this framework calls for an exploration of interlocking individual and environmental factors that frame experience and create organizational climates that become the breeding ground for complex DEI issues. This framework will be presented in-depth in the closing chapter, and its application to higher education spaces will be developed.

For now, it is important to note that this volume features sections coinciding with a social ecological perspective. By exploring tensions at *interpersonal*, *organizational*, and *community* and *structural* levels, this text illuminates how challenges at one level impact functions and outcomes at other levels. As you read the narratives and cases presented in this volume, I invite you to consider how our choices and practices at the personal level impact outcomes and processes at the organizational level and vice versa. As this chapter and volume reinforce, also consider how issues at the national level are impacting institutions and their internal stakeholders. Reflective of this, upcoming chapters will review the social and historical landscape that is shaping contemporary DEI trends and practices. The central claim in upcoming chapters and in this volume as a whole is that complex DEI problems require multilayered and comprehensive solutions.

CONCLUSION

Emerging conflicts magnify the need for continued interrogation of diversity work and practices. Importantly, they reflect ongoing tensions, contestation over long-held norms, and rejection of an in/out duality that has fostered alienation and feelings of disconnection among HMGs. There is a burgeoning resistance to this duality in contemporary higher education (Brown, 2019; Brown et al., 2016; Kelderman, 2019; Newkirk, 2019), there are counter-protests of this resistance (Brown, 2019; Mangan, 2019; Schmidt, 2008), and this tug-of-war is causing destabilization.

Speaking of her own experiences of an in-between place, and her rejection of its limits, Gloria Anzaldúa (1987) declared, "I will no longer be made to feel ashamed of existing… I will overcome the tradition of silence" (p. 40). The equality demands presented at colleges and universities across the nation, the sit-ins, hunger strikes, student, faculty and staff protests, and social media takeovers reflect how those traditionally defined as the "margin" (along with their majority allies) are attempting to break through the margins and speak into the silences that legitimize inequities and disparities.

The failed DEI moments featured in this chapter and volume suggest that a text like this is needed like never before. To positively impact the tone and tenor of institutions desiring to be a safe space for all, to support institutions attempting to foster a sense of belonging for all, to positively influence policies and practices implicated in the recruitment and retention of HMGs, and to raise levels of critical consciousness about diversity issues and strategies for enacting inclusivity and equitable outcomes, this text shines a spotlight on the state of affairs and the endless possibilities for change.

DISCUSSION QUESTIONS

1. Are there individuals on your campus who feel unsafe or like they do not belong because of their identities? What can you do to change this? What should your institution do?
2. What DEI incidents have occurred at your institution in the last three years? How have these incidents impacted your campus? In what ways have they impacted historically underrepresented or marginalized groups on your campus?
3. How is "diversity" performed as a "public relations" campaign? In general? At your institution?
4. In what ways are historically marginalized groups (HMGs) experiencing the in/out duality at your institution? In higher education in general? How can you address this in your daily practice as a student, faculty, or staff member? What one (tangible) thing can your institution begin to do to change this situation?
5. How are assumed centers legitimized through current DEI policies and practices at your institution?
6. In what ways has conditioned or socialized apathy sanctioned inequities in hiring, student outcomes, institutional responses to identity-based hate crimes, and general organizational practices?

REFERENCES

Ahmed, S. (2012). *On Being included: Racism and diversity in institutional life.* Durham, NC: Duke University Press.

Adserias, R. P., Charleston, L. J., & Jackson, J. F. L. (2017). What style of leadership is best suited to direct organizational change to fuel institutional diversity in higher education? *Race Ethnicity and Education*, 20(3), 315–331. https://doi.org/10.1080/13613324.2016.1260233

Anzaldúa, G. E. (1987). *Borderlands/La frontera: The New Mestiza.* San Francisco: Aunt Lute Books. https://rhetoricreadinggroup.files.wordpress.com/2015/04/anzaldua_from-borderlands.pdf

Bell, J. M., & Hartmann, D. (2007). Diversity in everyday discourse: The cultural ambiguities and consequences of "Happy Talk". *American Sociological Review*, 72, 895–914.

Bronfenbrenner, U. (1977). Toward an experimental ecology of human development. *American Psychologist*, 32, 513–531.

Brown, B. (2019). UNC'S chancellor was criticized as a consensus builder. How she departed may have changed everything. *The Chronicle of Higher Education.* https://www.chronicle.com/article/UNC-s-Chancellor-Was/245482

Brown, S., Mangan, K., & McMurtrie, B. (2016, May). At the end of a watershed year, can student activists sustain momentum? *Chronicle of Higher Education.* https://www.chronicle.com/article/At-the-End-of-a-Watershed/236577

CONTESTING MARGINALITY AND TRADITIONS OF SILENCE **13**

Denson, D., Jonas, A., & Stephenson, S. (2017). Archive of Pomona student petition. https://docs.google.com/document/d/1_y6NmxoIBLcZJxYkN9V1Yfa-PYzVSMKCA17PgBzz10wk/edit

Flaherty, C. (2019). Too taboo for class? *Inside Higher Ed.* https://www.insidehighered.com/news/2019/02/01/professor-suspended-using-n-word-class-discussion-language-James-Baldwin-essay

fnsnews. (2016). The racist seal controversy: What do the UNM kiva club and the RedNationwant?https://fnsnews.nmsu.edu/the-racist-seal-controversy-what-do-the-unm-kiva-club-and-the-red-nation-want/

Jenkins, W. (2019, October, 4). N.C. State professor is suspended after reportedly saying women 'are useless. *The Chronicle of Higher Education.* https://www.chronicle.com/article/NC-State-Professor-Is/247288

Kelderman, E. (2019, May 1). Disputes over presidential searches at 2 public universities. *The Chronicle of Higher Education.* https://www.chronicle.com/article/Disputes-Over-Diversity/246221

Kezar, A. (2008). Understanding leadership strategies for addressing the politics of diversity. *The Journal of Higher Education, 79*(4), 406–441.

Klein, K. J., Tosi, H., & Cannella, A. A. (1999). Multilevel theory building: Benefits, barriers, and new developments. *Academy of Management Review, 24,* 243–248.

Kramer, M. (2019). A timeline of key Supreme Court Cases on Affirmative Action. *New York Times.* https://www.nytimes.com/2019/03/30/us/affirmative-action-supreme-court.html

King, M. L. (1963). Letter from Birmingham Jail. https://www.africa.upenn.edu/Articles_Gen/Letter_Birmingham.html

Latham, W. (2016, October). Embracing campus diversity and addressing racial unrest. *University Business.com.* https://www.universitybusiness.com/article/embracing-campus-diversity-and-addressing-racial-unrest

Mangan, K. (2019, October 29). The University of Iowa keeps losing diversity officers. The turnover has raised alarms. *The Chronicle of Higher Education.* https://www.chronicle.com/article/The-U-of-Iowa-Keeps-Losing/247438

McIntosh, P. (1989). White privilege: Unpacking the invisible knapsack. *Peace and Freedom,* pp. 10–12.

McLeroy, K. R., Bibeau, D., Steckler, A., & Glanz, K. (1988). An ecological perspective on health promotion programs. *Health Education Quarterly, 15,* 351–377.

Mohanty, C. T. (1984). Under western eyes: Feminist scholarship and colonial discourses. *Boundary,* 2(12), 333–358. http://links.jstor.org/sici?sici=0190-3659%28198421%2F23%2912%3A3%3C333%3AUWEFSA%3E2.0.CO%3B2-Y

Neville, H. A., Gallardo, M. E., & Sue, D. W. (Eds.). (2016). *The myth of racial color blindness: Manifestations, dynamics, and impact.* Washington, DC, US: American Psychological Association.

Newkirk, P. (2019, November 6). Why diversity initiatives fail. *The Chronicle of Higher Education* https://www.chronicle.com/interactives/20191106-Newkirk

Oetzel, J., Dahr, S., & Kirschbaum, K. (2007). Intercultural conflict from a multi-level perspective: Trends, possibilities, and future directions. *Journal of Intercultural Communication Research, 36,* 183–204.

Oetzel, J., Ting-Toomey, S., & Rinderle, S. (2006). Conflict communication in contexts: A social ecological perspective. In J. Oetzel & S. Ting-Toomey (Eds.), *The Sage handbook of conflict communication* (pp. 727–739). Thousand Oaks, CA: Sage Publications.

14 HANNAH OLIHA-DONALDSON

Oliha-Donaldson, H., & Montgomery, G. (2019, November). Challenging the center: How can social justice education advance democratic sensibilities and raise levels of critical consciousness in the intercultural communication course? Paper presented at the *National Communication Association annual meeting*, Baltimore, MD.

Oliha-Donaldson, H. (2017). Let's talk: An exploration into student discourse about diversity and the implications for intercultural competence. *Howard Journal of Communications*. https://doi.org/10.1080/10646175.2017.1327379

Pappano, L. (2017, August). More diversity means more demands. *The New York Times*. https://www.nytimes.com/2017/08/04/education/edlife/protests-claremont-college-student-demands.html?mcubz=0

Shorman, J. (2016, September). College campuses across Kansas confront issues of race amid diversity efforts and racist threats. *The Topeka Capital Journal*. http://www.cjonline.com/news/2016-09-20/college-campuses-across-kansas-confront-issues-race-amid-diversity-efforts-and

University Business (2016, October 17). *Embracing campus diversity and addressing racial unrest*. Retrieved May 1, 2018, from https://universitybusiness.com/embracing-campus-diversity-and-addressing-racial-unrest/

U.S. Department of Justice (2019). *Hate crime statistics, 2018*. https://www.justice.gov/hatecrimes/hate-crime-statistics

Yant, K. M. (2017). *First not last: A not-so-modest proposal to support first-generation, low-income students at the University of Pennsylvania*. [Master's Thesis, University of Pennsylvania]. https://repository.upenn.edu/od_theses_msod/82

Chapter **2**

A Genealogy of "Diversity": From the 1960s to Problematic Diversity Agendas and Contemporary Activism

Hannah Oliha-Donaldson

> *Diversity and its management should be understood as forms of knowledge and discursive practices that are co-constructed through relations of power, and that constitute self and other.*
>
> (Ahonen et al., 2014, p. 2)

Since the 1960s, colleges and universities have tried, with various levels of success, to "nail down" (define and make manageable) and operationalize (make actionable) diversity in the context of a democratic society with a pluralistic self-image, yet it is evident that notions of diversity in U.S. institutions are complex, equity remains elusive, and inclusion is unfinished business ("Indicators of Equity," 2015; Bauman et al., 2005). In fact, the contemporary prominence of "diversity, equity, and inclusion" (DEI) as a framework in U.S. higher education and its attendant issues as fundamental talking points, organizing principles, and social agitators can be traced to critical moments of social activism, struggle, and contestation. This chapter illuminates these critical moments that have influenced and continue to shape talk, policy, and practice around DEI. If higher education professionals are to productively find solutions, we must understand how the past is shaping the present. This context is offered with a crucial claim in mind: understanding the emergence of the word "diversity" and its current iteration alongside the words "equity" and "inclusion" creates space to understand challenges facing contemporary institutions. To ignore these critical moments is to miss how and why institutions are experiencing a renaissance of the 1960s and new social justice demands. While this historical overview does not include the entire universe of factors implicated in emergence of the DEI framework, it does present four critical moments that changed and shaped discourse around educational access, equity,

16 HANNAH OLIHA-DONALDSON

inclusion, and diversity for many historically underrepresented and marginalized groups.

As will unfold shortly, this chapter locates the foundations of organizational "diversity practices" in the civil rights movement of the 1960s; because of this historical starting point, there is a necessary focus on race as a central marker in diversity talk and practices in this chapter. This is not to say that other identities do not matter and should not be considered; it is simply to review foundations of diversity frameworks while unpacking their structural, social, and political formations, which did and do center race, intersecting with class and gender.

FIRST WAVE: CIVIL RIGHTS MOVEMENT, GOVERNMENT REFORM, AND SELF DETERMINATION

From inception in U.S. institutions, the word "diversity" was, and in some circles, remains, a conduit of social justice ideals—even if only rhetorically. In 1946, President Truman was presented with a report detailing how financial assistance offered to veterans of World War II would continue to increase enrollments in postsecondary education. It was projected that two million young people would apply for enrollment in colleges and universities across the nation in the fall of 1946, the largest number up until that point. The report ended with a request that Truman appoint a commission to evaluate the state of higher education and review critical changes needed to ensure that institutions could "most effectively respond to the economic and political welfare of the country" (Snyder, 1946, as cited in Zook, 1947, p. 10).

Truman (1946) did indeed appoint the commission in July of 1946. In light of emerging shifts, he tasked the committee to "re-examine… higher education in terms of its objectives, methods, and facilities; and in light of the social role it has to play," (Truman, 1946). The commission was also to explore "ways and means of expanding educational opportunities for all able young people; [and] the adequacy of curricula, particularly in fields of international affairs and social understanding…" (President Truman, 1946, as cited in Zook, 1947, p. 11). This language was already signaling to a vision of higher education as an active social actor in fulfilling certain goals, including preparing students for global citizenship.

A year later, the Truman administration's 1947 Commission on Higher Education released a six-volume landmark report. Arguably, this report marked the beginnings of a large-scale awakening to the idea of social justice in higher education (Gilbert & Heller, 2010). The commission found access to postsecondary education was largely dependent on socioeconomic status, race, gender, and religious identity (Gilbert & Heller, 2010,

A GENEALOGY OF "DIVERSITY" **17**

p. 2). Critically, the commission shed light on a number of key issues impeding educational equity:

- Racial discrimination, of which "Negro" students were primary targets. The report noted that these students were also relegated to segregated institutions that received 3–42 times less funding than "institutions for whites" (The Department of State, 1947, Vol. II, p. 31). The commission reported that "educational facilities for Negros in segregated areas are inferior to those provided for whites" (The Department of State, 1947, Vol. II, p. 31). Comprising 10% of the population, African American students made up 3% of higher education attendance, and 85% of that number attended segregated institutions at the time of the report (The Department of State, 1947, Vol. II, p. 23);
- Religious discrimination, which largely impacted students of Jewish heritage at that time. These students were restricted in their choice of institutions and in certain areas of advanced study (The Department of State, 1947, Vol. II, p. 36);
- "Antifeminism," which impacted women's institutional options, and their educational outcomes in graduate and professional programs. Between 1939 and 1940, 8,317 men and 3,840 women obtained masters or second professional degrees, 1,244 men and 123 women received doctorates or third professional degrees, and only 10% of those in medical school between 1946 and 1947 were women (The Department of State, 1947, Vol. II, p. 40).

Speaking almost two decades before its time, the commission also stated:

> If we are to realize the *democratic principle* of *equality of opportunity in education,* new ways must be formed to translate this principle into practice. Fundamental to this effort must be a greatly increased will on the part of all American citizens to see that justice is done in educational institutions. There has been too much *tardiness* and *timidity*. It now seems clear that many institutions will change their policies only under legal compulsion.
>
>   (The Department of State, 1947, Vol. II, p. 43, emphasis added)

At the center of historical higher education discourse was a social justice mandate and an urgency to address socioeconomic, racial, gender, and religious injustices that were breeding educational limitations and boundaries. Despite the commission's efforts and sweeping recommendations, however, change in higher education would not come until 1964.

The Civil Rights Act of 1964,[1] initially proposed by President John F. Kennedy and later signed into law by his successor, President Lyndon

18 HANNAH OLIHA-DONALDSON

B. Johnson, on July 2, 1964, was a "crowning legislative achievement.... of the civil rights movement" ("Civil Rights," 2010, para. 1). Forceful enforcement of this law and the *Brown v. Board of Education* (1954) "decision as they applied to public higher education during the Kennedy and Johnson administrations" (Gilbert & Heller, 2010, p. 3) drastically changed the face of American higher education by creating opportunities for African Americans and other racial minorities that had previously been underrepresented (Gilbert & Heller, 2010). While the Truman Commission on Higher Education sparked a much-needed national debate, it was the civil rights era that ignited the first wave of equality measures and stirred social justice rhetoric in higher education to new heights.

This marks the beginnings of the first wave of "diversity" efforts. Yant (2017) notes that "The Civil Rights movement prodded elite institutions to actively recruit black, Hispanic, and female students, helping to 'pry open the gates that protected those long-exclusive institutions'" (Yant, 2017, p. 15; also citing Steinberg, 2002, p. xii). As the civil rights movement created a federal urgency to address and redress discrimination, the "face" of institutions slowly began changing (Gutierrez, 1994). The arrival of historically marginalized group (HMG) members "taxed the former habits and attitudes of institutions of higher education," forcing them to reevaluate institutional strongholds like curricula in light of the changing face of academia (Gutierrez, 1994, p. 157). Additionally, while the civil rights efforts of the 1940s and 1950s "sought slow, peaceful, change through assimilation, through petitions for governmental beneficence, and through appeals to white liberal guilt..." the 1960s took a sharp political turn as communities began to reject assimilation and agitate for "cultural autonomy" and "self-determination" (Gutierrez, 1994, p. 158).

These efforts coalesced in the late 1960s. At San Francisco State University in 1968, the Third World Liberation Front (TWLF), which was a coalition between the Black Student Union, select faculty and staff, and community members, launched a five-month strike advocating for inclusive admissions, a curriculum that would reflect lived experiences of indigenous communities and people of color, and an investment in faculty of color (College of Ethnic Studies, n.d.). The result was establishment of the first College of Ethnic Studies at San Francisco State University in March of 1969 (College of Ethnic Studies, n.d.). Other institutions across the nation experienced a similar phenomenon (see The Department of Ethnic Studies, n.d.).

Energized and inspired by the success of the civil rights movement (Clements, 2003), the women's liberation movement (WLM) was also birthed in that period and became part of second-wave feminism in the late 1960s and the early part of the 1970s (Bird, 2002). In academia, the movement was concerned with the untold stories and hidden perspectives of

A GENEALOGY OF "DIVERSITY" **19**

women, leading to the emergence of women's studies courses. These courses were so fiercely contested in the early days (Bird, 2002) that they were initially taught by graduate students in some instances, needed sponsorship from male allies, and generally faced resistance tactics (e.g., stalled committee approvals, questions of validity) when seeking an official space in the curriculum.

Between 1969 and 1982, 330 women's studies courses were established (Bird, 2002) and by the late 1970s, "professional associations such as the National Council of Black Studies, the National Association of Interdisciplinary Ethnic Studies, the National Association of Chicano Studies, and the Association for Asian American Studies" (Gutierrez, 1994, p. 159) had been birthed, helping to further shift the equity and inclusion conversation in academia.

The culmination of this first wave was the affirmative action policies of the early 1970s, which required institutions to take action to redress past discrimination by ensuring equal access for HMGs (Thomas, 1997).

SECOND WAVE: CALMING STORMS, VALUING DIFFERENCES, AND FOSTERING UNDERSTANDING

While the 1960s and 1970s ushered in affirmative action, equal access, and recognition of the contributions of HMGs, the late 1970s and 1980s ushered in charges of reverse discrimination by conservatives (Gutierrez, 1994). This backlash against social justice efforts of previous decades created space for resistance against affirmative action and ongoing efforts for equity and inclusion. In the midst of the backlash, affirmative action came under fire, as did all efforts to "level the playing field." Dissenters claimed these efforts were fostering disunity and giving unfair privileges to people of color (Omi & Winant, 1994).

In the landmark affirmative action case, *Regents v. Bakke* in 1978, a 35-year-old white man claimed he had been denied admission to medical school at the University of California at Davis due to the school's practice of setting aside 16 seats out of 100 for minority students (Harris, 2018). Justice Lewis Powell had the deciding opinion and declared that the only justification for affirmative action was for the educational benefits of a diverse student body. Further, race could only be used in concert with other factors to advance diversity. Finally, Justice Powell launched what is, debatably, the beginnings of a campaign for individual rights through his assertion that, "There is a measure of inequity in forcing innocent persons" like Bakke "to bear the burdens of redressing grievances not of their making" (Harris, 2018, para. 6; see also DiAngelo, 2011). McLaughlin et al. (2015) suggest that this decision, among others (Kramer, 2019), established the significance of a diverse student body and diversity as essential to institutional missions. However, Powell's opinion that race should only be factored into admissions decisions for the purpose and "benefits" of a diverse student body set the course for the definition and operationalization of diversity that continues to impact contemporary institutions (Harris, 2018; Newkirk, 2019). This landmark case *operationally* and *discursively* separated "diversity" as an organizational construct from considerations of social justice and equity in higher education (Harris, 2018).

In the midst of mounting dissension, proponents of equity and inclusion realized the work could not continue under the same discursive umbrella of "polarizing" efforts like affirmative action, nor could ethnic studies programs alone garner buy-in. Despite the incredible ways ethnic studies programs and affirmative action were helping to change the face of academia, these efforts spawned derision and distrust, and were actively resisted by some (McLaughlin et al., 2015). Evidence of these tensions were seen through a rash of racist and sexist incidents on campuses in the 1980s, punctuating "the tense relationship between efforts to diversify.... and those on campus who found these efforts threatening and disruptive to the status quo" (Bernstein, 2016, p. 26). Thus, it became apparent the movement had to rearticulate its values using new language.

The idea that rose to prominence in the 1990s was multiculturalism, which became the new framing for access, inclusion, and equity efforts. This shift represented the second wave of diversity efforts. The hallmark of multiculturalism was the importance of acknowledging and absorbing all forms of difference to produce a more democratic society. Cleckley (1997) suggests that multicultural ideals include "understanding, order, and peaceful coexistence" (p. 3). Central to this rearticulation of diversity efforts was the need to bring calm in the literal and figurative storm that ensued with the shifting demographic and curricular makeup of institutions.

Cleckley (1997) also acknowledged that while "demand for greater equality... has contributed to societal unrest and division," the aim of multiculturalism was "to engender respect for racial, cultural, and ethnic groups" (Cleckley, 1997, p. 4). Beyond easing tensions, central to this rearticulation of DEI efforts was engendering understanding and respect for differences. It was accepted in this wave that even if you don't like or understand the "other," there is a burden to at least "tolerate" them.

While accepting difference was part of this framing of equity and inclusion efforts, remedying structural inequity was often absent from the multiculturalism framework. If the first wave of equality and inclusion efforts was marked by action, the hallmark of this wave was the exact opposite. The "work," in this wave, was fostering respect, order, and positive change by understanding the "other," rather than by destabilizing structural inequities through direct action as in the civil rights era. Gender and race scholar Margaret Andersen (1999) noted "that in many discussions of multiculturalism, power is significantly absent from the conversation" (p. 13).

Unsurprisingly, while multiculturalism had many proponents (Stam & Shohat, 1994), by the middle of the 1990s, it was being problematized by its detractors as the greatest threat to unity in America on a national level; in academia, it was seen as a euphemism for "watering down the curriculum" to include "non-essential" works (Stam & Shohat, 1994). There were also progressive proponents of multicultural ideals who felt it was doomed to fail due to its oversimplification. Specifically, Wallace (1994) argued:

> Multiculturalism is not the promised land. As employed by universities, museums and advertising companies, the utopian ideal of a multicultural philosophy becomes a pragmatic institutional technique for neutralizing the myriad economic, political, and social demands of diversity…[M]ulticulturalism doesn't necessarily redistribute power or resources. (p. 258)

In short, scholars like Wallace (1994) and other higher education practitioners argued that multiculturalism was not suited to address social justice imperatives originally espoused by the civil rights movement, nor could it rival strides that were made by affirmative action and the self-determination movements of the 1960s. Therefore, by the mid-1990s, it was evident multiculturalism was not an adequate umbrella for capturing and actualizing the social justice agenda of the civil rights era in organizational equity and inclusion efforts.

THIRD WAVE: PLAYING IT SAFE WITH DIVERSITY

In light of the challenges to multiculturalism, the word "diversity" began to emerge as a new rhetorical framework in the mid- to late-1990s (Stiehm, 1994), representing the third wave of equity and inclusion efforts. While it was sometimes used interchangeably with multiculturalism, it was (and is) more widely accepted in academic and corporate circles for its simple avowal of difference (Ahonen et al., 2014). In general, it primarily represented the idea of valuing and celebrating difference (White, 1999).

Calls for social justice, access, and representation articulated through the work of affirmative action, ethnic studies programs, and to a lesser degree, multiculturalism, created an environment that was "too contentious," leading to retrenchment, retreat, and in some cases, abandonment of the social justice work that began in the 1950s. Diversity and "diversity talk" became a safe harbor. It became an acceptable, even if naïve, umbrella for capturing organizational equity and inclusion efforts. It was a way to

22 HANNAH OLIHA-DONALDSON

rhetorically signal the social justice imperatives of the 1960s without calling for a total change of the status quo or alienating those discomfited by the diversity, multiculturalism, and affirmative action "agenda" (Wallace, 1994). It is important to note that even today, "diversity" remains the dominant word used to capture institutional equity and inclusion efforts in corporate, nonprofit, religious, and higher education spaces.

FOURTH WAVE: EMERGENCE OF DIVERSITY, EQUITY, AND INCLUSION AS A CONSTRUCT

Beginning in the early 2000s, the word diversity was increasingly mobilized in conjunction with the words "equity" and "inclusion" in postsecondary institutions (Milem et al., 2005), representing a shift in the evolutionary life cycle of equity and inclusion efforts. This shift represents the fourth wave and solidly plants us in the present historical moment.

This framework is widely used in contemporary institutions. The DEI framework weaves in elements of every wave by: (1) using the language of the first wave and discursively mobilizing principles of access, representation, and social justice (often without the structural change focus or the necessary emphasis on racial, ethnic, religious, and gender minorities); and (2) calling for valuing and celebrating difference, like the second and third wave. While DEI has become the formalized institutional verbiage, however, the word "diversity" remains the primary object of focus and the general discursive umbrella for social justice efforts. As "diversity" remains the everyday verbiage, this chapter will follow this practice moving forward.

An underlying idea in this wave is that diversity is foundational (Smith, 2009). Overwhelmingly, diversity is articulated as central to institutional excellence, effectiveness, mission, and viability (Smith, 2009; see also Bauman et al., 2005). Generally, two dominant understandings of diversity shape institutional equity and inclusion practices in this wave. The first vision of equity and inclusion mobilized through the DEI framework is representational or categorical diversity. In fact, many institutions favor a definition of diversity as representation. Diversity is framed as a "business imperative" (Adserias et al., 2017), but beyond rhetoric, it often does not "do" anything (Ahmed, 2012). Included in this philosophy is the idea that diversity is an asset (Bernstein, 2016) that can and must be "managed" (Ahonen et al., 2014). This commodification of diversity represents a departure from activist thinking and acting (See Ahmed, 2012; Kirton et al., 2007). By simplifying diversity and its attendant issues and objectifying those framed as "diverse" as assets that can be acquired and controlled, this philosophy obfuscates the materiality of ongoing injustices.

In other institutions, diversity is more than representation; it is also an educational imperative, centering the values of intergroup mixing, exposure to "diversity" in all its forms, and "appreciation and respect for difference" and human rights. The goal is advancement of democratic ideals and active participation "in an increasingly complex and diverse society" (Ross, 2014, p. 871; see also Gurin et al., 2004). This view of diversity has existed since the Truman era and was featured prominently in the Truman Commission on Higher Education report (The Department of State, 1947):

> The American Nation is not only a union of 48 different States; it is also a union of an indefinite number of diverse groups of varying size. Of and among these diversities our free society seeks to create a dynamic unity. Where there is economic, cultural, or religious tension, we undertake to effect democratic reconciliation, so as to make of the national life one continuous process of interpersonal, intervocational, and intercultural cooperation. (p. 2)

This view of diversity has greatly impacted institutions, which are viewed as partners and resourcing sites in these efforts.

Sometimes comingled with these philosophies is the idea of "diversity for equity" (Owen, 2009, p. 187), which is concerned with institutions reflecting changing demographic trends and remedying historical and contemporary identity-based injustices—if not in deed, then at least in word (Adserias et al., 2017; Owen, 2009). Lack of actualization and performance of these ideals—often revealed through diversity statements—illustrates how diversity work is often just another form of "public relations" (Ahmed, 2012, p. 17), face-saving, and face-lifting for many organizations today. While many campuses now have a diversity course requirement or even opportunities for students to engage in intergroup dialogues, organizational structures are rarely, if ever, impacted. The "work" is left to organizational mission statements, symbolic figureheads that lack resources and power, individual faculty, or poorly funded programs (see Newkirk, 2019; Bauman et al., 2005; Milem et al., 2005; Williams et al., 2005). This brief genealogy demonstrates that sensemaking practices concerning diversity have implications, past, present, and future. As the upcoming section will demonstrate, they impact and continue to affect policy, practice, and experience.

CHALLENGES WITH NEW WAVE: IMPACT OF "DIVERSITY TALK" AND "DIVERSITY DISCOURSE"

> The domain of 'diversity' is informed by differing theoretical, political and practical ambitions, and diversity is used for divergent purposes, such as an idea, a taxonomical tool, or a mechanism for disciplining identities.
>
> (Ahonen et al., 2014, p. 8)

24 HANNAH OLIHA-DONALDSON

Today, many institutions now have a "diversity agenda" (Adserias et al., 2017) that weaves in some or all of the ideas of the fourth wave to varying degrees (see also Kezar, 2008). Central to the diversity agenda is talk of "weaving" and "embedding" diversity "widely" and "broadly" into the structure, fabric, and culture of institutions (See Adserias et al., 2017; see also Ahmed, 2012; Kezar & Eckel, 2008). Adserias et al. (2017) also note, "despite their symbolic significance as institutional policy and strategy artifacts, diversity agendas have high failure rates" (p. 316; see also Williams et al., 2005). While diversity agendas are commonplace (Kezar, 2008) and more institutions than not speak of institutionalizing diversity, there remain great institutional barriers delimiting the success of HMGs. Countless papers have been written and research projects conducted on the effects of campus culture, climate, and other institutional barriers impeding the success of HMGs (Howard-Hamilton, & Holmes, 2013; Johnson et al., 2014; Museus, 2011; Persico, 1990). Clearly, something is awry with how diversity and the DEI framework are being harnessed by institutions. Moving forward, three issues are addressed.

Absence of Equity and Inclusion

In this era, while equity and inclusion are woven into the diversity tagline and framework, functionally, what is often called DEI is the *diversity discourse* of the third wave coopting social justice language. While organizations mobilize the words *diversity, equity,* and *inclusion,* social justice ideals are seldom woven into the operationalization of DEI talk and practice in most institutions today. Ahonen et al. (2014) assert that "social justice has been lost in mainstream writings on diversity, as well as in some critical work. This… malaise is connected with the ways power and context have (not) been conceptualized and operationalized into research practice in the field" (p. 2). In many institutions, DEI work is dehistoricized, decontextualized, and disconnected from its social justice roots—the liberation movements of the 1950s and 1960s (Ahonen et al., 2014; Smith, 2009). Instead, differences are individuated, inequalities are concealed (Ahonen et al., 2014; see also Ahmed & Swan, 2006), and historical tensions and struggles between groups and their contemporary effects are often jettisoned, hiding structural inequities. Even in training contexts, the safety of keeping everyone comfortable and the content palatable (DiAngelo, 2011) has led to the superficial presentation and analysis of structural inequity and privilege—if these factors are even discussed for fear of "alienating," "offending," or "traumatizing" gender and racial majorities.

What we are left with in many institutions is "diversity talk"—rhetoric with no action or noteworthy impact. While "diversity" is established as something that adds value and its management is now central to organizational life, it "has replaced terms such as gender equality and anti-racism, masking its political and contested nature" and its social justice heritage and legacy (Ahonen et al., 2014 p. 9).

Diversity Means Everything and Nothing

The concept and object, diversity, is full of meaning. At the micro level, it means different things to different organizational members and is defined at the intersections of gender, race, and organizational identities, posing implications for practice (Oliha & Collier, 2010). In my own research investigating definitions of diversity among faculty, staff, administrators, and students, I found that diversity is conceptualized differently by different bodies: (1) illuminating the import and impact of social and cultural identities in organizations; (2) highlighting the problematically raced history and social practices of institutions; and (3) reflecting the organizational impact of differential levels of privilege, power, and opportunity (Oliha, 2010).

Also, in Bell and Hartmann's (2007) study exploring definitions of diversity among the general public, while people of color like African Americans and Hispanics defined diversity as a moral and civic responsibility and emphasized issues with inequality and intolerance primarily, white respondents "were mostly concerned about disunity and misunderstanding" (Bell & Hartmann, 2007, p. 909; see also Halualani, 2010; Oliha, 2010). While people of color were concerned with the material consequences of injustice, white respondents emphasized concerns over pluralism, often favoring assimilation. Further, a Ford foundation study delving into views of diversity revealed interesting tensions. Ninety-one percent of respondents agreed that, "Our society is multi-cultural. The more we know about each other, the better we will get along" ("The Court of Public Opinion," 1999, p. 19). Eighty-one percent agreed that "diversity education creates respect for differences and helps ease tensions between people" ("The Court of Public Opinion," 1999, p. 19), yet 47% agreed that "diversity education is added just to make some students *feel included*" and 58% agreed that "diversity education has a liberal agenda" ("The Court of Public Opinion," 1999, p. 19, emphasis added). Critically, 48% agreed that "diversity education, by emphasizing our differences and past abuses, can breed conflict," ("The Court of Public Opinion," 1999, p. 19). While the majority of respondents agreed that understanding others in multicultural communities is valuable and "diversity education is necessary," there was a split in perceptions with regard to the agenda and aims of diversity courses. Although over a decade apart, similar to Bell and Hartmann's (2007) study,

26 HANNAH OLIHA-DONALDSON

half of the participants favored a comfortable, non-challenging, nonthreatening, and dehistoricized form of diversity—what can be labeled as "diversity without oppression" (Andersen, 1999, p. 13; see also Andersen, 2001). This data reveal how diversity as *object* and *project* is perceived differently by different bodies.

At the organizational level, diversity means different things to institutions who typically mobilize the definition of diversity that suits emerging needs. Diversity has become a shifting signifier that can stand for whatever an organization needs; if it is inclusion of as much difference as possible, as evidence of a "diverse campus," it can be used to sanction representation. If it is needed for image repair after a failed diversity moment, it can be used discursively to reaffirm the identity of the institution as a place where diversity is "valued" and "where all are welcome" (Ahmed, 2012). It can be used as proof of institutional commitment to diversity, with diversity talk being the work itself, the action, and the change. In this way, *diversity talk* becomes the *substance* and *outcome* of institutional action. For diversity to be this malleable, it is often sanitized and emptied of historical context and inconvenient truths, allowing it to be harnessed as needed (see Newkirk, 2019). Symptomatic of this, Ahonen et al. (2014) note that diversity often "becomes everything and nothing, a signifier without a signified" (p. 10).

Reproducing a Center and Sanctioning a Racial and Gender Elite

> Moreover, the diversity discourse works to exoticize, criticize, trivialize, and compartmentalize the cultural objects of people of color as contributions to the enrichment of a presumably neutral 'us.'
>
> (Bell & Hartmann, 2007, p. 909)

> Women, people of color, and the poor cannot escape being partially defined by their social location for they are invariably marked by it, while middle- or upper-class White men can understand themselves as simply 'human.'
>
> (Owen, 2009, p. 189)

Diversity discourse has been used to codify some as nonnormative, diverse, different, and "bringing diversity" to institutions, authorizing an assumed center. This center is framed as normal, standard, acceptable, and already implicitly accepted. Current practices reify, reproduce, and punctuate this center. Early on, "the courts [through the Bakke case among others] laid the foundations for [the] inclusion of diversity as a primary educational goal" and a key part of institutional mission (McLaughlin et al., 2015, p. 224; See also Harris, 2018). While this framing of diversity as an educational imperative and matter of strategic importance (Williams, 2013; see also Owen, 2009) has led to positive gains for HMGs, it has also resulted in key challenges. Notably, the resulting operationalization of DEI efforts as being centered around "adding" diversity has not ultimately benefited these groups; instead, diversity—"their diversity"—becomes a tool used to "prepare" a racial and gender elite for the challenges of an increasingly multicultural world.

Bell and Hartman (2007) argue that "diversity discourse relies on assimilationist assumptions and employs linguistic tools that privilege white cultural norms and values while simultaneously naturalizing 'other' groups...as outside of (or 'addons' to) the white mainstream" (Bell & Hartmann, 2007, p. 909). Framing and operationalizing diversity in this way builds into the language of diversity assumed margins and centers. Some scholars assert that diversity discourse and practices cannot include evaluations of privilege, inequality, and power because of an assumed white center to which color and flavor are "harmoniously" and carefully added (Bell & Hartmann, 2007, p. 909). Consequently, those discursively constructed as "they," "other," or "addons," cannot be conceptualized as equals, nor are they ever truly included, given their adjunct and optional status.

This presents grave challenges for those labeled "diverse," who, because of their "diversity," are painfully and irrevocably marked (Owen, 2009). While racial and gender minorities are included, they still bear the burden of assimilating to a Eurocentric, male bias. By default, these individuals must employ tactics of communication and engagement that perpetuate ideas of a "normalized" way of being in organizations, which reinscribes a center to which they do not belong, also emphasizing their periphery and "marginal" status.

These practices reproduce an in/out duality that marks the experiences of HMGs. Consequently, students of color are still underperforming in comparison to their white counterparts, faculty and administrators identified as people of color or women remain underrepresented and marginalized in many institutional spaces or are only permitted to play token roles, and curricula continue to serve the needs of the center, alienating those defined as "other."

It is clear "diversity" does not necessarily make for equitable educational outcomes (Bauman et al., 2005). Similarly, more racial, ethnic, and gender minorities in more organizational spaces does not challenge the racial and gender hierarchy at the center of operation in most institutions (Goldberg, 1994; Tierney & Jackson, 2002). As the face of the U.S. continues change and HMG members continue to increase in institutions, interrogation of what diversity means and how it is being used (Ahmed, 2012) will remain foundational.

28 HANNAH OLIHA-DONALDSON

CLOSE

> Although recommendations, initiatives, and strategies proliferate, many segments of the national population continue to be grossly underrepresented on campus, and equity in education remains a much-sought-after goal.
>
> (Iverson, 2007, p. 587)

This chapter demonstrates that "diversity talk" or "diversity discourse" have become the "small talk" hiding the elephants in the room (Bell & Hartmann, 2007, p. 905, also citing Zerubavel, 2006), racial and gender inequalities, which remain "big structural elephants" in many institutions (Bell & Hartmann, 2007, p. 905). Consequently, organizations continue to struggle to meet the needs of HMGs at every level, and issues of access, inclusion, and equity continue to tax higher education systems and challenge educators (Bernstein, 2016; see also Iverson, 2007).

This chapter illustrates the ongoing centrality of intersecting identities of race, class, and gender in diversity talk and practices (Smith, 2009). Given the growing list of legitimate identity concerns to be addressed, in alignment with scholars like Smith (2009), I contend that the access and success of these HMGs will remain "the legacy and soul of diversity work today" (p. ix). This is so, not because these groups are more important, but because these identities often cannot be hidden, expose one to the cumulative effects of systemic institutional oppression, and irrevocably determine levels of access, success, and experience (see also Andersen, 1999). This does not and must not detract from other emerging and pressing identity concerns, rather, it warrants creativity in how to attend to critical needs.[2]

As this chapter reflects, the more diversity talk and practices are disassociated from the social justice efforts of the 1950s and 1960s, the more diversity becomes immaterial and intangible, able to be shaped and filled with any meaning. Ahonen et al. (2014) contend that diversity is now so highly malleable, it "can be deployed for various strategic purposes and with differing and shifting meanings" (p. 10). Diversity has become everything and nothing, and can be used representationally to stand for whatever an organization needs. Consequently, the cultures of institutions remain unchanged, leading to DEI challenges (like those presented in the introductory chapter and in this volume), convenient and easy solutions, and copious amounts of "goodwill" (Oliha, 2010), which leave problematically gendered and raced institutions intact. Without transformational changes that move beyond mere image repair, higher education will continue to function as a tool that reproduces social inequity.

In the larger context of this volume, this chapter makes a number of key claims. The turbulence we have seen between 2016 and 2019 are pushback against chronic race, gender, and class inequities, that over 70 years later, remain. Failed diversity moments in contemporary institutions reflect the problematic evolution of equity and inclusion discourse and practices, and the institutionalization of inequity in contemporary "diversity discourse." This genealogy of equity and inclusion discourse and practices shows that the more things change, the more they stay the same: major equity and inclusion shifts were the direct result of social movements in the 1960s and 1970s. In short, institutions were forced to change. Some of the narratives presented in this volume tell a similar tale. While we have perfected diversity talk, similar to institutions in the Truman era, many contemporary institutions are timid, reticent, and tardy in responding to the needs of this new generation of students, leading to the recent protests and equality demands. Importantly, backlash against these protests—evidenced through increased visibility of white supremacists on campuses and identity-based incidents of bias—reflect history.

Let me be clear, post-racial ideology has been irrevocably shattered, and despite the many gains, this chapter and volume remind us that there is tremendous work left to do. The last few years have shaken many higher education professionals out of their stupor by refocusing "attention on the unfinished business of diversity efforts begun in the '60s, when black students [and others] demanded more faculty of color and curricula that moved beyond a Eurocentric canon" (Newkirk, 2019, p. 9). Now we have an opportunity to move beyond reactivity to productivity. Institutions can continue to allow protests and identity-based hate crimes and incidents to take them by surprise and set the pace of institutional DEI reform, or institutions can begin engaging in critical dialogues and seeking multidimensional solutions to diversity issues. By teasing out the specific failures of diversity discourse, presenting productive definitions of DEI that set the stage for addressing inequities and disparities, offering narratives about impact, and presenting promising practices for change, this text is an invitation to pursue the latter.

DISCUSSION QUESTIONS

1. List the tangible ways diversity policies and practices are impacted by the historical evolution of the DEI framework at your institution.
2. What key challenges, if any, do you see with the "diversity agenda"?
3. How has the definition of "diversity" and the implementation of DEI practices changed over time at your institution?
4. What specific DEI policies and practices are in place at your institution to support historically marginalized groups? Are these policies and practices effective?

30 HANNAH OLIHA-DONALDSON

5. What key challenges, if any, do you see with the diversity program or plan at your institution?
6. What positive changes are you seeing in efforts to address racial and gender disparities and inequities at your institution? What lessons can be learned from the efforts and units/departments leading the efforts? How can your institution use these lessons in other areas?

NOTES

1. The Civil Rights Act of 1964 banned segregation based on race, religion, or national origin in public spaces, and it banned employment discrimination based on race, religion, national origin and gender. It also prohibited use of federal funds for discriminatory programs, while authorizing the Office of Education (now the Department of Education) to back school desegregation efforts ("Civil Rights," 2010).
2. This important question is being addressed by a number of scholars like Smith, 2009.

REFERENCES

Ahmed, S. (2012). *On Being included: Racism and diversity in institutional life.* Durham, NC: Duke University Press.

Ahmed, S., & Swan, E. (2006). Introduction: Doing diversity. *Policy Futures in Education,* 4(2), 96–100.

Adserias, R. P., Charleston, L. J., & Jackson J. F. L. (2017). What style of leadership is best suited to direct organizational change to fuel institutional diversity in higher education? *Race Ethnicity and Education,* 20(3), 315–331. DOI:10.1080/13 613324.2016.1260233

Ahonen, P., Tienari, J., Meriläinen, S., & Pullen, A. (2014). Hidden contexts and invisible power relations: A Foucauldian reading of diversity research. *Human Relations,* 67(3), 263–286. DOI:10.1177/0018726713491772

Andersen, M. L. (1999). Diversity without oppression: Race, ethnicity, identity and power. In M. Kenyatta, & R. T. Totowa (Eds.). *Critical ethnicity: Countering the waves of identity politics* (pp. 5–20). NJ: Rowman and Littlefield.

Andersen, M. L. (2001). Restructuring for whom? Race, class, gender, and the ideology of invisibility. *Sociological Forum,* 16(2), 181–201.

Bauman, G. L., Bustillos, L. T., Bensimon, E. M., Brown II, M. C., & Bartee, R. D. (2005). *Achieving equitable education outcomes with all students: The institution's roles and responsibilities.* [Online]. Washington, DC: Association of American Colleges and Universities. https://www.aacu.org/sites/default/files/files/mei/bauman_et_al.pdf

Bell, J. M., & Hartmann D. (2007). Diversity in everyday discourse: The cultural ambiguities and consequences of "Happy Talk". *American Sociological Review,* 72, 895–914.

Bernstein, A. R. (2016). Addressing diversity and inclusion on college campuses: Assessing a partnership between AAC&U and the Ford Foundation. *Liberal Education,* 102(2). https://www.aacu.org/liberaleducation/2016/spring/bernstein

A GENEALOGY OF "DIVERSITY" **31**

Bird, E. (2002). The academic arm of the women's liberation movement: Women's studies 1969–1999 in north America and the United kingdom. *Women's studies international forum,* 25(1), 139–149.

Civil Rights Act of 1964. (2010, June, 4). *History.com.* Retrieved February 1, 2020, from https://www.history.com/topics/black-history/civil-rights-act

Cleckley, B. J. (1997). Multiculturalism: A matter of essentiality. In L. Welch, B. Cleckley & M. McClure (Eds.), *Strategies for promoting pluralism and education in the workplace* (pp. 3–12). Westport, CT: Greenwood Praeger.

Clements, J. A. (2003). Participatory democracy: The bridge from civil rights to women's liberation. *The Public Purpose,* 1(1), 5–24.

College of Ethnic Studies: San Francisco State University. (n.d.). History. Retrieved March 1, 2020, from https://ethnicstudies.sfsu.edu/home2

The Court of Public Opinion. (1999). The Ford Foundation campus diversity initiative survey of voters on diversity in education and an interview with Edgar Beckham. *Equity & Excellence,* 32(2), 17–23. DOI:10.1080/1066568990320204

The Department of Ethnic Studies—UC Berkeley. (n.d.). History. https://ethnicstudies.berkeley.edu/about/history/

The Department of State of the United States of America (1947). Higher education for American democracy: A report of the president's commission on higher education. Washington: U.S. Govt. https://archive.org/stream/in.ernet.dli.2015.89917/2015.89917.Higher-Education-For-American-Democracy-A-Report-Of-The-Presidents-Commission-On-Higher-Education-Vol-I—Vi_djvu.txt

DiAngelo, R. (2011). White fragility. *International Journal of Critical Pedagogy,* 3(3), 54–70.

Gilbert, C., & Heller, D. (2010, November). The Truman commission and its impact on federal higher education policy from 1947 to 2010. *Paper presented at the Association for the Study of Higher Education annual meeting,* Indianapolis, IN.

Goldberg, D. T. (1994). Introduction: Multicultural conditions. In D. T. Goldberg (Ed.), *Multiculturalism: A critical reader* (pp. 1–41). Cambridge, MA: Basil Blackwell.

Gutierrez, R. A. (1994). Ethnic studies: Its evolution in American colleges and universities. In D.T. Goldberg (Ed.), *Multiculturalism: A critical reader* (pp. 157–167). Cambridge, MA: Blackwell.

Gurin, P., Nagda, B., & Lopez, G. E. (2004). The benefits of diversity in education for democratic citizenship. *Journal of Social Issues,* 60(1), 17–34.

Halualani, R. T. (2010). Intercultural interaction at a multicultural university: Students' definitions and sensemakings of intercultural interaction. *Journal of International and Intercultural Communication,* 3(4), 304–324.

Harris, A. (2018, October 13). The Supreme Court Justice who forever changed Affirmative Action *The Atlantic.* https://www.theatlantic.com/education/archive/2018/10/how-lewispowell-changed-affirmative-action/572938/

Howard-Hamilton, M., & Holmes, V. (2013). Review of creating campus cultures: Fostering success among racially diverse student populations. *Journal of College Student Development,* 54(4), 451–452.

Indicators of Equity. (2015). The Pell Institute. http://pellinstitute.org/downloads/publications-Indicators_of_Higher_Education_Equity_in_the_US_2019_Historical_Trend_Report.pdf

Iverson, S. V. (2007). Camouflaging power and privilege: A critical race analysis of university diversity policies. *Educational Administration Quarterly,* 43(5), 586–611.

Johnson, D. R., Wasserman, T. H., Yildirim, N., & Yonai, B. A. (2014). Examining the effects of stress and campus climate on the persistence of students of color and white students: An application of bean and Eaton's psychological model of retention. *Research in Higher Education,* 55(1), 75–100.

Kezar, A. (2008). Understanding leadership strategies for addressing the politics of diversity. *The Journal of Higher Education*, 79(4), 406–441.

Kezar, A. J., & Eckel, P. D. (2008). Advancing diversity agendas on campus: Examining transactional and transformational presidential leadership styles. *International Journal of Leadership in Education*, 11(4), 379–405.

Kramer, M. (2019). A timeline of key Supreme Court cases on affirmative action. *New York Times*. https://www.nytimes.com/2019/03/30/us/affirmative-action-supreme-court.html

Kirton, G., Greene, A., & Dean, D. (2007). British diversity professionals as change agents – radicals, tempered radicals or liberal reformers? *The International Journal of Human Resource Management*, 18(11), 1979–1994. DOI:10.1080/09585190701638226

McLaughlin, J. E., McLaughlin, G. W., & McLaughlin, J. (2015). Using composite metrics to measure student diversity in higher education. *Journal of Higher Education Policy and Management*, 37(2), 222–240. DOI: 10.1080/1360080X.2015.1019124

Milem, J. F., Chang, M. J., & Antonio. A. L. (2005). *Making diversity work on campus: A research-based perspective.* [Online]. Washington, DC: Association of American Colleges and Universities. https://www.aacu.org/sites/default/files/files/mei/MakingDiversityWork.pdf

Museus, S. D. (2011). Generating ethnic minority student success (GEMS): A qualitative analysis of high-performing institutions. *Journal of Diversity in Higher Education*, 4(3), 147–162.

Newkirk, P. (2019, November 6). Why diversity initiatives fail. *The Chronicle of Higher Education*. https://www.chronicle.com/interactives/20191106-Newkirk

Oliha, H. (2010). Discourses of diversity: Negotiating the boundaries for equity, inclusion and identity through the discourse of socially situated subjects [Doctoral dissertation]. University of New Mexico, Albuquerque, NM. http://hdl.handle.net/1928/11194

Oliha, H., & Collier, M. J. (2010). Bridging divergent diversity standpoints & ideologies: Organizational initiatives and trainings. *The International Journal of Diversity in Organizations, Communities, and Nations: Annual Review*, 10(4), 61–74. doi:10.18848/1447-9532/CGP/v10i04/39890

Omi, M., & Winant, H. (1994). *Racial formation in the United States: From the 1960s to the 1980s.* New York: Routledge.

Owen, D. S. (2009). Privileged social identities and diversity leadership. *The Review of Higher Education*, 32(2), 185–207.

Persico, C. F. (1990). Creating an institutional climate that honors diversity. In G. Stricker, E. Davis-Russell, E. Bourg, E. Duran, W. R. Hammond, J. McHolland, ... B. E. Vaughn (Eds.), (pp. 55–63). Washington, DC: American Psychological Association.

Ross, S. N. (2014). Diversity and intergroup contact in higher education: Exploring possibilities for democratization through social justice education. *Teaching in Higher Education*, 19(8), 870–881.

Smith, D. G. (2009). *Diversity's promise for higher education: Making it work.* Baltimore, MD: The Johns Hopkins University Press.

Stam, R., & Shohat, E. (1994). Contested histories: Eurocentricism, multiculturalism, and the media. In D. T. Goldberg (Ed.), *Multiculturalism: A critical reader* (pp. 296–324). Cambridge, MA: Blackwell.

Steinberg, J. (2002). *The gatekeepers: Inside the admissions process of a premier college.* New York: Penguin Group.

A GENEALOGY OF "DIVERSITY" **33**

Stiehm, J. (1994). Diversity's Diversity. In D. T. Goldberg (Ed.), *Multiculturalism: A critical reader* (pp. 140–156). Cambridge, MA: Basil Blackwell.

Thomas Jr. R. (1997). Barriers and facilitators to managing workplace diversity. In L. Welch, B. Cleckley & M. McClure (Eds.), *Strategies for promoting pluralism and education in The workplace* (pp. 43-58). Westport, CT: Greenwood Praeger.

Tierney, S., & Jackson II, R. L. (2002). Deconstructing whiteness ideology as a set of rhetorical fantasy themes: Implication for interracial alliance building in the United States. In M. J. Collier (Ed.), *Intercultural alliances: Critical transformation: International and intercultural communication annual* (pp. 81–106). Thousand Oaks, CA: Sage.

Truman, H. (1946, July 13). Letter of appointment of commission members. In *Higher Education for American Democracy* (1948). New York: Harper & Brothers.

Wallace, M. (1994). The search for the "good enough" mammy: Multiculturalism, popular culture, and psychoanalysis. In D. T. Goldberg (Ed.), *Multiculturalism: A critical reader* (pp. 45–74). Cambridge, MA: Blackwell.

White, R. D. (1999). Managing the diverse organization: The imperative for a new multicultural paradigm. *Public Administration & Management: An Interactive Journal*, 4(4), 469–493.

Williams, D. A. (2013). *Strategic diversity leadership: Activating change and transformation in higher education*. Sterling: Stylus Publishing.

Williams, D. A., Berger, J. B., & McClendon, S. A. (2005). *Toward a model of inclusive excellence and change in postsecondary institutions* [Online]. Washington, DC: Association of American Colleges and Universities. https://www.aacu.org/sites/default/files/files/mei/williams_et_al.pdf

Yant, K. M. (2017). First not last: A not-so-modest proposal to support first-generation, low-income students at the University of Pennsylvania. [Master's Thesis, University of Pennsylvania]. https://repository.upenn.edu/od_theses_msod/82

Zerubavel, E. (2006). *The Elephant in the room: The social organization of silence and denial*. Oxford, UK: Oxford University Press.

Zook, G. F. (1947). The president's commission on higher education. *Bulletin of the American Association of University Professors*, 33(1), 10–28.

Chapter 3

Dismantling the Trifecta of Diversity, Equity, and Inclusion: The Illusion of Heterogeneity

Tina M. Harris

A cursory review of my life—both professional and personal—reveals a specific theme: I have had a longtime interest in and commitment to issues of representation and equity. Unbeknownst to me, that interest was driven by what I believed was the inherent value of diversity. As a child (and even as an adult), I just could not process how people could be so wedded and committed to their prejudice, racism, and xenophobia. I could not fathom how and why someone could be so dismissive of someone who was of a different race, ethnicity, culture, or sexual orientation than themselves. I was bewildered by the *lack* of compassion, respect, and courtesy people showed each other. This way of thinking is something that I believe is not only in my DNA, but is also an extension of the values my parents instilled in my siblings and me throughout our lives.

My parents are from Griffin, Georgia, and were firsthand witnesses to (and victims of) the segregated South and the civil rights movement. Their parents and grandparents were primarily sharecroppers due to the impoverished South and, not surprisingly, consequences of the aftermath of slavery. Suffice it to say, they were keenly aware of the atrocities birthed from racism, whether it was Dad knowing to avoid direct eye contact with white women or Mom being forced to chop cotton at the age of 10 and be a domestic worker at the age of 12 for white people. They knew all too well of the racial hierarchy driving U.S. society, but they forged ahead and eventually became government employees (Office of Personnel Management and the Equal Employment Opportunity Commission) dedicated to fighting systemic oppression on behalf of the less powerful. While they have the emotional battle scars to prove it, their lives and those of our foreparents attest to the reality of racism and how measures need to be in place to safeguard against the continued harm that sadly remains an integral part of the moral fabric of our country.

When I was invited to write this book chapter, I literally welcomed the opportunity to be a part of this very important project. I definitely did not need yet another writing deadline to add to my already overloaded plate; however, I felt an urgency to produce an essay that would help me to articulate my thoughts on an issue that is very complex and has been a driving force behind why I do what I do. I am an endowed chair at an R1 in the south, a position which is the first of its kind in this country. I have worked hard throughout my career and am now reaping the harvest from all that I have sown in my various roles as professor, scholar, advisor, mentor, friend, colleague, and single woman who also happens to be Black. While there have been decades of tears, heartache, and pain mixed with joy and happiness, they have culminated into an amazing point in my career and life where I can see and enjoy the fruits of my labor. The barriers I experienced only served to make me stronger. Like a diamond that is refined through heat and pressure, so was I.

There were many moments where the pressure and stress of being subjected to racism, isolation, and tokenism were overwhelming, but with the support and love of family, friends, and some colleagues, I persisted. Those fires produced what I recognize now are best practices (or at least mine) for navigating the complex and messy nuances of academia. I am by no means perfect, and neither is the system; however, my epistemological viewpoint of higher education tells me the proverbial trifecta of diversity, equity, and inclusion (DEI) is fractured and in need of repair and long-term care. In this essay, I will identify the disconnect between diversity, equity, and inclusion, discuss examples of the types of barriers that contribute to and sustain this disconnect, and offer possible solutions for remedying the very problematic ways that higher education is failing its "shareholders." Ultimately, I hope to challenge all institutions to develop more integrative and sustainable strategies that offer a different and more refined prism through which to (1) reflect and embody true diversity, (2) create equity or equal access to opportunities and resources, and (3) foster inclusion or belongingness through quality interracial/intercultural interactions. I must first, however, provide a peek into my personal history so that you can best understand my positionality as a scholar–activist committed to doing my part to identify best practices for *true* DEI in academe and beyond.

When I reflect on my life's journey, I am always taken back to the time in my childhood where I had what I describe as incredibly transformative experiences living abroad. It was during this time that a seed was (metaphorically) planted in me that instilled an appreciation of racial, ethnic, and cultural differences as a result of living in Rota, Spain, as a Navy family for four-and-a-half years. We moved there when I was two-and-a-half years

36 TINA M. HARRIS

old, and while I am human and have biases like everyone else, I am convinced that being immersed in another culture, learning its traditions, and fluently speaking its language at an early age provided the foundation for who I have come to be (and continue to evolve into) as a person and all of my complexities. Moreover, this foundation has been at the core of how I identify as a cisgender, single, heterosexual African-American female who is also a professor at a predominately white institution (PWI).

In addition to my life abroad, there were other critical moments during adolescence (and beyond) that forced me to become keenly aware of diversity issues and racial tensions going on in my schools, neighborhood, community, and the country. My awareness of this racial divide occurred on a micro-level, and over time, I became more cognizant of the fact that these personal moments and experiences were the direct result of a macro-level seismic shift in racial tensions between whites[1] and Blacks[2] on a national level. I was witnessing white flight in my neighborhood and school, by extension, and was somewhat puzzled by the shrinking number of interracial friendships that my friends and I realized were slowly fading. White girls with whom I was friends began socializing amongst themselves, and the same occurred with us Black girls. Our interactions were limited to the classroom, and the likelihood of slumber parties and the forming of interracial childhood memories became a thing of the distant past.

I vaguely remember conversations with my parents and siblings about the racism that was directly impacting our school, neighborhood, family, and country, as I was not quite attuned to racial nuances of the schism that was shaping my reality. That changed when I was in ninth grade or so, and vividly recall a carload of my white peers whom I innocently thought were my friends, angrily yelling the n-word out of the window seemingly to anyone who would listen. I do not remember who was in the car with me, but I vividly remember being shocked, confused, and disappointed that my classmates were active racists. They were invested in hating people who looked like me. I was forced into the position of altering the way I viewed my world and that made me very sad.

Since those critical moments, I have had countless others that have had a more positive and profound impact on how I identify and how I navigate the world. Thus, I use the collective of my experiences to advance an argument regarding the importance of reframing how we think about and conceptualize DEI. These experiences have afforded me the opportunity to recognize how my intersectionality (race, gender, class, sexual orientation, and religion) has illuminated (for me) the many ways that being a member of multiple historically marginalized groups (HMG) is in direct response to systemic oppression, which is in the very DNA of our society. I use this essay as an opportunity to shatter the belief in a "bootstrap mentality" that valorizes merit and hard work, all the while hiding behind a thin veil disguising the racism, sexism, and heteronormativity that drive these very institutions. Scholarship, op-eds, and personal anecdotes are used to dispel the misconception that all organizations claiming a commitment to DEI have arrived. I argue that these institutional mantras are problematic and highlight the need for institutions to allocate the resources, leadership, and institutional commitment necessary for achieving *true* DEI (Lerner & Fulambarker, 2018).

THE DISCONNECT BETWEEN DIVERSITY, EQUITY, AND INCLUSION

The topic of diversity, equity, and inclusion (DEI) is typically critiqued within the context of colleges, universities, churches, and companies (Becker, 1998; Riddell, 2009; Wellin, 2008). There are certainly other contexts where DEI is a part of the rhetoric, and after doing considerable research on this topic, I strongly believe that the changing demographic landscape of these contexts is simultaneously viewed as both a positive and a negative shift in the organizational[3] culture (Gill et al., 2018). In other words, the change is recognized, but very little is done to truly adapt to this inevitability. There seemed to be a trend where DEI is deemed a positive because it suggests that the organization espouses a forward-thinking ideology in a rapidly changing society. In contrast, it is viewed as a negative because it is "forcing" difference onto the existing organizational culture and its members. Moreover, it means that the organization is undoubtedly going to experience change, which is a perceived threat to the organizational identity that has become all too familiar. As Wellin (2008) noted, "[c]olleges and universities are gateways to upward mobility and committed in principle to candid discourse and progressive policies on diversity" (p. 686). By extension, this can also be applied to the workplace and religious institutions.[4] Diversity is certainly creating change, but we must question whether the organization is *truly* ready to adapt to its inevitable and changing (read news) culture (Goethe & Colina, 2018; Joseph, 2017). Wellin also stressed that there are four issues that are important for organizations to prioritize as they move towards racial diversity. I will discuss each of those issues in greater detail later, but I want to initially offer a general summary of her main points, which contextualize my position on diversity. Wellin's general argument is that HMGs have complex identities (i.e., race, gender, sexual identity, individualism, collectivism) that come with them into the new culture. When they are people of color, the tension between these identities is heightened because they are trying to manage their marginalized status in a potentially unwelcoming environment. Thus, I argue that it is imperative that the organization be proactive in devising ways to best accommodate and adapt to diversity (Hartwell et al., 2017; Stanley

38 TINA M. HARRIS

et al., 2018), while also actively preventing the chilly or hostile climate many HMGs often face (Maranto & Griffin, 2011).

Schreiber (1996) spoke on this issue many years ago and identified "two avenues of guidance for organizations" (p. 459) for effectively and appropriately addressing diversity in a multicultural workforce. She stressed that businesses should, first, learn from academia and directly address "larger issues...revolving around sharing power and valuing difference." This also means avoiding the tokenization of these new members and actively creating a culture of inclusion. The second avenue involves "dismantl[ing] hierarchical structures in favor of participatory ones, [which] suggests ways of dissolving barriers and creating unity" (p. 459). I highlight her argument because she stressed the continued importance of organizations doing the hard work of being self-reflexive and then launching into the development of long-term, sustainable programs that transform organizational cultures into genuinely welcoming and inclusive spaces. Personally, I believe self-reflexivity is critical to DEI if institutions are truly going to change. They must face the hard reality that they were most likely founded on systemic oppression, and that requires changing ideologies such as biases, racism, and prejudice, which many are unwilling to admit. It is not until then that those individuals in power can experience the attitudinal and behavioral transformation required for institutional level change.

In researching for this chapter, I was elated to find the work of communication scholars Simmons and Wahl (2016), who echo my sentiments. They coordinated a forum on Diversity in Instructional Communication Research in the *Communication Education* journal and challenged "communication education scholars to engage in a moment of reflexive disciplinary intervention" (p. 532). They explained that using a self-reflexive approach requires that scholars directly address diversity issues in "mainstream communication education research" (p. 532) along with systemic problems related to diversity and inclusion programs at their respective institutions, particularly at the departmental level. The authors are, in my opinion, calling out scholars and other educators for failing to adequately address the issue of diversity in the scholarship being published and, more importantly, the departments within which the scholarship is produced. Personally, I like to say that we all need to "get in the trenches" and do the hard and dirty work necessary for change.

I often wonder, what exactly *are* programs doing to create a sense of belonging for members of HMGs? For example, Simmons and Wahl (2016) argue that "administrators at PWI[s] are failing to maintain productive relationships with African American students" (p. 232). My experience has been that this is true for them as well as other students of color, and even more so when they are graduate students. Graduate school requires more autonomy, and if someone is entering higher education with multiple cultural disadvantages, then they are being set up for failure if adequate support is not in place.

I am using "cultural disadvantage" to reference the lack of knowledge one has coming into an organizational culture, by no fault of their own. New members must learn how the organization functions, but if safeguards are not in place or the culture is uninviting, then the cultural disadvantage becomes weightier. They can also increase in number when a person has membership in one or more marginalized groups (see Bailey-Fakhoury & Frierson, 2014). Thus, when coupled with their general cultural disadvantage, the new member is destined to fail or barely survive. I can personally attest to the reality of these structural barriers that have been erected to impede the progress of HMGs. Low or no expectations of my/our success, (un)intentionally being excluded from social events, and being treated like a token are examples of some of the barriers that can render us invisible in these institutions. These and many other experiences are interpreted through an intersectional lens—raced, gendered, and classed—that whites often times cannot understand. Dare I say, some do not even want to attempt to do so. Unfortunately, HMGs are part of organizations that were not designed for our success; therefore, it should not be surprising that efforts to minimize or dismiss our experiences abound. Granted, some universities and businesses have established offices focused on DEI, but I cannot help but wonder if there is a genuine desire for equity and inclusion. Are they truly concerned with the possibility that faculty and students from HMGs often times suffer from imposter syndrome because assumptions are made about their very presence on campus? Are policies and procedures in place to help us cope with the microaggressions we frequently encounter from students and colleagues? Will perpetrators be held accountable if their microaggressions are reported? Better yet, when we report them, will we be believed or will our claims be dismissed? These are just a few examples of things HMGs think about on a daily basis as we attempt to navigate these organizational cultures where not much is done, beyond recruiting and hiring non-whites, to create a truly inclusive and supportive organizational culture.

While this does not apply to all organizations, many of them have what I call a "culture of resistance," whereby microcultural identities, or identities representative of nondominant and historically oppressed groups, are undervalued, which mirrors what is going on in larger society. Not surprisingly, this makes it difficult for those of us with multiple marginalized identities to acclimate and feel connected to the culture (Hotchkins, 2017; Hurtado, 2015). Matters are further complicated when the institution fails to implement safeguards that ensure our success and comfort (Ramasubramanian & Miles, 2018). My experience and research show that

40 TINA M. HARRIS

diversity, equity, and inclusion are treated as separate entities, if at all, which means that those safeguards may have never been an option.

Whenever I read anything related to DEI prior to working on this book chapter, I was flummoxed to see that the trifecta was treated as separate entities with little to no connection to each other. I pondered for quite some time to understand why that was the case, and it was after reading the work of scholars Putnam-Walkerly and Russell (2016) that my thoughts were crystallized. I recognized that many people were misusing and lacked a true understanding of the term DEI, and it is Putnam-Walkerly and Russell's essay that does what I believe is an excellent job in providing the clarity necessary for explaining what I believe are the intended definitions of these terms and the role they are expected to play in creating inclusive spaces. The authors used the Race Equity and Inclusion Action Guide (REIAG) developed by a philanthropic organization, the Annie E. Casey Foundation (2015), to make a compelling case for rearticulating the true essence of DEI. The REIAG stressed that "Building a proactive framework for addressing issues of race begins with having a clear understanding and vision of racial equity and inclusion" (n.p.). While they have limited their focus to race, I argue that the same position can be taken when it comes to gender, sexual orientation, class, and other marginalized statuses; however, because racism (and ethnocentrism) remains a volatile sociopolitical issue in the U.S., it is imperative that I use that prism to articulate a more nuanced understanding of DEI.

Diversity

For as long as I can recall, the word "diversity" has been a buzzword in many professional settings. Eventually, it began to ring hollow for people, thus lacking the fervor it was intended to have for inspiring and ultimately creating inclusive professional and personal spaces. Whether it be corporations or institutions of higher learning, the rhetoric communicated to society suggested that there was a commitment to having racially, ethnically, and culturally diverse spaces where the diversity was on visual display. In other words, the physical composition of the employees, customers, and others would reflect the diversity that exists in the world and/or local community. The public rhetoric used to promote or, at the very least, acknowledge a perceived interest in diversity carried a subtext that the organization was receptive to a cultural shift and ready to accept its new/future employees, leaders, and students from HMGs; however as Wade (2019) noted, there remains a sizable disconnect between the perception and reality of the relationship between diversity and inclusion.

On a very basic level, diversity refers to the "numerical representation of different types of people" (Putnam-Walkerly & Russell, 2016). Discovering this definition was a eureka moment for me because it helped me realize the disconnect between diversity, equity, and inclusion, a disconnect glaringly and painfully apparent to HMG members. In reviewing the literature and data on institutional and organizational diversity, I found that this is the "go-to" definition that many institutions are using to measure the racial/ethnic change occurring in their homogenous spaces. They boast of achieving certain diversity goals because of an increased number of applicants from these underrepresented groups, which engenders a sense of accomplishment that is heightened when those applicants become employees, students, and faculty. The assumption is that the institutions have achieved the daunting task of dismantling homogeneity through the mere act of shifting the demographic, which is problematic and disturbing. Equity and inclusion are part of the diversity discourse, and as my research has revealed, they are given minimal consideration, even when all three words are presented as part of a trifecta.

According to Roberson (2006), "diversity may be defined in terms of observable and nonobservable characteristics" (p. 214), with early definitions noting observable characteristics such as race, ethnicity, gender, and age. Over time, the definition has come to include non-observable characteristics that impact interaction, which Roberson identifies as being "cultural, cognitive, and technical differences" related to "education, functional background, organizational tenure, socioeconomic background, and personality" (p. 214). While these differences and qualities directly inform how people identify and define themselves, I believe it is paramount that we acknowledge the horrible reality that they also have the potential to signal biases, prejudices, and stereotypes held by some of the organizational members. These ideologies ultimately contribute to the preservation of the structural barriers that prevent the progress towards and evolution of organizations into diverse *and* inclusive spaces.

Equity

In doing a thorough, though not exhaustive, review of the literature on DEI, I found that "equity" was generally understood to mean "fairness." This "fairness" was reduced to the idea that, by merely having the opportunity to gain membership into an organization, microcultural group members have helped those organizations achieve their goal of equity. In other words, equity is a byproduct of diversity. Using a health context, the REIAG defines equity "as the absence of disparities in health (and in its key social determinants) that are systematically associated with social advantage/disadvantage" (n.p.). In order for there to be "absences," a plan by institutions must exist to first, identify and second, actively eliminate disparities between

42 TINA M. HARRIS

the macroculture (i.e., dominant group) and all other microcultures that are disenfranchised. Braveman (2014) offered a clear and more nuanced definition of equity that speaks to an active approach to leveling the playing field in a world where microcultures are perpetually at a disadvantage.

> Health equity is the principle underlying a commitment to reduce—and, ultimately, eliminate—disparities in health and in its determinants, including social determinants. Pursuing health equity means striving for the highest possible standard of health for all people and giving special attention to the needs of those at greatest risk of poor health, based on social conditions.

Using a health prism is one of the best ways to help people understand social injustices or inequities that are being ignored when it comes to DEI. People are able to understand the gravity and unfairness of health disparities when data reveal patterns in the lack of care marginalized communities are receiving. Their health is at risk due to a system designed to primarily benefit people of higher social status and the racial majority. The fact that this disparity oftentimes results in dire physical consequences (i.e., death, chronic illness) makes it somewhat easier for people to comprehend. I do want to stress, however, that because (in)equity in educational and workplace settings manifests differently, there are minimal expectations of a commitment to reduce disparities in these contexts. I use this lens to demonstrate how DEI is disconnected from an expectation that a plan is in place to help the organizational culture adapt to the changing landscape (emerging demographic shifts) that is evolving.

My experience and research have led me to conclude that self-reflexivity is an essential part of restructuring how we conceptualize and engage with DEI. Self-reflexivity is typically associated with qualitative research and the researcher's role in it (Palaganas et al. 2017). It means that the researcher has "a certain level of consciousness," is engaged in "self-awareness," and is "actively involved in the research process" (p. 427). In the context of DEI, I argue that the "researcher" is the organizational leader who has the responsibility to always engage in self-awareness of the role that they, the organization, and other leaders play in changing the culture. This means that they must do a considerable amount of work in developing and implementing "inclusive practices" (Becker, 1998, p. 451) that foster a sense of belonging and connection in microcultural group members. This also requires a considerable amount of self-reflection as well as a well-thought-out plan for determining to what extent each person is contributing directly or indirectly to the barriers preventing optimal DEI from being attained. Holding people accountable for their role in perpetuating systemic oppression is certainly uncomfortable, but it is vital to the ideal goals of DEI. Frankly, recognizing the role of accountability in this process is critical because it lessens the gap in the perception and reality of workplace inclusion and diversity

(Wade, 2019). Addressing these behaviors and attitudes while also putting processes and structures in place better positions the institution in creating a culture that is a safe and healthy space for microcultural group members.

My research revealed a disappointing yet unsurprising trend in how institutions view and understand the idea of fairness. Most institutions give very little consideration to the fairness that people of color (POC) experience once they have entrée into that space. I found it quite telling that, according to the data, it is generally presumed that equity exists because the marginalized person(s) has been admitted or hired based on their merit. This pattern prompted me to question the extent to which efforts being made *truly* foster fairness within the organizational culture. I have done research on racial microaggressions occurring on college campuses (Harris et al., 2018), and my findings further bolster longstanding arguments that POC are subjected to racist, prejudiced, discriminatory, and biased behaviors (Pettit, 2001) that have an adverse effect on their success and ability to thrive in their new environment. Depending on a variety of factors, students may either compartmentalize these experiences or view nearly all other experiences as being racial, thus making their matriculation through graduate school even more difficult than it typically should be. Being unfairly graded, unmentored, isolated, and stereotyped, among other acts (Ates & Eslami, 2012), are direct manifestations of the systemic oppression upon which these institutions were founded. These acts, individually and collectively, contribute to the failure of said institutions to ensure that they have done their due diligence in adapting the organizational culture to their diverse communities. They also contribute to racial battle fatigue (Hotchkins, 2017).

As Smith, Hung, and Franklin (2011) explain, "racism and racial microaggressions operate as psycho-pollutants in the social environment and add to the overall race-related stress for Black men, Black women, and other racially marginalized groups" (p. 67). I can personally attest to the toll these infractions and oppressions can have on your whole being. They can be debilitating to your mind, body, and spirit, and having to deal with all of that on your own and in a toxic environment is a devastating and harsh reality many are either unwilling or refuse to face due to voluntary or involuntary complicity. My colleagues of color and I have experienced (and continue to experience) racial microaggressions (RMAs) firsthand as graduate students, faculty, and administrators, and, despite being "on the battlefield" for quite some time, we have survived our wounds and continue the fight for social justice in these spaces, even when we face inevitable resistance. We are keenly aware that, by doing nothing or very little to change the organizational culture, the powers that be and other conforming community members are actively and systematically contributing to a toxic work or educational environment that is having a profoundly adverse effect (Ramasubramanian & Miles, 2018). We also know that our presence is superficially accepted, which means that we must grapple with the reality that institutions are doing nearly nothing to ensure that we are included and given access to opportunities and resources traditionally denied us. This oversight can hinder our success and ultimately leads to feelings of isolation, which is directly tied to the idea of exclusion (i.e., need for inclusion) (Razzante & Tracy, 2019). As the next section will demonstrate, inclusion is much like diversity and equity in that it is treated as a separate entity and conceptualized in equally troubling ways.

Inclusion

According to Putnam-Walkerly and Russell (2016), the REIAG defines inclusion as "the action or state of including or being included within a group or structure ... [Unlike diversity,] inclusion involves an authentic and empowered participation and a true sense of belonging." Inclusion is the third piece of the trifecta that many institutions proclaim they are embracing and promoting. Research tells us that there are far more institutions that fail at creating an inclusive environment than those who have successfully done so. In order to reverse this, I strongly believe that there needs to be a commitment to social justice (Charity-Hudley, 2018) on a much deeper and more meaningful level. Riddell (2009) notes that, in the case of other underrepresented groups, such as students with "learning disabilities and social emotional and behavioural difficulties," schools do not have the adequate resources "to support mainstreaming" (p. 283) these populations into the existing organizational culture. "Mainstreaming" here is used to reference an assimilation to the dominant culture and is directly tied to behaviors over which a person has no control. These aspects of their identities are immutable and deemed a barrier to their ability to function in society, which is similar to how their raced and gendered peers are minimally socialized into the culture. As HMGs, we are expected to assimilate because our racial and gender differences are viewed as physical characteristics having no impact on our identities, lived experiences, or worldviews. There is an assumption that we are to completely immerse ourselves into the dominant culture, thus denying our race, ethnicity, and culture. This way of thinking would not be problematic if said culture were not steeped in white supremacist ideological frameworks where Whiteness[5] was normalized and the standard by which all others are measured (Asante, 2019). Thus, as members of HMGs, we are subjected to pressures and issues that White and (fe)male peers are not.

Wellin (2008) identified four specific issues that these circumstances create for marginalized groups and, relatedly, the institution in question.

DISMANTLING THE TRIFECTA **45**

I would like to stress that these issues become amplified and potentially introduce others when institutions ignore them or do very little to address them in response to its changing demographic landscape and culture. As previously noted, issue one speaks to the failure of institutions to critique the meaning of demographic shifts. An influx of HMG members requires the institution to redefine itself, since its very identity is changing. Similarly, the tension between individualist and collectivist cultures, which is the second issue, resides within all organization members. The organization reflects a collectivistic culture, and the tension arises when the new HMG member enters, for example. They are a person negotiating their individual identity that is separate from their professional identity in hopes of meshing with the collective identity and culture. This tension ultimately leads to the third issue, which is the pressure to reconcile those competing identities. Unfortunately, the institution forces HMG members into the difficult position of having to deal with multiple fears and stressors (Wellin, 2008) that their white peers do not. Lastly, HMG members bring communication styles to the culture that very likely are different from those of dominant group members, increasing the likelihood of intercultural conflict. Rather than recognize this tension as a manifestation of diversity, institutions frame it as a call for assimilation. Assimilation is the expectation that new cultural group members (i.e., outgroup members) will adapt to the dominant culture and minimize connections to their group of origin. In this case, HMGs are often times expected downplay their identities.

In short, a schism remains between diversity, equity, and inclusion. Institutions are treating them as if they are individual entities and organizational ideologies that need to be addressed as such. While the literature demonstrates that there is a basic understanding of what these concepts are, we are still missing the mark. Institutions and powers that be are either unable or unwilling to connect the proverbial dots, which I argue requires a racial social justice lens. In order to get there, it is imperative that there be genuine interest in restructuring the organization to adapt to its internal changes. Organizations must engage in serious self-reflexivity on individual and institutional levels in order to achieve the goal of truly being multicultural.

INTEGRATING DEI

Sison (2017) identified a very serious issue in how organizations deal with diversity. A negative outcome has been that diversity has achieved the exact opposite of what it is allegedly trying to achieve: exclusion and perceived bias. She further stated that "organizations need to refocus on

46 TINA M. HARRIS

inclusion [in order] to gain the full advantages of diversity" (p. 130); however, she explained that the data continue to demonstrate that organizations with a focus on diversity are directing very little attention to inclusion, "partly because of the lack of clarity about inclusion, from academic and workplace experts" (p. 132). The definition that I believe best captures and resolves the issue of the disconnect between the three concepts is the one offered by accounting firm, Deloitte (2013). Inclusion is described as an "active process of change or integration, as well as an outcome, such as a feeling of belonging," and, according to their own research, inclusion is achieved when employees perceive "fairness and respect" and "value and belonging" being fostered within the organization (p. 12). Their research bolsters my assertion of a disconnect within the trifecta (Robertson, 2006), and that organizational self-reflexivity can actually create a welcoming climate with "inclusive elements" in conjunction with diversity. Such is the case with Deloitte, who concluded that this can lead to higher employee engagement, which is really what all organizations are striving for.

According to Pasztor (2019), how organizations frame diversity is a contributing factor to the schism. After conducting a summative content analysis and framing analysis of 15 of the top 20 corporate websites recognized as "top-ranked" in the area of diversity management, she found that organizations use three primary approaches in how diversity and isolation are framed:

> First, as an organizational asset promoted and preserved through its human resources and corporate values; second, as a driver of business excellence and competitive advantage; and finally, as a structural mechanism supported by diversity and inclusion initiatives such as employee mentoring, networking, diversity training, and institutionalized governance. (p. 455)

Pasztor concluded that these websites are symbolic and critical to "contemporary representations of impression management among stakeholders, stockholders, and employees" (p. 455). The organizations and their members are successful in embodying the true essence of DEI by (assumedly) management and other power figures actively engaging in the process of adapting to changing demographics. This also requires that organizational members on all levels be involved in order to ensure that change is going to occur and be sustainable. They are putting into action ways of thinking about and responding to diversity that others are not. In the case of Deloitte, they have recognized and moved on the fact that social inclusion is a vital ingredient in the process of fostering new and inclusive spaces (Becker, 1998). This process has also included organizations being attuned and responsive to the perceptions that employees have of these diversity climates (Roberson, 2006).

WHERE DO WE GO FROM HERE?

In reviewing the literature and data on DEI, I am disappointed yet encouraged that there were no clear or consistent solutions for solving this pervasive social issue. I am disappointed because there has been a history of lip service. Diversity has been a buzzword for decades, and while the general public seems to have a basic understanding of what it means, the same can be said for institutions throughout the world. The ideological framework for organizational change has been extended to include equity and inclusion; however, more must be done in order to synthesize these concepts and transform them from being an idea to a process (Becker, 1998; Deloitte, 2013; Roberson, 2006). Thus, I am using the Race Equity and Inclusion Action Guide (REIAG) developed by the private philanthropic organization, Annie E. Casey Foundation. (While there is a clear focus on race here, I extend this to include gender, culture, ethnicity, sexual orientation, and other social identities contributing to inequities and other forms of systemic oppression.) It describes itself as an organization that "creates brighter futures for the nation's children by developing solutions to strengthen families, building paths to economic opportunity and transforming struggling communities into safer and healthier places to live, work and grow" (n.p.). In their document, they have a statement explaining the purpose of the guide, which was written "in partnership with Terry Keleher, thought leadership and practice specialist at Race Forward: The Center for Racial Justice Innovations" (n.p.). They also explain that the Foundation and Keleher have both developed and are using tools to help them advance their goals of promoting race equity. Their guide outlines seven steps that should be followed in order to achieve *true* diversity, equity, and inclusion that goes beyond characteristics, alleged fairness, and exclusion.

The first step involves an institution *establish[ing] an understanding of race equity and inclusion principles* (p. 1), and that requires all invested parties or institutional members having a shared understanding of what these various concepts mean. The guide explains that a challenge of effective interracial communication "is to move people from the narrow and individualized definition of racism to a more comprehensive and systemic awareness. To illuminate racism, we need to 'name it, frame it and explain it'" (p. 4). This approach is in keeping with how my co-author, Mark Orbe, and I (2015) define and conceptualize racism for our readers. Racial differences sometimes become a salient issue for people during everyday conversations, and when at least one person defines or understands racism as being "racial prejudice + societal power," then achieving race equity and inclusion is impossible. I have witnessed many colleagues professing a commitment to DEI, but then choosing to purposely erect barriers for

48 TINA M. HARRIS

HMG members in very subtle yet disturbing ways. Somehow, the rules of the game change without warning, and the graduate student or faculty member is forced to learn the new rules however they can, despite how unfair it may be. I have expended considerable emotional labor mentoring and counseling people through these traumatic events, while keeping a wary eye on a colleague. I resigned myself to the fact that calling out racism sometimes is in vain, as the perpetrator will never admit their egregious behavior; therefore, I "get in the trenches" with the violated and do whatever I can to demonstrate that other strategies for inclusion exist that oftentimes come from others similarly oppressed. Inclusion involves informal wellness checks, occasional emails of support, and career advice and encouragement.

The REIAG further explains that investors should have a shared language to be used to create a narrative that makes it easier "to communicate the commitment to racial equity, both internally and externally" (p. 1). Shared language also "creates a platform for coordinated work toward equitable outcomes" (p. 1). Dialogues about race can be very difficult and generate negative feelings, such as guilt, anger, and shame (Orbe & Harris, 2015), as well as grievances (REIAG, n.d.); therefore, it is imperative that organizations have these difficult conversations about the "causes, effects, systems and solutions" (p. 4). The REIAG identifies five basic elements that contribute to effective issue framing, which are: (1) shared values at stake; (2) the problem; (3) the cause; (4) the solution; and (5) the action needed. Collectively, they achieve the goal of establishing the race equity and inclusion principles for the organization. It has been my experience that, when committees convene around the issue of DEI, it is the same people sitting at the table and includes a few faculty from one or more HMGs who feel tokenized. These efforts sometimes fail because we are "preaching to the choir," and DEI have become "buzzwords" with little to no meaning. To bring about true transformation, we have to remain in the trenches and diligent in all efforts to directly address systemic oppression, even if it means making some people uncomfortable.

The second step is pretty straightforward and commonsensical, yet it seems to be a considerable oversight: *engage affected populations and stakeholders.* The REIAG stresses how critical it is to include POC, particularly since they can speak to how systemic racism, or what they refer to as "systemic racialization," has functioned to exclude them from essential aspects of the organizational culture, such as "decision making, civic participation and power" (p. 4). It further describes POC as being "the most direct stakeholders" in the fight to eliminate racism, who have insider knowledge of and personal experiences with the impact of systemic racism on their very being. As such, the REIAG argues that POC "must have a role in social-change efforts along with whites" (p. 4). Inclusion in the early stages allows the organization to directly benefit from engaging diverse stakeholders with active and authentic connections to the different communities of which they are a part. Such an investment works to "ensure meaningful participation, voice and ownership," while also increasing the speed with which the organization can move from "theory to practice" in the creation of equitable opportunities that will be of direct benefit to the communities they are serving.

As the nation's first endowed chair of race, media, and cultural literacy, I am being connected with a number of people in positions of power and influence who have a genuine interest in DEI. Their interest translates into meaningful discussions about how to be a part of the change they want to see. This part excites me because it allows me to translate theory into practice by using my research to make a difference in the world in real time.

Step three, *gather[ing] and analyz [ing] disaggregated data*, requires that institutions gather data on themselves that is broken up across demographics, including but not limited to race, gender, and class. This is a form of self-reflexivity that allows institutions to determine how they can best achieve DEI by creating "improvement efforts, quality assurance, supervision and accountability processes" (p. 7) that directly benefit the communities they are serving. The REIAG also stresses that "it is critical to design a set of research questions that will help to identify the type of data needed" for a given institution. I have decades of anecdotal evidence to support many of the claims regarding the disconnected trifecta, but it is my current research project that is generating data exemplary of this specific principle. I am conducting in-depth interviews with students of color (SOC) about race issues on campus and in the local community. A recurring theme is that there are currently no programs in place designed to make them feel connected to the university. The students explained that there are groups and programs targeted to them, but they are in name only. They feel that they are being seen and treated as if they are monolithic, all belonging to one race. There was a cry, per se, for the university to do its homework (i.e., gather data) and make concerted efforts to truly understand the interests and needs of its student body.

Step four requires that an organization *conduct systems analysis of root causes of inequities* (p. 8), which requires it to get at "the root causes of differential outcomes" and "takes into account the convergence of race, place, class and history" (p. 8). While all of the steps are valuable and essential, this step is more so because it challenges organizational members to adopt a structural perspective that draws attention to the existent policies and practices that either unintentionally or intentionally perpetuate systemic racism, thus reproducing racial inequities. The REIAG further stresses that this knowledge can lead to "informed and strategic decisions about how to interrupt and change inequitable patterns" (p. 8). This involves a holistic

50 TINA M. HARRIS

approach to addressing and tackling systemic racism, with the end goal being to identify the causes and offer transformative solutions to such inequities.

I taught an undergraduate interracial communication class one semester that addressed this very issue. A group chose to address the issue of DEI by addressing their outrage with the university's history with slavery through a proposed program or initiative to rename buildings dedicated to racists, slaveowners, and confederates. The group was primarily concerned with what they believed was the university's failure to hold up its alleged commitment to inclusion. Although it claimed to have achieved diversity and equity by admitting SOC, the institution continued to fail in acknowledging this racist legacy and how it serves as an enduring reminder to SOC that they do not belong.

Step five moves the institution closer to its own inequities by *identify[ing] strategies and target resources to address root causes of inequities* to reduce racial disparities while "increasing racial equity" (p. 9). This step is a difficult but important one. There are so many different ways that these inequities manifest themselves, and even more reasons for why addressing them is essential, but the resources to do so are limited. Thus, it is imperative that institutions do the dirty work (i.e., work in the trenches) necessary for remedying these institutional wrongs. For example, what can be done to address the pay inequity when there are two faculty of the same rank, status, and gender, but the only difference is race? Is the white faculty member benefiting from her privilege? Is the faculty member of color being penalized because of her race? Quite frankly, I have asked myself these questions throughout my career, and my gut tells me the answer is "yes." Administrators may explain away the issue by producing budget data and other information to rebut the presumption of discrimination; however, the issue remains. While it may be hard to pinpoint specific behaviors contributing to them, those in power need to be willing to face the hard truths and actively seek change.

Step six requires that an organization *conduct Race Equity Impact Assessment for all policies and decision-making*. The REIAG describes this as "a systematic examination of how a proposed action or decision will likely affect different racial and ethnic groups" (p. 10).

This step directly addresses the void in the literature on DEI and the issues with initiatives by centering on policies that impact HMGs. This involves evaluating the impact such strategies have on dismantling systemic oppression. If programs and policies have been implemented, then are they *really* creating a more welcoming environment? Can a unit or department honestly do a self-assessment and expect that the feedback is accurate? Will organizational members be open to sharing how they truly feel about the program, not to mention those who have power over them? This is where having external firms not affiliated with the institution or the unit gathering the data is vital. They are a neutral third-party with no vested interest, which may engender trustworthiness amongst all parties and increase the likelihood that real change and transformation can occur.

Step seven is a long-term strategy and involves institutions engaging the process to *continuously evaluate effectiveness and adapt strategies*, which means it will be in what I am calling a perpetual state of self-reflexivity. The REIAG's description of this stage provides hope that institutional change is possible. It explains that, in an effort to remove the barriers that are systemically negatively impacting HMGs, institutions should be adopting, implementing, and refining strategies that were created to "promote policy change, system reform and program delivery" (REIAG, p. 12). Doing so will get them closer to achieving equity and sustainable outcomes. The guide also stresses that this step should be repeated on a consistent basis, thus allowing the institution to determine whether or not its racial equity goals are being achieved and making the necessary adjustments towards that end. Organizations must recognize the value in regular self-assessment and self-reflexivity if truly dedicated to DEI and creating inclusive climates. If this step is to occur, institutions must be ready for the emotional and material labor that comes with self-reflexivity. Yes, this means facing hard truths that are difficult to accept, and energies must be exerted on changing the organizational culture so that its traditions, beliefs, and values are reflective of the diversity that defines it.

FINAL THOUGHTS

Implementing a process where DEI is a true priority is a reasonable and appropriate one that can lead to organizational transformation. Moreover, it can be a catalyst for success for members of HMGs who have been denied access to certain resources (Bailey-Fakhoury & Frierson, 2014) and are negatively impacted by systemic oppression on micro and macro levels. This seven-step process stresses the importance of dialogue and collaboration as being pivotal to institutions making connections between diversity, equity, and inclusion. While many people, including myself, hail from diverse backgrounds and are subjected to systemic oppression, there are even more who are direct benefactors thereof. Thus, I believe it is imperative that all institutional members be involved—down in the trenches—in every phase of the development, implementation, and assessment of strategies, programs, or policies designed to promote DEI on a deeper and more impactful level. It is only through these efforts that true change can occur.

As noted earlier, Schreiber (1996) stressed how businesses should, first, learn from academia and directly address "larger issues…revolving around sharing power and valuing difference." Personally, I cannot stress enough how hard institutions and their members must work to actively avoid

52 TINA M. HARRIS

tokenizing new members and create a *true* culture of inclusion. This also means that, according to the second issue, there must be a commitment to the establishment of participatory hierarchical structures that ultimately dismantle systemic racism by "dissolving barriers and creating unity" (p. 459). While I cannot offer solutions, this chapter has at least laid the foundation upon which to build an argument for a reconceptualization of what DEI means and how it can be achieved. This requires that all organizations must first take a hard look in the mirror and identify their failings in how they conceptualize DEI and treat them as three separate entities. Once that hard work has begun, it can then engage and inspire all members to delve deeper into how HMG members are acclimating to the culture. Above all else, I believe that these efforts must be guided by a dedication and commitment to social justice through the creation of an inclusive organization whose purpose is to dismantle racism and other forms of systemic oppression in powerful and substantive ways.

Following the lead of Deloitte (2013), I believe all members of these institutions, in this case, higher education—including administrators, staff, faculty, and students—can play a critical role in producing valuable DEI initiatives, programs, and scholarship that eventually create sustainable processes for organizational transformation and adaptation in an ever-changing world. It is the historically marginalized who remain incredibly vulnerable to the various hierarchies guiding and defining our society; thus, I challenge us *all* to remain committed to dismantling metaphorical ideological monuments that preserve the racial disparities continuing to plague the oppressed in very troubling and problematic ways.

DISCUSSION QUESTIONS

1. What is my university doing to foster diversity, equity, and inclusion?
2. In reviewing the mission statement and other public documents, how are they aligning with actions of my university? Are they "walking the walk"?
3. How can my department or university overcome its reputation for being exclusionary?
4. What process is in place that can allow students, faculty, and staff to address behaviors that contribute to a hostile work environment without fear of retribution?
5. What resources are available to help institutions implement programs that can facilitate and encourage intergroup dialogue about these important issues?

6. What is the most effective way to correct prejudiced and discriminatory behavior? How likely is it to lead to long-term success?

7. As a student, what kinds of changes would you like to see happen on your campus? How likely are they to bring the change that is needed to make everyone feel included?

8. What are some successful strategies you have seen your university use to address the issue of isolation for its students? What is being done to make students feel connected and reduce the likelihood of attrition?

NOTES

1. I am capitalizing Blacks and using lower case for whites to acknowledge the continued power imbalance and unequal treatment across racial lines that continues to exist in society, as per Toure in Who's Afraid of Post-Blackness? What It Means to Be Black.

2. As a woman who identifies interchangeably as Black and African American, I am choosing to capitalize Black as a formal connection to this aspect of my identity.

3. I will be using "organization" and "institution" interchangeably, since the literature refers to these contexts frequently in addressing DEI. Their interchangeableness is an acknowledgement that both contexts are equally important.

4. The terms "institution" and "organization" will be used as a general term to collectively reference colleges, universities, businesses, and religious institutions.

5. I prefer to capitalize Blackness in order to recognize the rich complexities of a people group who have been rendered cultureless; therefore, I use Whiteness for the purpose of parity.

REFERENCES

Annie E. Casey Foundation (2015, January 8). Race equity and inclusion action guide. *The Annie E. Casey Foundation.* Retrieved from https://ssir.org/articles/entry/what_the_heck_does_equity_mean

Asante, G. A. (2019). #RhetoricSoWhite and US centered: Reflections on challenges and opportunities. *Quarterly Journal of Speech,* 105(4), 484–488. https://doi-org.libezp.lib.lsu.edu/10.1080/00335630.2019.1669892

Ates, B., & Eslami, Z. (2012). An analysis of non-native English-speaking graduate teaching assistants' online journal entries. *Language & Education: An International Journal,* 26(6), 537–552. https://doi-org.libezp.lib.lsu.edu/10.1080/09500782.2012.669766

Bailey-Fakhoury, C. & Frierson, C. M. (2014). White institutions: Fostering their academic success using african american motherwork strategies. *Journal of Progressive Policy & Practice,* 2(3), 213-228.

54 TINA M. HARRIS

Becker, P. E. (1998). Making inclusive communities: Congregations and the "problem" of race. *Social Problems*, 45(4), 451–472. https://doi-org.libezp.lib.lsu.edu/10.2307/3097207

Braveman, P. (2014). What are health disparities and health equity? We need to be clear. *Public Health Reports*, 129(1_suppl2), 5–8. https://doi.org/10.1177/00333549141291S203

Charity-Hudley, A. H. (2018). Engaging and supporting underrepresented undergraduate students in Linguistic Research and across the University. *Journal of English Linguistics*, 46(3), 199–214. https://doi-org.libezp.lib.lsu.edu/10.1177/0075424218783445

Deloitte (2013). Waiter, is that inclusion in my soup? A new recipe to improve business performance. Retrieved from Sydney: http://www2.deloitte.com/content/dam/Deloitte/au/Documents/human-capital/deloitte-au-hc-diversity-inclusion-soup-0513.pdf

Gill, G. K., McNally, M. J., & Berman, V. (2018). Effective diversity, equity, and inclusion practices. *Healthcare Management Forum*, 31(5), 196–199. https://doi.org/10.1177/0840470418773785

Goethe, E. V., & Colina, C. M. (2018). Taking advantage of diversity within the classroom. *Journal of Chemical Education*, 95(2), 189–192. https://doi.org/10.1021/acs.jchemed.7b00510

Hartwell, E. E., Cole, K., Donovan, S. K., Greene, R. L., Burrell Storms, S. L., & Williams, T. (2017). Breaking down silos: Teaching for equity, diversity, and inclusion across disciplines. *Humboldt Journal of Social Relations*, 39, 143–162.

Harris, T. M., Janovec, A., Murray, S., Gubbala, S., & Robinson, A. (2018). Communicating racism: A study of racial microaggressions in a southern university and the local community. *Southern Communication Journal*, 84(2), 72–84, https://doi.org/10.1080/1041794X.2018.1492008

Hotchkins, B. (2017). Black women students at predominantly White universities: Narratives of identity politics, well-being and leadership mobility. *NASPA Journal About Women in Higher Education*. https://doi.org/10.1080/19407882.2017.1326943

Hurtado, S. (2015). Thinking about race: The salience of racial identity at two- and four-year colleges and the climate for diversity. *The Journal of Higher Education*, 86(1), 127–155. https://doi.org/10.1353/jhe.2015.0000

Joseph, R. L. (2017). What's the difference with "difference"? Equity, communication, and the politics of difference. *International Journal of Communication*, 11, 21.

Lerner, J. E., & Fulambarker, A. (2018). Beyond diversity and inclusion: Creating a social justice agenda in the classroom. *Journal of Teaching in Social Work*, 38(1), 43–53. https://doi.org/10.1080/08841233.2017.1398198

Maranto, C. L., & Griffin, A. E. (2011). The antecedents of a 'chilly climate' for women faculty in higher education. *Human Relations*, 64(2), 139–159. https://doi-org.libezp.lib.lsu.edu/10.1177/0018726710377932

Orbe, M., & Harris, T. M. (2015). *Interracial communication: Theory to practice* (3rd ed.).Thousand Oaks, CA: Sage Publications.

Palaganas, E. C., Sanchez, M. C., Molintas, M. P., & Caricativo, R. D. (2017). Reflexivity in qualitative research: A journey of learning. *The Qualitative Report*, 22(2), 426–438. Retrieved from https://nsuworks.nova.edu/tqr/vol22/iss2/5.

Pasztor, S. K. (2019). Exploring the framing of diversity rhetoric in "Top-Rated in Diversity" organizations. *International Journal of Business Communication*, 56(4), 455–475. https://doi-org.libezp.lib.lsu.edu/10.1177/2329488416664175

Pettit, S. (2011). Teachers' beliefs about English language learners in the mainstream classroom: A review of the literature. *International Multilingual Research Journal*, 5(2), 123–147. https://doi-org.libezp.lib.lsu.edu/10.1080/19313152.2011.594357

Putnam-Walkerly, K., & Russell, E. (2016, September 15). What the heck does 'equity' mean? *Stanford Social Innovation Review*. Retrieved from https://ssir.org/articles/entry/what_the_heck_does_equity_mean

Riddell, S. (2009). Social justice, equality and inclusion in Scottish education. *Discourse: Studies in the Cultural Politics of Education*, 30(3), 283–296. https://doi-org.libezp.lib.lsu.edu/10.1080/01596300903036889

Roberson, Q. M. (2006). Disentangling the meanings of diversity and inclusion in organizations. *Group & Organization Management*, 31(2), 212–236. https://doi-org.libezp.lib.lsu.edu/10.1177/1059601104273064

Ramasubramanian, S., & Miles, C. (2018). White Nationalist Rhetoric, Neoliberal Multiculturalism and Colour Blind Racism: Decolonial critique of Richard Spencer's Campus Visit. *Javnost - The Public*. https://doi.org/10.1080/13183222.2018.1463352

Razzante, R., & Tracy, S. (2019). Co-cultural theory: Performing emotional labor from a position of exclusion. In C. Liberman (Ed.), *Casing communication theory* (pp. 117–130). Dubuque, IA: Kendall Hunt.

Schreiber, E. J. (1996). Muddles and huddles: Facilitating a multicultural workforce through team management theory. *Journal of Business Communication*, 33(4), 459–473. https://doi-org.libezp.lib.lsu.edu/10.1177/002194369603300406

Simmons, J., & Wahl, S. T. (2016). Rethinking inclusion and diversity in communication education research. *Communication Education*, 65(2), 232–235. https://doi-org.libezp.lib.lsu.edu/10.1080/03634523.2015.1098711.

Sison, M. D. (2017). Communicating across, within and between, cultures: Toward inclusion and social change. *Public Relations Review*, 43(1), 130–132. https://doi-org.libezp.lib.lsu.edu/10.1016/j.pubrev.2016.10.015

Smith, W., Hung, M., & Franklin, J. (2011). Racial battle fatigue and the miseducation of Black men: Racial microaggressions, societal problems, and environmental stress. *The Journal of Negro Education*, 80(1), 63–82.

Stanley, C. A., Watson, K. L., Reyes, J. M., & Varela, K. S. (2018). Organizational change and the chief diversity officer: A case study of institutionalizing a diversity plan. *Journal of Diversity in Higher Education*. https://doi.org/10.1037/dhe0000099

Wade, R. (2019). How to craft an informative, actionable and measurable conversation about inclusion and diversity. *Communication World*, 1–3.

Wellin, C. (2008). Telling tales out of school: Dilemmas of race and inclusiveness in the liberal academy. *American Behavioral Scientist*, 51(5), 686–708. https://doi-org.libezp.lib.lsu.edu/10.1177/0002764207307750

PART II

INTERPERSONAL CONTEXT: CRITICAL CONVERSATIONS

II

Chapter 4

Scholar-Mothers Navigating Maternal Microaggressions in the Academy: "You Should Be Home Snuggling Your Baby"

Lisa S. Kaler, Leah N. Fulton, Zer Vang, and Michael J. Stebleton

The parallels between motherhood and graduate study conceal themselves from the casual observer. How could raising a child mirror the experiences of learning to think critically, research ethically, and write academically? Both journeys, however, involve uncertainty, the completion of unfamiliar tasks, high levels of stress, and requirements to meet milestones. It should, therefore, feel natural for mothers to pursue graduate degrees. They should be welcomed into the academy and appreciated for the strengths that their mothering skills foster, for their perspective, and for their insight. This is often not the case. Instead, mothers are marginalized, regarded as individuals who do not belong in graduate programs, and judged for choosing to spend time away from their children in a selfish pursuit.

This chapter explores the experiences of three mothers in a higher education doctoral program: Zer, Lisa, and Leah. They share stories of entanglement between motherhood and graduate study, highlighting the many failed diversity moments that threaten to make them feel unwanted in the academy. Fortunately, one of the many gifts that motherhood bestows is resilience. Despite the repeated marginalizing interactions, these women, like many others, are determined to earn their degrees. Their scholarly achievements demonstrate their capabilities while refuting the societal norms that marginalize scholar-mothers.

Each scholar-mother in this chapter chose a different path to degree completion, from full-time student to full-time employment. Their children are preschool-aged or younger, and they have all been pregnant during the doctoral journey. Their differing racial and ethnic identities

60 LISA S. KALER ET AL.

contribute to the diversity of their experiences and perspectives. Their experiences as mothers of young children while pursuing doctoral degrees at a research university create a sense of unity in their diversity. These women recognize that their identities as cisgender, heterosexual, married, biological mothers afford a measure of privilege and do not represent the full spectrum of parenting or mothering pathways and experiences. Together, they have been subjected to assumptions about the role of mothers in rearing children and questions about their place in the academy. Each of their experiences reinforce the racialized nature of motherhood, compounded in academia (DePouw, 2018). Mothers are subjected to a variety of social judgments and expectations. Within the academy, a mother's relationship to race, class, and an assortment of other social identities contributes to differential perceptions and treatment (Anaya, 2011). Rather than presenting a single failed diversity and equity incident, this chapter describes a compilation of incidents and explores their complex effects.

INSTITUTIONAL CONTEXT AND CHAPTER DEVELOPMENT

The Department of Organizational Leadership, Policy, and Development (OLPD) at the University of Minnesota – Twin Cities is part of the College of Education and Human Development. OLPD offers a Ph.D. in higher education in which Zer, Lisa, and Leah are all third-year students. The higher education program's model for graduate students does not follow a traditional cohort model; therefore, students in the same year may reach doctoral milestones at different times. Nonetheless, students in the same year often refer to themselves as a cohort. To accommodate students working full- or part-time, most classes are offered in the evening.

Zer, Lisa, and Leah are the only mothers in their cohort. Throughout their journey, they have exchanged stories, validating and empowering each other to overcome obstacles that arise. When the opportunity to write about failed diversity moments arose, it felt timely to co-author this chapter and share these experiences, which are particularly troubling because they take place in an education program. Education research and practice frequently espouse aspirational ideals in regard to progressive views, equity, and social justice (Harris & Patton, 2018). Nonetheless, praxis within higher education continually fails to achieve these aspirational goals, as demonstrated by persistent gaps in the literature and the negative experiences of marginalized groups (Anaya, 2011).

Mike is an associate professor and coordinator of Higher Education in OLPD. He is the proud father of two children, ages 12 and 8. His partner is also a faculty member at the institution. During his pre-tenure years, he and his partner struggled with the common challenges in dual-career relationships, including parenting young children. Although he did not encounter the same experiences as Zer, Lisa, and Leah, he navigated his own experiences around work-life role demands and balance in the academy. Mike's research interests focus on college student development, including the role of student-faculty interactions on engagement and student success. Mike became interested in this topic of graduate "scholar-mothers" after several conversations with Lisa, who works as a graduate research assistant with Mike and identifies as a scholar-mother. Applying this lens of positive student-faculty engagement, Mike's objective is to encourage other faculty and higher education professionals to be more mindful and supportive of scholar-mothers (and fathers) in the academy.

The writing team for this text held four meetings to discuss the doctoral experience thus far. In these meetings, Zer, Lisa, and Leah shared accounts of their experiences as mothers and graduate students. Mike attended, listened, and synthesized his experience as a faculty-parent and father. These meetings served as opportunities to make sense of challenging incidents that have punctuated graduate school. Based on the stories shared in these meetings, each scholar-mother wrote a narrative account of her graduate studies, focusing on interpersonal interactions that marginalized her; the team considers each of these interactions a failed diversity moment.

Below, we briefly describe literature related to motherhood and academia, offering a theoretical framework through which Zer, Lisa, and Leah interpret their experiences. Each student tells the story of her scholar-mother journey, describing the context in which they arrive on campus each day, the moments of failed diversity, and the effects that the patriarchal academic system and these interactions have on their mental health and their academic and career choices. Then, the team offers a perspective on the connections between these stories, focusing on three main recurring themes. Essential to the meaning-making process was a recognition of the discord between the layers of the ecological systems within which scholar-mothers exist. For example, the question of attending school while mothering evokes multiple (and conflicting) attitudes and behaviors within and between cultural communities, families, classmates, professional settings, and society at large. Mike offers insights from the perspective of a faculty member in the department, developed in conversations with Zer, Lisa, and Leah. The team collaborated to interpret themes across each scholar-mothers' experiences and to offer recommendations for faculty and departmental leaders to encourage the inclusivity of mothers in the academy and in their graduate programs.

62 LISA S. KALER ET AL.

A HISTORY OF TENSION BETWEEN MOTHERHOOD AND ACADEMIA

Scholarship scrutinizing the experiences of mothers in academia dates back several decades. Ward and Wolf-Wendel (2012) explored tensions between motherhood and academia in a 10-year study that followed faculty mothers through their early to mid-careers. Their study highlighted the presence of role conflicts, specifically struggles between the mothering role and faculty role, for mothers in the academy. Although roleconflict theory may be considered a more traditionalist view of gender and work (Barnett & Hyde, 2001), it situates experiences in academia well (Ward & Wolf-Wendel, 2004). The creation of academia by and for cis-hetero, White men reverberates through the ivory tower today, reinforced through traditionalist, racist, and patriarchal structures students must navigate (Harris & Patton, 2018; Mason et al., 2013).

Barnett and Hyde (2001) posited that multiple roles are, in fact, beneficial for both men and women. Reasons for this beneficial relationship include increased opportunities to experience success, increased self-complexity, and an expanded frame of reference. Barnett and Hyde emphasized that while certain conditions make multiple roles beneficial, beyond certain limits, overload and distress may occur.

In Ward and Wolf-Wendel's (2004) study of scholar-mother faculty members, they explored the nature of role conflicts for participants. These women shared stories about the joys of academic work and challenges they faced due to the "greedy" nature of academia and family life. They also felt they never had enough time, despite the flexibility and autonomy of a faculty appointment. Ward and Wolf-Wendel claimed that conflicts do exist between the dual roles of mother and faculty member. Mother-faculty often feel both stress and guilt, as both roles have unending expectations and a short supply of time. Conversely, women in the study shared the benefits of being both mothers and faculty members, echoing Barnett and Hyde's (2001) ideas concerning the positive impacts of multiple roles. Again, there were limits to these benefits: "when either work or home life is threatened or added to, disequilibria, stress, and nonproductivity are likely" (Ward & Wolf-Wendel, 2004, p. 254).

More recently, scholars have explored the experiences of graduate-student mothers as they navigate the academy. Lynch (2008) highlighted the symbolic nature of both mothers and students, examining the interactions of these roles. She also illuminated challenges that graduate-student mothers face, including advisors calling into question a woman's decision to have children during graduate school. Another study emphasized not only challenges within the academy, but familial and relational obstacles that arise for scholar-mothers (Carter et al., 2013). Women in that study shared repeated advice from others that they should terminate their doctoral studies when an obstacle arose. Abetz (2016, 2019) explored discursive struggles and uncertainty faced by scholar-mothers. She emphasized the double standards scholar-mothers face, centering incidents where others question or judge scholar-mothers for pursuing a doctoral degree while having children (Abetz, 2016).

The experiences of the women in Abetz's (2016) study resonate with Zer, Lisa, and Leah's own experiences of feeling questioned and judged for pursuing a Ph.D. while mothering young children. High representation of women in both undergraduate and graduate degree programs contributes to a false perception that the environment is progressive and inclusive (Mason et al., 2013). Marginal treatment of mothers, recounted in this chapter and depicted throughout the literature, demonstrates a more accurate narrative. Zer, Leah, and Lisa's cohort also includes several fathers, and their experiences show that treatment of mothers varies greatly from the treatment of fathers (Carter et al., 2013). This chapter, therefore, gives voices to scholar-mothers, whose ambitions are questioned while their male peers' ambitions are celebrated.

MATERNAL MICROAGGRESSIONS

The interpersonal interactions described in this chapter, which represent failed diversity moments, often take the form of microaggressions (Sue et al., 2007; Torres et al., 2010). Originally associated with insults toward People of Color, Sue et al. (2007) defined microaggressions as "brief, everyday exchanges that send denigrating messages to People of Color because they belong to a racial minority group" (p. 273). Microaggressions have been applied to a number of minoritized identities based on race, ethnicity, citizenship status, abilities, language, age, and gender (Harper, 2013; Lewis et al., 2016; Wong-Padoongpatt et al., 2017). After dialoguing for this chapter, microaggressions surfaced as a common thread in the experiences of Zer, Lisa, and Leah as mothers within academic settings, which led to the formation of our framework: maternal microaggressions.

We named these interactions "maternal microaggressions" because this captures the denigrating nature of comments that individuals make based on the status of scholar-mother. Our goal is not to appropriate the term "microaggressions." Instead, our use of the term describes and gives meaning to the layered and nuanced nature of comments individuals make towards mothers, which often integrate both gendered and racial assumptions. While we focus on interactions in this chapter, we recognize that environments may perpetuate maternal microaggressions via silence, representation or lack thereof, assumptions, etc. According to Sue et al. (2007), microaggressions can take the form of microassaults, microinsults,

64 LISA S. KALER ET AL.

and microinvalidations. Microassaults represent explicit derogatory comments meant to hurt the victim. Microinsults convey rudeness and demean a person's identity; in the case of a maternal microaggression, the communication demeans someone as a mother. In the context of academia, this may include questioning the presence of mothers in a scholarly environment. Finally, microinvalidations exclude or invalidate the thoughts, feelings, and experiences of victims (Sue et al., 2007). Microinvalidations towards mothers may take the form of telling a pregnant woman that she "hides [pregnancy] well," thereby invalidating her experience of carrying a child and implying that she should be hiding her pregnancy.

As we have stated, the perception that the institution of higher education is progressive masks the reality of cultural norms that permeate the environment, particularly related to motherhood. As the literature demonstrates, conflicts between a scholar-mother's roles and identities may arise during graduate school (Abetz, 2016, 2019; Lynch, 2008; Ward & Wolf Wendel, 2004, 2012). Because of social norms dictating what mothers should be and should do (Lynch, 2008), people perpetuate maternal microaggressions based on the assumption that scholar-mothers occupy conflicting roles. These maternal microaggressions then exacerbate a scholar-mother's feeling that her dual roles as scholar and mother conflict with one another. The result is the persistent message that scholar-mothers are unwelcome, inept, and unqualified to attend graduate school.

Though many of Zer, Lisa, and Leah's interpersonal interactions with faculty, administrators, and colleagues have been positive, the nature of microaggressions are such that they can take shape through climate. Consequently, even positive encounters can be inadequate in combating the ubiquity of maternal microaggressions. The narratives below provide examples of each type of maternal microaggression. Zer, Lisa, and Leah reflect on the continuous experience of maternal microaggressions in the form of questions, judgments, unsolicited advice, and rude comments, and the subsequent impacts on their studies, identities, and overall well-being.

ZER

As a Hmong mother of two children (two years old and five weeks old), a first-generation doctoral student, and one of few Women of Color in my place of work, I struggle with imposter syndrome, navigating multiple identities, and role conflict. I also worry about how my varied roles and identities impact the way others perceive my commitment to each of my pursuits.

An example of this experience came at the beginning of my graduate program. I had just started a new full-time job on campus when I learned I was pregnant with my first child and had also been accepted into a Ph.D.

program. To my surprise, my first reaction was, "how am I going to share this news with my supervisor and how will my supervisor react?" I was worried and unsure of how she might respond to this news and whether she would be supportive. Most of my concerns were related to her perception of my ability to perform my job while balancing these new roles. As a new employee, a Woman of Color, and now a pregnant woman, it was hard not to think about what assumptions my new supervisor and colleagues might make about me.

These concerns arose due to my awareness of racial stereotypes about Asian-American women and, in particular, Hmong-American women. Additionally, I grappled with the boundaries (visible and invisible) that culture places on us all. As a Hmong woman, I am assumed to be the primary caregiver and to bear many children. My culture expects a passive, well-disciplined, and tradition-following daughter and daughter-in-law, which can be contradictory to how White Americans might view women in the workplace and at home. I did not want my new supervisor and colleagues to assume that I was not committed to my work and that I would be distracted by the many roles I was occupying. I also carried a heavy burden by worrying that they would assume that I would have more children, and thus be on maternity leave, subsequently leaving more work for them.

Due to my concerns about how others might perceive me, I began doubting my capacity to perform the responsibilities required in my new roles. I struggled for months with doubts and even considered postponing or discontinuing my pursuit of a doctoral degree. With these doubts, my imposter syndrome deepened. As I continued to consult with close colleagues and mentors, I was encouraged to take a leave of absence from my program because of the challenges of being a new mom. I ultimately postponed my entry into the program by one year.

The challenges of playing multiple roles during my academic and professional journey increased during the second year of my doctoral program when I became pregnant with my second child. I felt that this pregnancy was frowned upon by others. While I was excited about having another child, it was difficult to shake the feeling that others judged my decision to do so. At an event on campus, a colleague whom I had not seen in over a year exclaimed, "you're pregnant again!" This made me feel ashamed, as if I had done something wrong. I was unsure how to respond, so I smiled and left the conversation with a sense of guilt and discomfort. I assumed that others may have held similar perceptions of me. I began trying to justify my actions and then questioned myself for feeling the need to justify them.

Furthermore, as a member of a collectivist culture that values family (and having large families), I was experiencing the opposite sentiment at home, where extended family members often asked why I was not having more children. They urged me to have more children every time I saw them, and those conversations added a different kind of guilt to what I was already

66 LISA S. KALER ET AL.

experiencing in my school and professional life. I felt like I had failed everyone and struggled with these feelings throughout my pregnancy.

Throughout my second pregnancy, a variety of experiences caused me to feel extremely insecure professionally, personally, and as a graduate student. In my first pregnancy, I gained over fifty pounds and my child was born almost two months early due to a complication. In my second pregnancy, I was gaining weight rapidly and began to feel very insecure about my appearance. On top of feeling like I needed to work harder to prove that I am capable of doing it all, I now worried about my body. During my seventh month of pregnancy, a male faculty member commented about my physical appearance. He told me that every time he saw me, I looked different. I initially questioned what he was saying by wondering "did he just comment on my body!?", which led me to feel embarrassed and ashamed. I already felt uncomfortable, fatigued, and exhausted. Upon hearing this, I was mentally and emotionally crushed. To add to this, a male colleague commented on how I walked, saying that I waddled. He even imitated my walk. He seemed unaware of my internal struggle and the additional pain and discomfort he caused. These hurtful experiences were maternal microaggressions, which made me question my ability to be a working mother in the academy. The nature of these microinsults (Sue et al., 2007) that I experienced demeaned me as a pregnant student and professional.

These experiences of feeling guilty, having to prove to others and myself that I am doing enough, and feeling conflicted about my many roles have made this journey in my academic and professional career more challenging. My experiences with imposter syndrome, navigating multiple identities, maternal microaggressions, and doubting my abilities to be a good mom, student, and employee are thoughts that I carry with me daily. These feelings and thoughts mentally and emotionally drain me. When people make unsolicited comments, I often do not have the energy to respond. I am, however, fortunate to have supportive people around me. I have an amazing, supportive partner, siblings who remind me that I am a wonderful mother, parents who understand and support me, an advisor who is also a Woman of Color, a cohort that I can connect with about these issues, and a community of mentors and colleagues who are uplifting and encouraging, and who remind me that I am worthy and capable. I am reminded of this often and this community keeps me going.

LISA

I learned that I was admitted into a one-year master's program six days after learning I was pregnant. In the first conversation that I had with my master's advisor, who is now my doctoral advisor, I apologized multiple times for getting pregnant and questioned whether I would still be able to get a master's degree. Fortunately, she was reassuring, excited, supportive, and flexible. Her continued support throughout my graduate studies has been critical to my success. My goal even before I applied to the master's program was to pursue a Ph.D., so a master's degree was only step one in my plan. But the reality my husband and I now saw as we gazed down the path leading to my terminal degree involved raising a child; this was not a hurdle that we anticipated so early on the path. Nonetheless, we decided that I would remain in the one-year master's program and apply to begin the Ph.D. program the following year.

As graduate students often do, my peers in the master's program frequently asked about my plans upon graduation. Perhaps I got this question more than others when I was visibly pregnant. Each time I was queried, I replied that I was applying to the Ph.D. program because that had always been my goal. One male student in my cohort often heard this conversation. Every time, he would chide me, "Lisa, you're going to have a baby, you should be home snuggling your baby." He would smile, fold his arms over, and pantomime rocking a baby back and forth. Each time I laughed and reminded him that a master's degree was just the middle of my education; I had bigger ambitions. What I wondered to myself was whether my classmates agreed with him. Did everyone think I should stay home to "snuggle my baby" instead of going on to a doctoral program? No one ever asked my husband what his plans were after the baby came. Obviously, he would continue working. His ambitions would not be interrupted by the birth of a child because the ambitions of fathers are rarely pierced by the cries of an infant. I was also hurt that my classmate thought the end of my pregnancy also signaled the end of my scholarly and career ambitions. Reflecting on this experience through our discussions for this chapter, that was a microinsult (Sue et al., 2007). With a smile on his face, he demeaned my identity as a mother and told me where he felt I would soon belong: at home.

Partly because of that repeated, insulting encounter during my master's studies, I entered my doctoral program feeling I had something to prove. In every class, when I introduced myself, I announced that I had a nine-month-old at home, that I was a full-time mom and a full-time doctoral student, plus I was fortunate to have a research assistantship. I did not share that I was also struggling with postpartum depression and that I was neither happy at home nor in school because I always felt that I should be in the place I was not, doing more than I could, doing better than I was. I felt that I had to hide the reality of life for a new mother in a doctoral program. As I reflect on this experience, I recognize how my actions, and what I did and did not choose to disclose, reflected a desire to portray the White mother "supermom" stereotype (Anaya, 2011). So while I was open about my roles as mother and scholar, I was not transparent about the challenges I was negotiating daily.

The first two-and-a-half years of our daughter's life, the reality I hid was a challenging one. My husband travels frequently for work. In the final semester of my master's and for the first two years of my doctoral program, I was often the sole caregiver until a nanny arrived at our house five minutes before I left for school. Daycare was not an option because OLPD classes are offered in the evening. I was still breastfeeding, so I pumped on campus and I pumped while sitting at the computer when I got home from class. On weekends, I went to the library to write. I worked at night when necessary, but often collapsed on the couch shortly after our daughter went to bed, exhausted from splitting my brain between academia and mothering. This schedule got us through two years of doctoral coursework and my preliminary exams. Now that I am a candidate and I have finished classes, we have more flexibility, and I finally feel the vice grip dictating my family's schedule so forcefully has been loosened. Nonetheless, ripples of the interpersonal encounters questioning my place in a doctoral program continue to affect me.

I once had a meeting with a male faculty member who asked about my timeline to degree. Upon hearing my four-year goal, his response was, "How do you have time to be a mommy, a student, and a wife? When do you see your husband?" The word "mommy" stung, it felt pejorative. It felt like when my classmate told me I should be home snuggling my baby. Mothers I know often refer to each other as "mama"; it is a term of empowerment. Being called a "mommy" and having my marriage questioned by a faculty member was not empowering, it was a maternal microaggression. The truth is, I have limited capacity to be "mommy," student, and wife. One, if not all of the three, is always suffering. For two-and-a-half years of evening classes (master's and doctoral), I saw my husband little, especially when I went to the library on weekends. I am with our daughter during the week, thinking of all the schoolwork I could be doing. When I am doing schoolwork, I worry about whether she is happy, safe, well cared for.

I push myself to finish my degree quickly so that I may return to work full-time, ideally as an assistant professor. I also push myself because I want to prove that I am capable of earning a Ph.D. while also learning to be a mother. When I was in the accelerated master's program, I gave birth during winter break. I returned to class two weeks later and graduated on time. When I reflect on those achievements, I am reminded that I am capable of achieving my goals. But when I experience maternal microaggressions, I doubt my goals, myself, and my value in a doctoral program.

I know that my experiences are also shaped by unearned privileges I am afforded as a White woman. In the conversations with Zer and Leah, I heard the distinct contrast in how Leah and I felt about sharing that we had children. I felt compelled to let everyone in my department know that I had a child because being a mother is an enormous part of my identity now. As a White mother, I do not face the same stereotypical judgments that Women of Color face. Writing this chapter enlightened me as to how my own actions may have marginalized other mothers, and I am so grateful to Zer and Leah for sharing their wisdom and experience with me, and for being so generous in their understanding and support. Furthermore, I recognize how my privilege as a White mother allows me to merely reflect on the role of race in my experience in the past tense, and often in relation to Mothers of Color.

LEAH

I recently saw a social media post that says society expects women to work like they do not have children and parent as if they do not work. I resonate with that sentiment. When I began to consider enrolling in a doctoral program, people asked if it was good timing and how I would manage everything. None of my male colleagues describe encounters like those, but other scholar-mothers do.

Life at the intersection of two independently demanding experiences—motherhood and graduate school—triggers a role conflict. The conflict is not inherent, as evidenced by affirmations received by male colleagues who are also parents. Instead, it is instigated by cultural norms that frame good motherhood in exclusive terms that are practically impossible for any mother to live up to. All the while, those who were never included in the frame (read Mothers of Color) or choose not to opt in (read mothers who work outside of the home or attend school) are penalized.

Motherhood is also a racialized phenomenon. Though I have a sense of solidarity with mothers from a variety of backgrounds, my experience as a Black mother has its own particularities, including "gendered racial microaggressions that objectify Black women and reduce them to their race and gender" (Lewis et al., 2016, p. 773). Being a Black mother comes with centuries-old tropes and stereotypes about fertility, hypersexuality, and responsible parenting that further complicate matters. Role conflict perpetuates social reprimands for us deviant mothers, which result in "maternal microaggressions." When negative racial stereotypes are also factored in, a challenging experience—graduate school—can sometimes feel impossible. For scholar-mothers like myself, Lisa, and Zer, maternal microaggressions have personal, emotional, relational, and psychological consequences that materialize within the academy.

It is not easy to recount negative experiences I have had with peers, faculty, and administrators. They represent exchanges with people with whom

70 LISA S. KALER ET AL.

I have valued relationships. I also recount positive experiences as a testament of the ways that faculty have helped to affirm me as a mother-scholar. While it is important to highlight the positive impact faculty can have on students at the doctoral level, it is inadequate to expect individual acts of kindness to drive the necessary changes in higher education towards the inclusion of student-mothers. As is characteristic of microaggressions, each interaction obliges a mental and emotional reckoning of whether I disclose the impact of their words on me or not. Confession of the hurt presents the risk of social isolation, conflict, dismissal of my feelings, broken relationships, or navigating the emotions of someone who has hurt me. The need to calculate the cost of vulnerability adds to the mental load of being a scholar-mother. My anecdotes evidence the ways that social messages—both implicit and explicit—have facilitated maternal microaggressions during my doctoral student experience. Sharing them is, perhaps, a tool of catharsis.

During my doctoral program information-gathering process, I disclosed that I had small children to a university administrator. His response was to ask, "Why would you want to get a Ph.D. right now? Is this a good time?" I could not help but wonder if my partner would have faced the same scrutiny. I wish that this was an 'isolated' encounter, but it was not. More comments and interactions further perpetuated racial and gender tropes that isolated me from colleagues and administrators.

Upon meeting my three-year-old for the first time, a colleague asked him if he would be an athlete when he grew up. I struggled for months about whether I would address the incident or not. My angst around my colleague's comments is rooted in the long-standing narrative about Black boys as athletes, coupled with higher education's pernicious number of Black men who are recruited to make money for colleges and universities. The not-so-subtle implication of my colleague's comment is that my child was seen through tropes and stereotypes about Black boys. What does it mean for the future if emerging leaders engage across differences using presumptive, racist tropes? In this instance, my identity as a Black mother needing to protect her son from negative racial stereotypes stood in opposition to my identity as a graduate student needing to get along with a colleague. I am not interested in maintaining relationships where I have to sustain a high level of vigilance or where I am constantly expected to correct well-intentioned racist gestures or comments. As I also do not want to internalize the racialized stress that comes with carrying these hurts alone, decisions about self-disclosure have been a constant source of negotiation since beginning my studies.

Upon acceptance into my Ph.D. program, I was advised not to disclose my parental status. I was grateful to receive insider knowledge from another Woman of Color who also completed her doctoral studies as a mom.

I understood her advice as a protective measure against a university ecology that would perpetuate more explicit, poignant, targeted maternal microaggressive behavior against me if they knew that I was a mother. Her caution was that the rules for Mothers of Color are different than they are for White moms, a microcosm of broader social dynamics. She said, "They will hold it against you." My experiences in the academy had already begun to suggest that she was right, but I could not shake the feeling of resentment as I watched my classmates talk about their children while I shared trivial facts about myself. I later chose to disclose my parental status, and it has been a humanizing experience that also facilitated the birth of my dissertation topic. Sharing my story on my terms has contributed to the quality of my experience, though there have been unexpected consequences.

During my first year, I disclosed my parental status to a faculty member with whom I would have regular interactions. Her response was, "Damnnnn!" I spent the next year speculating, "Did she say that because they are so young? Because I have multiples? Because they are so close in age? Does she think I shouldn't be here? Does she think I'll be overwhelmed? Does she think I won't be able to keep up with the workload?" My fears were so deep-seated that I dreamt about the interaction. To say the least, I felt insecure. When I recounted our first meeting to her some time later, she apologized for any stress she may have caused and shared that the source and meaning of her comment stemmed from her own mothering journey. Seemingly ambiguous or theoretically neutral comments can take on a very specific meaning for a graduate student Mother of Color in an environment that questions or ignores your presence. Though on-campus interpersonal interactions related to my status as a graduate student Mother of Color have been largely neutral, if not positive, the difficult experiences are disproportionately formative.

The consequences of being a Black student-mother are diverse and abundant. I am often pulled in so many directions that I fall short of the kind of mother and student that I aspire to be. I do not have as much time to commit to scholarly endeavors as I would like, but my family inspires much of my research agenda. I have missed more deadlines than ever before in my academic career, but I am learning how to choose the things that are most important to me. My studies leave me feeling enraged about the state of race and education, and well-aware of the possibility that people may see me as an Angry Black Woman, but I also feel empowered to produce knowledge and create social change. The intellectual rigor of a graduate degree is assumed, but I was not prepared for the emotional rigor that accompanies the process. Whether I reconcile the tensions or live within them, my mental health bears the effect of role conflicts surrounding my identity as a scholar-mother as I navigate maternal microaggressions in the academy.

72 LISA S. KALER ET AL.

IMPLICATIONS AND LESSONS LEARNED

Based on these narratives, it is clear that both challenges and opportunities exist to improve and enrich the experiences of scholar-mothers in graduate programs in the academy. Ward and Wolf-Wendel (2012) discussed the dominant narratives of academic motherhood as being marked by negativity, challenge, and constraint. Work by Abetz (2016, 2019) and Augustine et al. (2018) echoed the uncertainty that women doctoral students experienced in graduate programs. The narratives in this chapter reflect similar sentiments and ambivalent feelings about the experience of scholar-mothers. In this section, we summarize and analyze three main themes of Zer, Lisa, and Leah's narratives. Additionally, Mike offers some practical implications and suggestions from faculty and administrative perspectives developed through conversations with the scholar-mothers. Finally, Zer, Lisa, and Leah reflect on how they envision a graduate education that fosters a sense of wholeness as scholar-mothers. An overarching theme of the implications and recommendations is the need for a capacious narrative about motherhood (in general and in the academy specifically), which makes space for the recognition of race, culture, class, and other important contextual realities. Policies, practices, and scholarship that fail to address difference often reify higher-education's motherhood discourse as (implicitly) White.

Maternal Microaggressions

First, all three students in this chapter experienced maternal microaggressions from peers, faculty members, and others in their lives. Frequently, these slights were overt (e.g., a direct comment from a classmate or faculty member). As a result, the three students in this chapter often experienced doubt, anger, and resentment based on the treatment they received from others. The students all experienced "critical moments" where they felt challenged by these comments or assumptions from others. In some cases, supervisors or well-intended faculty members made comments that disparaged students as new or expecting mothers.

Seeking Wholeness

Second, Zer, Lisa, and Leah all hoped for greater inclusivity and acceptance of their intersecting identities as scholar-mothers. Abetz (2019) noted how the graduate students in her study experienced both silence and uncertainty. She mentioned that the scholar-mother identity seemed incompatible and "created an anticipated concern that seeking wholeness was a risky act" (p. 83). Each scholar-mother in this chapter wanted to be in learning environments where they could share their full selves and be recognized and accepted as scholars and mothers.

All three of the students discussed concerns that if they shared their full selves, they would be perceived as less committed to their scholarly endeavors. Other student mothers in the work of Abetz (2019) and Fothergill and Feltey (2003) parallel these fears. For scholar-Mothers of Color, in particular, socially constructed ideals of a good mother, modeled off of White mothers, and a good student conflict with one another (Anaya, 2011). In the case of Leah, she was advised (by a scholar-Mother of Color) not to share with others that she was a mother of three because of the social implications for her scholarly life as a Black woman. Silence as a coping strategy can lead to incongruence and a lack of wholeness, which can exacerbate imposter syndrome, dissonance, and stress.

Unrealistic Expectations

Third, all three narratives discussed the feeling of "never doing enough" and experiencing the multiple pressures of meeting personal expectations as a mother and scholar (Augustine et al., 2018). Often, these pressures stem from internal expectations, yet reflect larger societal views about gender norms (Hodges & Park, 2013; Wolf-Wendel & Ward, 2006). Meeting the expectations of the ideal mother and professional becomes unrealistic; this challenge is well-supported by Ward and Wolf-Wendel (2017) and their scholarly inquiry on academic motherhood. Based on the work of Bronfenbrenner (1979, 2005), these messages about "a good mother" are distal messages from the exosystem and macrosystem levels that interact with the students to shape their experiences.

PROMISING PRACTICES FOR CHANGE: TRANSFORMING THE ACADEMIC EXPERIENCE FOR SCHOLAR-MOTHERS

Leaders in higher education need to do a much better job of supporting scholar-mothers. These narratives represent a collection of critical incidents that call for fostering environments and spaces where scholar-mothers feel empowered rather than minimized and demoralized by others.

Normalize Parenthood

First, academic administrators and faculty can include parenthood as part of graduate-school life. They can normalize parenthood through proactive acknowledgment of this status, and by making scholarly considerations when

74 LISA S. KALER ET AL.

relevant. These conversations can take place individually with students and advisors and/or more openly in orientations and other programmatic events. For example, faculty members who are parents themselves can mentor students and share personal experiences about the challenges and rewards of balancing work and children; this can help facilitate a more welcoming and open space for scholar-mothers. Grenier and Burke (2008) discovered that the academic department makes a significant difference in the support provided by faculty members. We argue that non-faculty institutional agents could extend this support as well (e.g., advisors, student-affairs professionals, among others). The message should be intersectional and clear: scholar-parents of all gender identities are welcome in this space; moreover, the message should emphasize a culture of acceptance and openness rather than silence.

The lack of discussion about graduate student-mothers creates a sense of invisibility and devaluation. Even among progressive faculty and students, mothers are often overlooked as an identity group, and this leads to the sense that the status of motherhood is not valued in the academy. These discussions can begin and be normalized in recruitment and orientation materials, both in terms of listing resources available for student parents, peer-mentoring opportunities, conceptualizing the classroom for student-parents, and including photos of mothers with their children participating in graduate events.

Faculty can support scholar-mothers through affirming their scholarly ideas, offering academic resources related to their areas of research, and recognizing the significance of parental status on the graduate-student experience. Leah had a professor embody these principles by validating both her drive and her need for rest.

Policies Specific to Scholar-Mothers

Second, many programs and institutions fail to develop and implement specific policies that support and protect scholar-mothers (Abetz, 2019). Policies around funding and leave options should be identified and communicated to all students, not just scholar-mothers. Mothers and fathers should have access to family-friendly support services that provide provisions for parents (Lester & Sallee, 2009). Moreover, evidence suggests that employees (including students) often feel reluctant to use these benefits even if they are available. A culture needs to exist where there are no repercussions—whether real or perceived—for using these benefits. Again, initiatives should be targeted at both scholar-mothers and scholar-fathers enrolled in academic programs. Additionally, networks of support for students must be developed in order to "create structures that sustain them through stressful situations and devise ways to meet the challenge of graduate studies" (Grenier & Burke, 2008, p. 599).

Include Mothers in Equity and Diversity Trainings

Third, it is clear that some faculty members and other staff (often male-identified) are insensitive to expecting mothers and scholar mothers. This manifests through the various maternal microaggressions Zer, Lisa, and Leah describe. Whether due to awkwardness or lack of tact, this behavior is unacceptable. Ongoing professional development and training opportunities should exist in these cases; these modules could be added to existing programs around diversity, equity, and inclusion on campus. This recommendation does not suggest adding a new group to diversity, equity, and inclusion spaces, but rather adding the dimension of motherhood to ongoing conversations about race, gender, and student status. Normalizing the presence of mothers in graduate programs through the first two suggestions can also address this issue. By including scholar-mothers in conversations, including those about diversity, equity, and inclusion, individuals may become more aware of the impact of their words and actions on mothers.

Listen to Scholar-Mothers' Needs

Finally, administrators and faculty members need to do a better job of listening to the needs, issues, challenges, and assets that scholar-mothers bring to the academy. For a host of reasons, these conversations are not regularly taking place on our campuses, as evidenced by the three student voices in this chapter. Intentional actions need to be developed in order for our learning spaces to become more welcoming and accepting.

Zer, Lisa, and Leah's Hopes for Academia

Zer, Lisa, and Leah met during the editing process to discuss their hopes for new, more inclusive paradigms in graduate programs for scholar-mothers. If microaggressions perpetuate fragmentation and indignities, then the authors' hopes were to explore institutional and scholarly strategies that help create wholeness. The list they generated was extensive and is briefly outlined here. For graduate student-mothers to experience a sense of dignity and wholeness in the academy, they need freedom to bring their full selves to the campus and the classroom. Representation in the discussion of motherhood in academia that acknowledges issues of race, culture, gender expression, class, familial structure, abilities, sexual orientation, and a host of other factors that inform each mother's needs are vital for facilitating a more robust narrative about academic motherhood.

Furthermore, rather than questioning how mothers "manage it all" or "balance school, family and work," faculty, staff, and peers can provide

76 LISA S. KALER ET AL.

encouraging words or offer support. Not only do such comments reify the role-conflict narrative, but they are also loaded with racial, classist, and gendered assumptions about what financial, community, and familial resources a mother does or does not have. Finally, pregnant and postpartum women are not performing pregnancy or postpartum for an audience. While the visibility of pregnancy and breastfeeding may cause individuals to feel entitled to comment on women's bodies, they must not. No scholar-mother, or woman, should ever be subjected to comments about their body by an individual in a professional or academic setting.

CONCLUSION

Scholar-mothers attending U.S. graduate institutions represent an increasing demographic and scholarly inquiry on their experiences continues to grow (Abetz, 2019). While the rhetoric within the academy points to the value of their presence and contributions, policy and practice frequently demonstrate deficiencies. The narratives shared in this chapter bolster the argument that more work needs to be done to support scholar-mothers in postsecondary-education contexts. Women's resilience and the kind acts of a select few faculty members, staff, or classmates do not remedy the macrolevel responsibilities facing faculty and administration to mitigate the microaggressive environments that scholar-mothers face. Higher-education stakeholders—including administrators, faculty, and student-affairs professionals—need to work in collaboration to confront the conditions that produce maternal microaggressions. In doing so, these failed diversity moments have the potential to become learning moments for change and opportunity at every layer of the ecological system. More importantly, increased attention to the issues facing scholar-mothers will ideally foster a more positive and inclusive graduate-school experience, both inside and outside the classroom.

DISCUSSION QUESTIONS

1. Faculty members in graduate programs are uniquely positioned to influence the experience of scholar-mothers. In your context, what professional development can occur to help faculty recognize their roles in supporting scholar-mothers? How can you support your department in encouraging more positive interactions between faculty and scholar-mothers?
2. Think about your own department (e.g., academic or work setting). What structures are in place to support the needs and interests of scholar-mothers and/or other parents that have childcare responsibilities? What policies, procedures, or structures might be initiated to meet these needs in the future?

3. Emerging literature describes microinterventions as rehearsed scripts that marginalized people can use to resist microaggressions. What kinds of microinterventions might you develop to navigate the academy or other spaces where you experience maternal microaggressions?
4. Parenthood is a racialized and gendered phenomenon. How does your student-parent curriculum or student services incorporate intersectionality? What opportunities exist to better meet the needs of student-parents from minoritized backgrounds?
5. Explore and think through how your program and/or institution are or are not normalizing parenthood. What are some strategies your program and/or institution can employ to create a sense of inclusivity and normalization of parenthood?
6. What strategies could you implement in your respective academic programs to advance equity and inclusion in engaging mother-scholars in research, professional development, and in other learning spaces?
7. How are scholar-mothers represented, or not, in your curriculum? What opportunities exist to incorporate parental status into larger conversations about equity and inclusion?

REFERENCES

Abetz, J.S. (2016). "You can be anything but you can't have it all": Discursive struggles of career ambition during doctoral candidacy. *Western Journal of Communication,* 80(5), 539–558. doi: 10.1080/10570314.2016.1186825.

Abetz, J.S. (2019). "I want to be both, but is that possible?": Communicating mother-scholar uncertainty during doctoral candidacy. *Journal of Women and Gender in Higher Education,* 12(1), 70–87. doi: 10.1080/19407882.2018.1501582

Anaya, R. (2011). Graduate student mothers of color: The intersectionality between graduate student, motherhood, and women of color in higher education. *Gender & Social Justice,* 9, 13–31.

Augustine, J.M., Prickett, K.C., & Negraia, D.V. (2018). Doing it all? Mothers' college enrollment, time use, and affective well-being. *Journal of Marriage and Family,* 80(4), 963–974. doi: 10.1111/jomf.12477

Barnett, R.C., & Hyde, J.S. (2001). Women, men, work, and family: An expansionist theory. *American Psychologist,* 56(10), 781–796. doi: 10.1037//0003-066X.56.10.781

Bronfenbrenner, U. (1979). *The ecology of human development.* Cambridge, MA: Harvard University Press.

Bronfenbrenner, U. (Ed.). (2005). *Making human beings human: Bioecological perspectives on human development.* Thousand Oaks, CA: SAGE.

Carter, S., Blumenstein, M., & Cook, C. (2013). Different for women? The challenges of doctoral studies. *Teaching in Higher Education,* 18(4), 339–351. doi: 10.1080/13562517.2012.719159

DePouw, C. (2018). Intersectionality and critical race parenting. *International Journal of Qualitative Studies in Education,* 31(1), 55–69. doi: 10.1080/09518398.2017.1379620

78 LISA S. KALER ET AL.

Fothergill, A., & Feltey, K. (2003). 'I've worked very hard and slept very little': Mothers on the tenure track in academia. *Journal of the Association for Research on Mothering*, 5(2), 7–19. Retrieved from https://jarm.journals.yorku.ca/index.php/jarm/article/view/1995

Grenier, R.S., & Burke, M.C. (2008). No margin for error: A study of two women balancing motherhood and Ph.D. studies. *The Qualitative Report*, 13(4), 581–604. Retrieved from https://nsuworks.nova.edu/tqr/vol13/iss4/4

Harper, S.R. (2013). Am I my brother's teacher? Black undergraduates, racial socialization, and peer pedagogies in predominantly white postsecondary contexts. *Review of Research in Education*, 37(1), 183–211. doi: 10.3102/0091732x12471300

Harris, J.C., & Patton, L.D. (2018). Un/doing intersectionality through higher education research. *The Journal of Higher Education*, 90(3), 347–372. doi: 10.1080/00221546.2018.1536936

Hodges, A.J., & Park, B. (2013). Oppositional identities: Dissimilarities in how women and men experience parent versus professional roles. *Journal of Personality & Social Psychology*, 105, 193–216. doi:10.1037/a0032681

Lester, J., & Sallee, M. (2009). *Establishing the family-friendly campus: Models for effective practice*. Sterling, VA: Stylus.

Lewis, J.A., Mendenhall, R., Harwood, S.A., & Browne Huntt, M. (2016). "Ain't I a woman?": Perceived gendered racial microaggressions experienced by Black women. *The Counseling Psychologist*, 44(5), 758–780. doi: 10.1177/0011000016641193

Lynch, K.D. (2008). Gender roles and the American academe: A case study of graduate student mothers. *Gender and Education*, 20(6), 585–605. doi: 10.1080/09540250802213099

Mason, M.A., Wolfinger, N.H., & Goulden, M. (2013). The graduate school years: New demographics, old thinking. In M.A. Mason (Ed.) *Do babies matter?: Gender and family in the ivory tower* (pp. 8–25). New Brunswick, NJ: Rutgers University Press.

Sue, D.W., Capodilupo, C.M., Torino, G.C., Bucceri, J.M., Holder, A.M.B., Nadal, K.L., & Esquilin, M. (2007). Racial microaggressions in everyday life: Implications for clinical practice. *American Psychologist*, 62(4), 271–286. doi: 10.1037/0003-066X.62.4.271

Torres, L., Driscoll, M.W., & Burrow, A.L. (2010). Racial microaggressions and psychological functioning among highly achieving African-Americans: A mixed-methods approach. *Journal of Social and Clinical Psychology*, 29(10), 1074–1099. doi: 10.1521/jscp.2010.29.10.1074

Ward, K. & Wolf-Wendel, L. (2004). Academic motherhood: Managing complex roles in research universities. *The Review of Higher Education*, 27(2), 233–257. doi: 10.1353/rhe.2003.0079

Ward, K., & Wolf-Wendel, L. (2012). *Academic motherhood: How faculty manage work and family*. New Brunswick, NJ: Rutgers University Press.

Ward, K., & Wolf-Wendel, L. (2017). Mothering and professing: Critical choices and the academic career. *NASPA Journal About Women in Higher Education*, 10(3), 229–244. doi: 10.1080/19407882.2017.1351995

Wolf-Wendel, L.E., & Ward, K. (2006). Academic life and motherhood: Variations by institutional type. *Higher Education*, 52(3), 487–521. doi: 10.1007/s10734-005-0364-4

Wong-Padoongpatt, G., Zane, N., Okazaki, S., & Saw, A. (2017). Decreases in implicit self-esteem explain the racial impact of microaggressions among Asian Americans. *Journal of Counseling Psychology*, 64(5), 574–583. doi: 10.1037/cou0000217

Chapter 5

Managing the Classroom as a Military Veteran and Graduate Instructor: "Please Don't Call Me by My First Name"

Dianna N. Watkins-Dickerson

Incidents characterized as failed diversity and inclusion moments in a university setting are experienced by Black women on an almost daily basis, whether directly or indirectly. They vary between poor course evaluations due to racialized notions, to lack of institutional advancement to full professorship and administrative leadership (Ross, 2013). Black female academics also tend to have increased service expectations and perform a disproportionate amount of invisible labor while experiencing general overwork and more, especially at Predominantly White Institutions (PWIs) of higher learning (Collins, 1986; Hendrix, 1997). Harley (2008) contends, "[u]nlike the white female counterparts in the academy, the experiences of Black women cannot and should not be e-raced or driven into narratives considering sexism without deciphering the ways in which race colors their realities" (p. 20). This is to say that not considering the intersections of race, class, and gender takes away from the complexity of the tensions they face. Dismissing race eradicates the particularities of Black women's experiences.

To this end, Harley (2008) continues by saying, "[to] be deprivileged illustrates why African American women faculty are metaphorically referred to as the *maids of academe*" (p. 20). Citing McKay (1997) and Kawewe (1997), Harley contends that the:

> Maid syndrome becomes more evident when African American women remain at PWIS, where many abuses constantly beset their sensitiveness. In PWIs, misconceptions and stereotypes about race and gender lead to the (mis)treatment of and interaction with African American women as a label, thus devaluing the real person behind the stigma and encouraging self-fulfilling prophesies by the gender and race that hold power. Specifically, African American women are subjected to 'gendered racism.' (p. 20)

80 DIANNA N. WATKINS-DICKERSON

The erasure and e-racing of Black women not only hampers their ability to be seen as subject-matter experts (SME) in their fields and credible truth-tellers, but lessens the effects of anti-Black racism and misogynoir— the intersection of misogynist and sexist violence superimposed upon Black women (Bailey & Trudy, 2018).

Inside and outside higher education, the various challenges to Black women's agency are complicated and diverse. As a military veteran still serving as an officer in the reserve component, I am well aware of the way in which structural racism and sexism devalue women and people of color. However, as a Black female graduate student and instructor who balances the familial responsibilities of wife and mother, navigating the labyrinth of academia has proven more defaming and destructive than many experiences I have lived through and beyond in the Armed Services. As Harley (2008) makes clear, "[i]ndividually and collectively, African American women at PWIs suffer from a form of race fatigue as a result of being over extended and undervalued" (p. 19). I contend that Black women's rhetorical agency is inhibited by daily microaggressions, forcing some into rhetorical silence as an inculcated phenomenon of strategic survival in the academy. Others, like myself, choose to be vocal, which comes with its own set of challenges.

One of my primary introductory statements in a new class is that students refer to me as "Professor Watkins-Dickerson" or "Mrs. Watkins-Dickerson."[1] Due to the historically documented and empirically proven ways Black women have been economically, politically, socially, and rhetorically undermined professionally, I open my course by asking students to respect me in this way at the beginning of each semester. I stress that I *ask* my students to do this (adding a syrupy-sweet "please" and smile with the request), because demanding such respect would be immediately characterized as rude, harsh, uptight, or as Hendrix (2007) articulates, "trippin" (p. 85). While people have failed to render a salute while in uniform, the bounds of discipline and redress for such affronts in the military are as clear-cut and traditional as the same racism and sexism I sometimes experience in that space. However, in the "liberal" academy, such corrections are harder to exact, and at times, come with negative effects for underrepresented minorities.

Essentially, with the institutionalized, neoliberal ideologies already thwarted upon workers in colleges across the country, the price of Black women's success quite often comes at the cost of their silence and submission to racialized repression and sexist suppression, all further optimized by classist oppression based on the hierarchies of the academy. Therefore, in this paper, I offer two instances in which I have been called by my first name by White male students when I politely asked (and then reminded) them not to do so. I utilize critical race theory (CRT) to conceptualize these incidents and unpack their effect on my teaching.

CRT considers racism to be a central component of our culture. Legal scholar and primary CRT theorist Derrick Bell (1992) argues that racism remains a fixture of American life. This theoretical perspective also values the epistemological purview of marginalized persons of color and the wisdom gained from their experiences. Finally, it challenges White supremacist norms and the ways in which they are centered in various social systems, leading to oppressive, repressive, and depressive social spaces.

Through CRT, I consider the misogynoir and anti-Black sexism inflicted upon me during my time as a graduate teaching instructor at a southern PWI. I will contextualize this university space while offering highlights of its historical evolution with regards to race and gender dynamics. Finally, I detail diversity and inclusion challenges facing Black female graduate students serving as instructors and teaching assistants. This is just one story among many.

LITERATURE REVIEW

Theorizing through Deborah King's multiple jeopardy (1988), I contend Black women who serve as graduate teaching instructors in the academy must not only *ask* students not to call them by their first name (among other requests), but must unfairly work through various forms of classroom conflict and disorder in ways White graduate students do not. Even Black male graduate teaching instructors can deploy their masculinity in ways inaccessible to Black women. Scholars like King assert that Black women's experiences of sexism are multiplied by racism, thereby making both of their physical categories classed.

Leading Black feminist scholars Patricia Hill Collins (1986) and bell hooks (1989) have noted the ways in which Black women are not only "othered" but suffer rampantly under the guise of neoliberal ideologies. Although misogynoir has not been carefully considered in the field of communication, let alone within issues of diversity and inclusion in the university setting, I argue it fits squarely into this space (Bailey & Trudy, 2018). Bailey and Trudy's (2018) concept of misogynoir, in the context of this paper, focuses on how Whiteness presumes women are inferior, and Black women, in particular, are rhetorically reviled when they are not servicing White society within the confines of the traditional cultural trope of *mammy*, entertaining them, or stoking sexual desires and fetishes as "*jezebel*" (Cartier, 2014). Due to this, problematic issues with diversity and inclusion in the academy persist when Black women are working outside of service roles. When they are in positions traditionally read as highly intellectual requiring above-average educational attainment, social status, and a higher class affiliation, students, faculty, and others who subscribe to White supremacist

82 DIANNA N. WATKINS-DICKERSON

ideals reject their authority and ability to lead. White supremacy and anti-Black racism perpetuate this stigmatization and belief, whether carried by students or faculty. In her essay, "A Phenomenology of Whiteness," Sara Ahmed (2007) explains, "[w]hiteness could be described as an ongoing and unfinished history, which orientates bodies in specific directions, affecting how they 'take up' space, and what they 'can do'" (p. 149).

Data from a 2017 study coordinated by the National Center for Education Statistics show that "of the 1.5 million faculty in degree-granting postsecondary institutions," White men and women account for 76% of those in full time positions in the United States (U.S. Department of Education, 2019, para 1). Consequently, Black graduate student instructors in general, and those visibly ascribed a Black female identity specifically, trudge through an uncompromisingly difficult social terrain and may receive little support from academic advisors who fully understand the unique challenges they face or who have experienced the same treatment. Experience and research suggest that Black women do not always have the opportunity and support to speak up about daily microaggressions (Ross, 2013). Even within what should be the liberty of their very own classrooms, these provocations and limited institutional support shame Black women into deeper silence and apprehension.

In her article "The Angry Black Woman Scholar," Charmaine Williams (2001) describes her disillusionment as a graduate student in her autoethnographical account. She describes acts of racism and sexism against her by a well-known academic figure in her department. In spite of her complaints and witnesses supporting her claims of injustice, nothing was done to protect her position or reputation. Even after reporting these activities to a university official, nothing was done. In many ways, the protections of an organization, such as a higher learning institution dedicated to valuing diversity and inclusion, seem like empty words when not enacted for the protection of all. For example, when students are told, "I didn't see racism or sexism influencing your evaluations," as in my experience, we are left with little to no recourse. In other instances, our scrupulous documentation of events seem only to take up storage on a bookshelf or personal computer.

In the military, troops are taught that documentation is important. In fact, it is often said, "if it isn't written, it doesn't exist." Such a retort is also a learning tool the academy reinforces in written and oral composition: evidence is key. Despite this, Black women are not believed, nor are they consistently supported.

While the direct quantitative research studying the numbers of Black women working as graduate teaching assistants and instructors is not readily available, Wilder et al. (2013) remind us that "Black women faculty account for only 3 percent of all faculty nationwide, and face a myriad of

MANAGING THE CLASSROOM **83**

challenges related to their social location" (p. 27). With this in mind, rhetorical provocations shaming them into silence and apprehension, even when they are the leader in a space, warrant illumination. Harley (2008) contends,

> [I]n general, African American faculty must cope with cultural insensitivity and sometimes just plain stupidity from students, colleagues, administrators, and staff in the academy... As an already marginalized population, African American women faculty members are more often reprimanded by their dean and criticized by colleagues based on supposition, misperceptions, and on information without merit. Whenever such responses occur they compromise the professional integrity of African Americans, contaminate their professional experiences, and further highlight the politics of being an African American woman in higher education. (p. 24)

Quite simply, Black women in all levels of the university classroom are forced to weigh the risk versus the benefit of sharing our testimony—even with those that should support us. Like Hamer's testimony, when our embodied truths are put on display for one audience or another, there is always the risk for more trauma if one is not believed or told that those experiences "aren't that serious" or don't "matter."

Smith (2002) asserts that Black female graduate instructors may not be judged fairly, heard justly, nor treated with respect. Considering the ways in which race and gender have been studied in the field of sociology and labor studies, Smith argues:

> The study of ascriptive differences in authority, along with the processes that generate such differences, has been the primary concern of authority researchers over the last 20 years. In this line of research, two consistent findings transcend authority measures, data, and research foci: Women have less authority than men, and minorities have less authority than whites. Moreover, when minorities and women do have authority, it is largely at lower levels of authority and mainly when they supervise the work of other minorities and women. (p. 535)

As a workplace context, the classroom remains a space where some Black women struggle to wield authority. This situation is further complicated by the lack of diversity in the administrative, tenured faculty, and staff ranks in non-historically Black institutions. These challenges are far more dire for Black women at Predominantly White Institutions (PWI).

In her online blog and digital archive of experiences during graduate studies, Amanda Armstrong's "Adventures of a Black Woman in Academia" articulates the complexities of being a triply oppressed individual in academic settings. While negotiating role marginality and strain as graduate instructors (see Evans et al., 2018), they must deal with gender and racial bias. In her entry titled "Mental Health in Graduate School," Armstrong

(2018) notes: "I have had to make a committed decision. I have decided no one cares about my mental health as much as I do so I have to create boundaries and take care of myself" (para. 5).

Of note, Hendrix et al. (2007) acknowledge that White men have an easier time in the classroom in comparison to their peers who are marginalized by the social signifiers of race and gender (Hendrix et al., 2007). While Evans et al. (2018) consider ways in which the wider university community, departments, and even advisors can help diminish role disparities experienced by graduate students, individuals on the margins of the graduate experience, to include those that are gender non-conforming, persons of color, and in this case, Black women, experience still far greater differences based on their identities, impacting their overall experience.

CONTEXTUAL BACKGROUND

With the motto "Driven by Doing," the University of Memphis markets itself as a research institution located in the heart of Memphis, Tennessee, "driven by making a difference" (University of Memphis, 2019). It was founded in 1912 and hosts undergraduate and graduate students primarily hailing from surrounding areas of the greater metropolitan region, but representing 72 countries (University of Memphis, 2019). Visually, pamphlets and website materials boast a diverse makeup that in many ways overshadows the history of racism, sexism, and class domination that made the city famous for the sanitation strikes that ended with the assassination of Dr. Martin Luther King, Jr. Demonstrating this rich and complicated history is a placard on campus calling attention to the story of the Memphis State Eight. These eight Black students integrated the then all-white campus in 1959, only five years after *Brown v. Board of Education.*

From the school's newspaper *The Daily Helmsman,* student writer Raven Copeland's essay "Memphis State Eight's Legacy Lives on at the U of M" discusses the challenges these students faced and restrictions imposed upon them by the administration. While Copeland notes that numbers from the enrollment office detail that almost one-third of the 19,897 students enrolled in the school are African American, with added diversity among administration, faculty, and staff, several conclusions from such numbers can be misleading because they do not account for personal experiences (Copeland, 2018). Although the 2018 article did not cite the words and experiences of the Black women of the Memphis State Eight, I imagine their experiences were much like, if not far worse, than the men we do have the opportunity to witness and sight/cite.

Copeland writes that Sammie Johnson, one of the eight, was noted as saying, "I felt like I was invisible" during a 2006 interview. He continued, "the white students were unwelcoming, and it was clear that they weren't excited we were there" (Copeland, 2018). Copeland later writes, "Ralph Prater said the uninviting behavior of some white students made him feel isolated" (Copeland, 2018). In the 2006 WKNO interview, Prater commented that, "Students didn't speak to me, and they wouldn't sit by me in the classrooms—there would be vacant seats on both sides... [i]f I ever sat at a table with students, they would all leave" (Copeland, 2018).

Likewise, as a student and instructor, I have experienced a certain sense of exclusion while on campus, though my story is not foregrounded with the same limitations as the Memphis State Eight. However, as with the Memphis State Eight, who articulated a sense of loneliness and racism during their first few years at the school, Black women's multiplied experiences reveal that we are not far enough removed from some of the same insensitivities of a dark, racist past. Further, although this upcoming generation has now lived in the reality of a Black commander-in-chief, there are still living memories of lunch counter sit-ins, segregation, and firsthand accounts of violence where diversity and inclusion were not simply failed, but refused. Through my lived experience, I illuminate some of the challenges that remain and that face Black women in higher education classrooms as instructors, tenured or not.

SO WHAT HAD HAPPENED WAS...: FROM RETELLING AND REMEMBERING TO RE-TELLING AND RE-MEMBERING

As I imagine most instructors would, I begin the school year by reviewing the syllabus on the first day of class. As any instructor, tenured with rank, graduate student, or otherwise, I review relevant assignments and field questions students may have. I introduce a few key concepts to ensure students can leave with an idea of my teaching style and the material before dismissal. However, I follow in the footsteps of Black faculty mentors of the past and present, requiring all students address me by a title. I accept the titles "Ms." and "Mrs.," and prefer "Professor." While some professors around college campuses agree to be called by their first names, my military experience and identity as a Black woman dictate otherwise. As a military officer, I am quite used to outranking the majority of individuals in my company. Unless we are in public or exceptionally close (yet never in uniform), I am never called by my first name. In fact, I return this level of respect by referring to my troops by their title and last name as well. This is a fundamental rule of the rank structure within the military, but also a practice signifying respect in the Black community as well, where the history of naming is particularly important.

86 DIANNA N. WATKINS-DICKERSON

Due to the lack of respect offered to Black men and women before, during, and after enslavement, many African Americans have tirelessly worked towards building a persona that engenders this basic moral right. Even into Jim/Jane Crow and amid civil rights, leaders, members of the clergy, in particular, and other professionals within the community were reserved particular spaces of authority and respect (Honey, 2007). In fact, while not more important than other members of the community, the doctor, the preacher, the lawyer, and the teacher functioned as leaders pacing the beat of progress. Yet, despite constant reminders of the rules regarding titles and naming and the rationale behind this request, students have referred to me as "Dianna," "Miss Dianna," or *even* "Professor Dianna."

In one of these cases, I corrected a student because I was addressed as "Professor Dianna" when I corrected him for calling me "Dianna." I initially redirected him privately, actually ignoring it briefly. I wanted to show sympathy for a family loss. Despite class being in session for some time, and his awareness of my preferred title, this student insisted on calling me what he preferred.

The second incident came, again in the middle of the semester. I was giving instructions for the day and a student had a question. In order to obtain my attention, he called, "Miss Dianna." At no point in time had he ever called me this, and for some reason, this "mental slip" occurred. He explained, "well, I didn't mean any harm, but we are in the South." All of this was after this particular student was admonished for overstepping the bounds for freedom of religion and expression while in class.

Whereas the free expression of religion, faith, belief or lack of either is a right I swore to protect in my military service, and furthermore agree to accommodate and support as a chaplain, this student's efforts to proselytize during two class presentations were problematic given his approach and the context. After much consideration, I addressed the class, and though I did not denounce the student's beliefs, I did remind the group to be careful of proselytization in the classroom and respecting faith diversity in a public university.

More incredulous was the audacity this student displayed in "pulling me to the side" to assert, not only his beliefs but articulate his ultimate surprise that I did not "stand behind" him in sharing the "Gospel of Jesus Christ" during his final speech assignment as "we are both Christians." What is more, "you are a [military] chaplain," he claimed. The insolence, disrespect, defiance, and privilege displayed in those few moments captured the history of Black women refused respect and called "auntie," or violated because their bodies were not deemed worthy of liberation, even as it was preached that Jesus Christ came to save us all. While some might question tracing his temerity to the original mishandling of my name and title, and my correction of it, Smith's (2002) essay about authority in the workplace

MANAGING THE CLASSROOM **87**

rings true here. It contends that Black women do not consistently have access to upper echelons of privilege in American society, and the lack of respect they receive is proof of this (Smith, 2002), leading to various assaults on their efficacy in the workplace.

With both students, I addressed the first instances in which they called me by my first name in a passive manner. Although frustrated with what seemed to be an indignant and direct push against my authority, I ignored the missteps, assuming that these students would think critically about their behavior by observing the example of others and through indirect reminders of my preferences. In the end, this was not the case. Whether confronted by White male students and other colleagues, in my listed and unlisted experiences, some Black women like myself are forced to accommodate or even acquiesce to the racist and sexist demands of some students in their classroom. This is particularly true with White students levying complaints and trumped-up grievances that do not exist. Feeling the pressure to "survive" in higher education, Black female instructors often find that they must stroke the ego of White male students while also dealing with the politically correct smiles of White female students, forcing them into the *mammy* trope. On our evaluations and even in feedback during class, students' words and nonverbal cues, respectively, speak volumes, demonstrating the ways in which Whiteness yet reigns supreme despite one's official title or record of leadership (Ross, 2013).

This was expressed by Rev. Henry Logan Starks in Michael K. Honey's *Going Down Jericho Road: The Memphis Strike, Martin Luther King's Last Campaign.* Rev. Starks was one of the prominent Memphis pastors heavily involved with organizing and leading the community. Honey writes that an officer was reprimanding Starks, saying, "'Get along, boy. Go on, boy. Move it, boy.' And I remember Rev. Starks saying, 'I'm not a boy. I am the Rev. Mr. Henry Starks and if you call me 'boy' just one more time you are going to arrest me for assault'" (Honey, 2007, p. 264). Within this text, Honey offers a number of other accounts of Black leaders, clergy, and others, faced with blatant, racist disrespect by the White community.

To be clear, my experiences of anti-Black sexism and misogynoir are nowhere near the same as Hamer or Starks. However, the issue of respect, and what bodies are seen as credible and "worthy" of inhabiting the space of "teacher," continues to weigh heavily on efforts to diversify the teaching ranks and include voices and bodies historically underrepresented in those hallowed roles. To hear my voice as a reputable leader in the classroom and to respect my title as instructor holds great importance for the teaching and learning process and for interrupting the faulty assumption that only *some* bodies can function in that role.

In the classroom, instructors should be seen as credible SMEs worthy of respect. Yet research suggests that Black instructors, women in particular,

88 DIANNA N. WATKINS-DICKERSON

and graduate instructors even more so, struggle with receiving these basic niceties. When respect, a necessary part of the equation for successfully managing a classroom, is conditionally tied to race and gender, it is neither easily acquired or maintained.

IMPLICATIONS AND LESSONS LEARNED

In a basic-level course, and without the protections and exemptions of faculty standing or tenure, the construction of my syllabi must match, in great part, the 'course shell' approved by the department. Yet, despite the standardization of course materials and lesson plans, the students that remain registered after the first day of class (quite possibly realizing their fate to have a Black female instructor with a "non-revealing name") incessantly challenge my instructor status the entire semester. They refuse to take seriously my standards as stated in the syllabus, challenge my grading, and reject my correctives. In reviews, they speak of my "distance," as though I should be a close friend, and though I do not teach argumentation and debate, I would have no problem with the subject matter due to my practice of well-polished retorts. No matter how intimidating the crowds I have conquered in my preaching and speaking, or the 20,000+ military and Department of Defense members I served on deployment, once my body shows up, my worth as a legitimate instructor fades.

Correcting these issues is quite difficult without adequate support from faculty supervisors and advocates with rank. Whether pulled to the side (in my case) or the occasional outburst, Black female university instructors are faced with disadvantages in every area of course construction and classroom management, highlighting the importance of hypervigilance and copious amounts of transparency while fulfilling administrative functions, like grading, to avoid push back (Smith, 2002).

Lessons Learned: What Can Be Taken Away from This Incident?

Taking into consideration these accounts, Black female graduate student instructors need an overwhelming amount of support to be successful in the classroom. As they develop their own scholarly identity and wrestle with managing the expectations of the university, department, and undergraduates, they need advocates who are ready to actively resist the anti-Black sexism and misogynoir they will face at almost every turn. Although this task includes both invisible and visible labor, it can be done with proper attention to detail. Simply believing these incidents is a first step.

Likewise, our acceptance and equal investment with such mentors or advocates has to be considered thoroughly and carefully. Citing Derrida and the like should not be a prerequisite for believing in a graduate student, their smarts, ability to teach, or worth. I need an ally that acknowledges and understands that my positionality as a Black woman brings with it particular phenomenological truths and an enduring existential quandary, adding complexity to my experiences as a military Veteran, doctoral student, wife, and mother. They must be willing to acknowledge that despite being the "instructor of record," as a graduate student instructor, I have been presented with challenges to my productivity in teaching, assignment construction, and authority. Even though all students present challenges, my main difficulties and challenges are typically presented by White, heterosexual male and female students. Importantly, my space in the classroom has also been challenged by White female faculty (who should be advocates) in front of my students. While this may not be everyone's experience, it is, indeed, mine. With this in mind, faculty allies must understand that Black women, with their bodies automatically labeled by systemic histories of racist, sexist, capitalistic productions in the neoliberal academy, are not only living in the intersection of their identities as both Black and female, they are being hit by additional blows as they come to voice in the classroom. Scholars like Armstrong (2018) have described the ways Black women are forced, at times, to 'choose sides' between their Blackness and their womanhood. Advocates that support Black women, regardless of race or gender, must not make Black women choose to *only* center their gendered or their race-based experiences. Rather, they must understand the unique challenges facing Black female graduates and support them in resolving the daily challenges they face in academic spaces.

PROMISING PRACTICES FOR CHANGE: "WHERE DO WE GO FROM HERE?"

When faced with challenges in the military, we often suggest an individual 'adapt and overcome' to meet the difficulty. In this case, adapting only leads to accepting anti-Black, sexist treatment. Thus, with more and more Black women entering graduate school, the academy must change. Conforming to these norms also situates us within the problem and further forces us to internalize unhealthy microaggressions while positioning female academics to potentially fall prey to hazing and racially motivated physical violence—both of which I have survived in the academy.

Without spending more than a moment on the statement, I make it clear I do NOT want to be called by my first name. Yet, the matter is never *if* it happens, because it *always* happens. Such episodes of direct disparagement are often covert presentations of craftily constructed, "innocent" insult hiding behind what Eduardo Bonilla-Silva (2003) calls "colorblind

90 DIANNA N. WATKINS-DICKERSON

racism." In his text, *Racism Without Racists,* Bonilla-Silva describes this color-blind racism as "the dominant form of racism that persists in the post–Civil Rights era" (Bonilla-Silva, 2003, p. 9). He explains that "[l]ike the systematic brutal racism in the pre–Civil Rights era, colorblind racism functions to reinforce "the totality of the social relations and practices that reinforce white privilege" (Bonilla-Silva, 2003, p. 9). This is different from the overt nature of traditional racism I have seen firsthand in the military, where comments about my hair in relation to my White female counterparts, or even racist and misogynist jokes, are all part of military culture. Instead, Zamudio and Rios (2006) suggest that some may deem colorblind racism as "racism lite" or "discrimination with a smile" (p. 483).

In years to come, there will be more Black female graduate teaching instructors and faculty as institutions become more diverse. Yet, we, as academicians, must realize what attorney and diversity and inclusion expert Vernā Myers is well-known for saying, "Diversity is being invited to the party; Inclusion is being asked to dance" (Brown, 2017, para. 9). I, too, have been inadvertently left off of distribution lists, not included in email chains, and not offered the chance to dance, figuratively and metaphorically. It is not a good feeling, and an apology does not come close to the failed diversity and inclusion moment it creates. These failed instances demonstrate the ways in which Black women are ignored and strategically erased and e-raced, with apologies given only after the fact. In the same way, disrespect in the classroom only reinforces the additional issues outside of teaching. In light of these challenges, I offer two pathways forward.

Tear Down and Build Up

These challenges must be met with advocates that work tirelessly to include Black women's voices. This does not mean faculty and administrators tokenize them in an effort to optimize optics, but truly to dismantle institutionalized ideals and policies that acknowledge diversity and inclusion efforts have failed Black women only after someone brings it up. Importantly, respective colleges and departments of the institution must form their own affirming policies with the help of equal opportunity specialists inside and outside of the university.

Allies—Crucial MVPs

A first-level solution for those experiencing failed diversity and inclusion moments is to have their experiences believed. Black female graduate students need respectful, responsive, and racially diverse professional advocates in the department and administration who are willing to come alongside, support, mentor, and 'go to bat for' them. Whether teaching independently or as a teaching assistant, Black women's narratives of racist, sexist micro- and macroaggressions against them shape their views of the academy. In addition, their power (or lack of power) to respond and live through these circumstances is affected, particularly when they work to defend themselves unsupported by those with power.

As Harley (2008) contends, "Many institutions focus primarily on recruiting African American faculty and fail to have a plan for retention. It is as if once African American faculty members arrive on campus, university administrators feel as if they have accomplished their goal" (p. 33–34). The same can be true with Black female graduate students. Once we arrive, the failed diversity and inclusion moments begin. Hence, the main way for the academy to move forward is to believe, support, and continue to invest in ways to dismantle racist, sexist, and classist behavior against Black women. Because our skin and gender are visibly present or assumed, our ability to navigate systemic oppression is quite difficult, if not impossible, with little to no power in the hierarchical structure.

CONCLUSION

My great-grandmother and my great-grandfather, in spite of their education status as school principals and relative good standing as tithe-giving, tax-paying, home-owning, passing the "brown paper bag test," law-abiding citizens, in no way assuaged White audiences that saw them as fit for nothing more than sweeping their floors or driving them around town. Despite their efforts to advance the educational dreams of little Black and brown boys and girls in their small community of land-owing entrepreneurs just outside of Memphis, Tennessee, they were daily subjected to racial indignities, among which was the pronouncement of the label "boy" or "gal," which was used to erase their intelligence, worth, contributions, and competence. This is an erasure I must still resist in this twenty-first-century moment. Although far more subtle, the racial ideology that delegitimizes the credibility and worth of Black people persists. In those instances when I am called "Miss Dianna," I am reminded of this.

When I remind students, like a Black female mentor and professor reminded her predominantly White, cisgendered, Protestant, and male seminary audience, that her first name was reserved for the people that knew her and loved her, not those that were to be graded by her, I am reminding my class that they do not want "Miss Dianna" to judge their speeches. While fair, Dianna is not the instructor. Dianna prefers being at home with her three-year-old son. Dianna would rather spend quality time with her husband. However, Mrs. Watkins-Dickerson is expected to teach you public speaking and ensure you are a confident and competent citizen, able to engage in argument and persuasion at a basic level.

Every semester, I must make sure I am not being 'too aggressive,' even when it comes to receiving the simple levels of respect necessary for doing my job. When White students refuse to respect my wishes or 'stumble' and forget, I am either forced to ignore these moments of disrespect to ensure "good evaluations," or correct them, risking tensions in the classroom. In either case, I am forced to forgive. When excuses are made or when students 'laugh off' these slights, it only intensifies the tension between accepting and resisting the behavior. So you see, I am not angry. I am beyond rage. Quite simply, Dianna is not your friend and never will be. So above all else you do in my classroom, please, don't call me by my first name.

DISCUSSION QUESTIONS

1. In what ways can institutions empower colleges/departments with adequate training to ensure graduate students of color are equipped and supported as both students *and* instructors?

2. If there are no Black women faculty available in the department/college, how can course coordinators and/or department leads advocate for and/or mentor Black women who are graduate instructors without dismissing their specifically raced and gendered concerns?

3. How do we hear, listen, empathize, and extend goodwill towards graduate teaching instructors without rushing to find solutions? How do we support them by simply *believing* their story?

4. Outside of CRT or Black feminist theory, what other theories can help us move towards ethical communicative strategies that center Black women's voices?

5. How can faculty remain open to receiving honest feedback from colleagues (both junior and senior) about their negative attitudes or behaviors towards graduate students of color? What strategies could diminish defensive responses while generating receptivity to inclusive practices?

6. What can we learn from diverse experiences graduate instructors may have that broaden or challenge academic perspectives or knowledge bases? Are there ways in which real-world experiences supersede our theoretically based understandings of communication?

7. In what ways, if any, have you inadvertently participated in the devaluation of a graduate instructor's authority and autonomy in the classroom?

MANAGING THE CLASSROOM **93**

8. How can we acknowledge, understand, and interpret inherent bias in course feedback and evaluation, specifically when we "don't see race/gender" as a factor?

9. In what ways have neoliberal ethics of consumerism driven our classroom management style, and how does this unfairly position graduate instructors? Graduate instructors of color? Women of color? Black women specifically? Veterans?

NOTE

1. At the time of writing this essay, I am a doctoral candidate in my fourth year of studies. The title of Professor is acceptable for instructors with a master's degree. I have a Master of Divinity, and therefore prefer this title.

BIBLIOGRAPHY

University of Memphis (2019, August). Retrieved from University of Memphis: memphis.edu

Ahmed, S. (2007). A Phenomenology of Whiteness. *Feminist Theory*, 8(2), 149–168.

Armstrong, A. (2018). Retrieved from Adventures of a Black Woman in Academia: https://adventuresofablackwomaninacademia.com/

Asante, M. K., & Atwater, D. (1986). The Rhetorical Condition As Symbolic Structure in Discourse. *Communication Quarterly*, 34(2), 170–177.

Bailey, M., & Trudy (2018) On misogynoir: Citation, erasure, and plagiarism. *Feminist Media Studies*, 18(4), 762–768.

Bell, D. (1992). *Faces at the bottom of the well*. New York: Basic Books.

Bonilla-Silva, E. (2003). *Racism without racists: Color-blind racism and the persistence of racial inequality in the United States*. Lanham, MD: Rowman & Littlefield.

Brown, N. (Writer), & Mabry, T. (Director). (2017). *Chapter IV [Motion Picture]*. USA.

Cartier, N. (2014). Black Women On-Screen as Future Texts: A New Look at Black Pop Culture Representations. *Cinema Journal*, 53(4),150–157.

Collins, P. H. (1986). Learning from the outsider within: The sociological significance of black feminist thought A. *Social Problems*, 33(6), S14–S32.

Copeland, R. (2018, February 8). *Memphis State Eight's legacy lives on at the U of M*. Retrieved from The Daily Helmsman: http://www.dailyhelmsman.com/news/memphis-state-eight-s-legacy-lives-on-at-the-u/article_eb7d7a04-0d30-11e8-ad2e-772ad1d61d2d.html

Education, U. D. (2019). *Characteristics of Postsecondary Faculty*. Retrieved from Statistics, National Center for Education: https://nces.ed.gov/fastfacts/display.asp?id=61

Evans, T. M., Bira, L., Gastelum, J. B., Weiss, L., & Vanderford, N. L. (2018). Evidence for a Mental Health Crisis in Graduate Education. *Nature Biotechnology*, 36(3), 282–284.

Harley, D. A. (2008). Maids of Academe: African American Women Faculty at Predominately White Institutions. *Journal of African American Studies*, 12(1), 19–36.

Hendrix, K. G. (1997). Student Perceptions of Verbal and Non-verbal Cues Leading to Images of Black and White Professor Credibility. *The Howard Journal of Communications*, 8(3), 251–273.

Hendrix, K. G. (2007). "She must be trippin:'" The Secret of Disrespect from Students of Color toward Faculty of Color. *New Directions for Teaching and Learning*, 110, 85–96.

Hendrix, K. G., Hebbani, A., & Johnson, O. (2007). The "other TA": An exploratory investigation of graduate teaching assistants of color (GTACs). *International and Intercultural Communication Annual*, 30, 51–82.

Honey, M. K. (2007). *Going Down Jericho Road: The Memphis Strike, Martin Luther King's Last Campaign*. New York: W.W. Norton & Company, Inc.

hooks, b. (1989). *Talking back: Thinking feminist, thinking Black*. Boston: South End Press.

Kawewe, S. M. (1997). Black women in diverse academic settings: Gender and racial crimes of commission and omission in academia. In L. Benjamin (Ed.), *Black women in the academy: Promises and perils* (pp. 263–269). Gainesville, FL: University Press of Florida.

McKay, N. (1997). A troubled peace: Black women in the halls of the white academy. In L. Benjamin (Ed.), *Black women in the academy: Promises and perils* (pp. 11–222). Gainesville, FL: University Press of Florida.

Ross, S. N. (2013). The Politics of Politeness: Theorizing Race, Gender, and Education in White Southern Space. *Counterpoints*, 412, 143–159.

Smith, R. A. (2002). Race, Gender, and Authority in the Workplace: Theory and Research. *Annual Review of Sociology*, 28(1), 509–542.

U.S. Department of Education, National Center for Education Statistics. (2019). *The Condition of Education 2019* (NCES 2019-144). https://nces.ed.gov/programs/coe/indicator_csc.asp

Wilder, J., Jones, T. B., & Osborne-Lampkin, L. (2013). A Profile of Black Women in the 21st Century Academy: Still Learning from the "Outsider-Within". *Journal of Research Initiatives*, 1(1), 27–38.

Williams, C. C. (2001). The Angry Black Woman Scholar . *NWSA Journal*, 13(2), 87–97.

Witte, E. (2008). "Because Our Lives Be Threatened Daily": A Rhetorical Analysis of Fannie Lou Hamer's Testimony at the DNC. *National Communication Association. Conference Preceedings–Conference Papers*.

Zamudio, M. M., & Rios, F. (2006). From Traditional to Liberal Racism: Living Racism in the Everyday. *Sociological Perspectives*, 49(4), 483–501.

PART **III**

ORGANIZATIONAL CONTEXT: PEDAGOGICAL LIMITATIONS AND OPPORTUNITIES

III

Chapter **6**

Pedagogical Failures: Challenging Assumed Centers and Engendering Community Through Personal and Pedagogical Reflexivity

Meggie Mapes

bell hooks (1994) describes education as the practice of freedom. As a method of empowerment, consciousness-raising, and liberation, Giroux (2014) argues that education was once a utopian ideal meant to educate persons to be "reflexive, critical, and socially engaged agents" (p. 31). I, too, have identified with the pedagogical possibilities inherent in conversing with college students in and through formalized educational settings. Put simply, I view education as a public good—as a community-oriented mechanism that provides students critical-thinking skills to participate constructively in the public sphere. The goal of this educational framework is, for me, to underscore the public and community aspects of education, and to move students towards a more complex understanding of power, culture, and communication.

Unfortunately, neoliberal culture has deflated the community and critically oriented nature of democratically aimed educational institutions, stripping education of empowerment-based ideals by transforming schools "into a private rather than public good" (Giroux, 2014, p. 35). A privatized and consumer model of education reframes students as individualized consumers, and education becomes a means to support their own social standing in the long-term. Giroux (2015) summarizes the relationship between the neoliberal turn and consumerism:

The public is urged to become consumers, customers and highly competitive while taught that the only interest that matters are individual interests, almost always measured by monetary considerations. Under such

98 MEGGIE MAPES

circumstances, social and communal bonds have been shredded, important modes of solidarity attacked and a war has been waged against any institution that embraces the values, practices and social relations endemic to a democracy.

Rather than a democratically facing public good, neoliberalism transforms schooling into a privatized practice and, in turn, students become focused on themselves, detached from investigating their identities in relation to larger publics, structures, and institutions.

Education, then, functions as a tool within neoliberal markets to secure a narrative that all individuals are equally capable of success, creating the illusion that oppressive hierarchies around race, class, gender, nationality, and ability are nonexistent. Benny LeMaster (2015) argues that "neoliberalism rhetorically frames subjects as equally capable of realizing freedom if they make effective life choices to resemble a mythical normative center (e.g., White, cisgender, heterosexual, able-bodied, and so forth)" (p. 169–170). LeMaster's description highlights the ways in which the normative center—or mythical norm—is always already the standard for neoliberal success, limiting critical possibilities towards diversity work. Our once community-facing ideals are flattened into the singularity of an individual. Giroux (2015) warns that students' inability to see their suffering in relation to larger issues is a clear effect of neoliberal ideology in education.

As a communication studies scholar and Introductory Course Director, I can read Giroux with skepticism and cognitive dissonance. After all, I can and do confidently point to the foundational communication course, public speaking, as evidence that education still supports a democratically oriented empowerment model that facilitates diversity work. Troup (2002) argues that public-speaking courses "appear to be a prime site for equipping our students to do the practical work of rehabilitating the public square in America" (p. 2), with public speaking emerging as a key cultural lynchpin to uphold democratic values over tyrannical leadership. Public speaking, advocates argue, facilitates practiced civic engagement whereby citizens identify relevant information that a discrete (i.e., present) audience can learn from or act upon. In turn, teaching public speaking may offer an outlet for individuals to locate important concerns and empower groups to confidently and competently deliver necessary insights to better the community. Upon first glance, a communication curriculum that foregrounds public speaking may appear to uphold the utopian educational ideals that opened this chapter and resist the critical failures inherent in Giroux's description of education embedded in a neoliberal ideology.

Despite the promise of equitable empowerment through access to education, assumptions inherent to public speaking's disciplinary history reveal curricular practices may actually uphold the mythical norm. Nakayama and Krizek (1995) summarize:

> Historically, the development of the study of communication has followed a focus on the center. Plato and Aristotle, from a privileged class, were not interested in theorizing or empowering ways that women, slaves, or other culturally marginalized people might speak. The rhetor was always already assumed to be a member of the center. (pp. 292–293)

Nakayama and Krizek (1995) foreground engagement with curricular practices that allow assumptions of "centeredness" to remain "intact and unquestioned" (p. 293). If our historical curricular underpinnings are grounded in the center, and if the current neoliberal model encourages the individualization of content whereby students learn to always and only advocate for the self, are we merely empowering students to succeed in and through normativity? How can we enable discipline-specific reflexivity that challenges individualized frameworks that disallow a community approach toward empowerment?

These questions emerged for me through failure—when my knowledge of critical engagement and diversity ideals lost to the curricular underpinnings of my discipline's historicity. I erred on the side of tradition. I erred on the side of the center. This chapter engages with one such moment of diversity failure. First, through a first-person narrative lens, I detail the failed classroom moment, using public speaking as a curricular case study to reflect on failure. Second, I outline the implications of the communicative act before offering pedagogical possibilities that expand curricular engagement beyond the normative center. Failure functions praxiologically, and I am hopeful that narrating these experiences will lead to additional innovations that can alter individual, systemic, and cultural diversity practices throughout our courses.

Failure: A Case Study

A White student walks to the front of the classroom to present a public speech, and he gently places a lacrosse stick on the upright computer station. The goal of the speech is to inform his audience, constituted by his peers, and to increase their understanding about an idea. Grounded in a communication-studies curriculum, the student selected his hobby as a speech topic, a selection based on teachings that a good speech is often located in a speakers' individual passions, and he's meant to relate that content to his audience in an interesting way. Dressed in his team's attire, he smiles, beginning his speech by narrating his interest in and connection with the sport of lacrosse. I begin taking note of his delivery techniques, his

100 MEGGIE MAPES

organizational strategy, and the effectiveness of his crafted content by asking, "Does the speaker connect his topic to the audience that is present?" As I look around, I mentally note the predominantly White and U.S.-based audience that surrounds me.

With a quick transition, he begins his first main point, which focuses on the history of the game. "Lacrosse was actually invented by Native American communities in the United States," he explains. "When Europeans migrated over, Native Americans taught them the sport, and they maintained friendly relationships—Native American and European groups regularly had pleasant game-play experiences. Later on, Europeans updated and formalized the rules, making the game what we know today."

With every word, I become increasingly aware of the dominant colonialist narrative and, as every second passes, I realize that the speaker will not return to trouble the Whitewashed history that has permeated his claims and the classroom. I try to quickly process the narrative as my mind begins to question the initial interpretation of his language: "What did I hear? Did I decode that correctly?" I look at my screen as the small cursor blinks in anticipation of my next move. Reflections of seated students appear on my white screen as I wonder, "Should I stop the speech?" "Is this history pulled from a 'research' article?" Looking over my shoulder, the class of White students appear nonverbally engaged as they laugh at the speaker's well-placed jokes.

"Wow, what a really interesting history," a student-peer shares at the conclusion of the speech, informally complimenting the speaker as he takes his seat. He beams confidently as he places his lacrosse stick on the floor with a thud.

As every second passes, a pressing failure begins to seep in. I have failed. And as every second passes, I wait for my ability to articulate a feeling—a feeling of failure and failing to find language that articulates the previous happening. Students begin filing out of the classroom at the conclusion of our class, and I am left to sit in the familiarity of failure and the residual impact of White supremacy.

IMPLICATIONS AND LESSONS LEARNED

In this section, I reflect on my failed diversity moment, arguing that the student's narrative recenters a colonialist, White-supremacist ontological telling of the history of lacrosse. Teasing out the implications of such an act, I ground my analysis by asking, "How did this happen?", linking curricular and cultural impacts of my pedagogical failure.

First, the communicative act exemplifies White supremacy by centering a European narrative of the sport's historicity. Deeper research describes a

PEDAGOGICAL FAILURES **101**

Native-focused perspective that differs greatly from the friendly, European-focused framing that was provided in the initial speech. Research does seemingly agree that the initial roots of lacrosse were formed within Indigenous communities, and Europeans were part of game-play, but Root (2016) provides further insight into the racist outcomes, noting that, after teams were formed in lacrosse,

> The conclusion drawn by white lacrosse enthusiasts was that many of the players were simply not gentlemen, and were unfit for formal competition. This attitude was especially directed at the presence of Native American players, who played for money, and were believed to be incapable of becoming gentlemen themselves due to their racial inferiority. (p. 42)

Rather than friendly play, Root's historical retelling describes how Europeans co-opted the otherwise Native sport, excluding Indigenous players on racial grounds.

This example of White-supremacist historicity demonstrates how colonialism has become banal and everyday, where "the continued centralization of European narrativization suggests that White supremacy's command of ontological truth continues unabated" (Smith, 2014). For students in my public-speaking course, such European narrativization becomes affirmed, and a now popular U.S. sport is attributed through Whiteness, valorizing White cultural contributions (Smith, 2014). Because alternative historical tellings are often absent, non-White students lose opportunities to learn about cultural phenomena that center their ethnic or racialized identities. Minoritized students on campus and in our classrooms become inconsequential to the White supremacist and neoliberal enterprise that privilege colonialist, normative realities.

Reflecting on the racialized implications of colonial storytelling, I can't help but ask, "How did this happen?" In response, I turned to disciplinary and pedagogical scholarship for support. Unfortunately, I quickly realized that neoliberal logics of individualization and normativity permeate communication studies and public-speaking literature, as students are encouraged to choose topics based on their individual passions and beliefs. "Select a topic that you're interested in!", I would explain in class, linking to classroom texts. "If you aren't passionate about a topic, the audience can tell, and they'll likely become poor listeners." Unsurprisingly, the lacrosse student—informed to look inward and locate his own passion—selected a hobby that had always already been informed through his White experiences. This resulted in the public good becoming defined through *his* community—a primarily White community that tells a primarily White historical narrative. As social justice educational advocates, we often teach students to empower themselves, but at who's expense? What about when empowerment is defined through the center? The questions of who and

102 MEGGIE MAPES

what become significant: that is, who benefits from this curriculum, who can listen (or audience) it, and what is commonly spoken about? As a faculty member at a predominantly White institution (PWI), I wonder what implications arise when White, privileged speakers are taught that civic participation is grounded in expressions of democratic futurity based, primarily, on their individual passions—informed in and through Whiteness—to a discrete audience of (oftentimes) likeminded individuals?

Unfortunately, as the opening paragraphs of this section demonstrate, White supremacy emerges as a core implication. But audiences are also relevant to reflecting on my failed diversity moment. In communication studies, a good speaker is defined by the ability to take note of observable audience characteristics including, for example, race, to "create messages appropriate to the audience, purpose, and context" (Broeckelman-Post & Ruiz-Mesa, 2018, p. 7–8), where the audience "consists of the people who are listening to your speech" (Floyd, 2019, p. 55). The lacrosse speaker's audience was seemingly similar in their demographic characteristics, with similar majors and predominantly from the same geographic region. So, if a White speaker is speaking to a largely White audience, does a European-centric narrative constitute well-crafted content? Put differently, when the White male student stood and, in front of discrete peers, normalized a colonialist history whereby Europeans "updated" a game after "friendly relations" with Indigenous communities that were later displaced from their lands, does this approach reward and refocus the center? If audiences are defined through discreteness, are we failing to account for the impact that a speaker's rhetorical choices have on groups that may not be represented in their immediate audiences? I would argue yes; we are failing.

It seems, then, that my disciplinary and curricular history, too, had failed me. Turning to central public-speaking texts provided little curricular guidance as I reflected on my failure. Beyond often vague references to ethical communication or condemnations of explicit racist language, many foundational texts seemingly supported the inclusion of historical narratives that privileged a European-focused historical narrative of lacrosse. In fact, the student may have, arguably, provided an exemplary telling based on the curricular tools that I provided. If students are only responsible for changing the minds of those present, speakers are allowed a level of detachment from how their language can affirm beliefs, values, or stereotypes that influence larger communities and the public good.

In an era of Trumpian rhetorical practices that are deemed persuasive (Goldhill, 2017; Kapoutsis & Volkema, 2019), how can we—advocates of democratic educational ideals – more deeply reflect on our failure to situate the implications of our rhetoric beyond the discrete context? Giroux (2015) argues that we are in a moment where "the emptying out of

PEDAGOGICAL FAILURES **103**

language is nourished by the assault on the civic imagination" (p. 95), with Trumpian appeals mobilizing neofascists movements. Trump is successful, in part, by appealing to the values of key discrete audiences without accountability towards other groups or communities that are referenced or implicated in his rhetorical frameworks. From a pedagogical perspective, it's important to ask, how do our own curricular and pedagogical practices enable the normative center by teaching in and through individualized and neoliberal models? To engage with this question—born out of my failure—I explore promising pedagogical practices below.

PROMISING PRACTICES FOR CHANGE: FAILURE AS INNOVATION

In this section, I work to map pedagogical possibilities. While grounded in communication studies, I view these praxiological suggestions as interdisciplinary by altering curricular decisions from an individualized approach towards a broad, community-focused framework, whereby students are encouraged to consider the implications of their communicative choices beyond the physicality of the classroom. I posit that communication as constitutive expands students' accountability of their rhetorical choices. Or, as I argue elsewhere, "how we talk about who we're talking about: how we're talking about the groups that are either represented and/or affected by our message" (Mapes, 2019, ch. 2). I believe that a focus on larger community members requires students to be reflexive in how their communicative acts and rhetorical framing may impact others beyond the discrete listeners present. To demonstrate, I offer a brief reflexive rereading of the lacrosse speech to demonstrate how communication, as constitutive, and reflexivity function—both prior to and after the completion of the speech—to intervene in an otherwise colonialist narrative of lacrosse.

A constitutive view of communication posits that communication is world-making because subjects are always constituted through rhetoric. For Charland (2016), this means that audiences and communities are not extra-rhetorical; instead, rhetorical acts "inscribe real social actors within its textualized structure of motives, and then inserts them into the world of practice" (p. 389). Subjects are rendered through the ideological subscription of meaning in communicative acts, so what rhetoric infers—explicitly or implicitly—about groups, cultures, or subjects matters. In a curricular context, constitutive communication means that students are responsible for the reality described and created through the selection and presentation of information to *explicit* audiences—those discrete listeners located in the physical space of the classroom—and the *implied* audiences and cultural groups that messages are speaking to or about. Without this focus, students can lack reflexivity about the type of ideologies being supported,

104 MEGGIE MAPES

and they are only accountable for the explicit group of listeners present. Grounding communication as constitutive becomes pedagogically fruitful by expanding student advocacy beyond their individualized experiences and passions, and connecting those experiences towards a community-oriented approach.

In addition to integrating the notion of communication as constitutive, reflexivity functions as a second promising pedagogical practice—a process of continually questioning the assumptions and ideological underpinnings of our communication acts. I'm drawn to teacher Brian Smith's (2014) suggestion, where he describes his own reflective practices: "I implore students to re-engage with a narrative that is perceived to have been settled, asking them to consider what might be significant for those who are generally absent from the common narrative of national history." This reengagement requires a reflexive and investigatory ethos for students, particularly students who inhabit identities that have contextual privilege. Without this reflexivity, speakers and audiences alike may fail to understand diverse community concerns. Chakravartty et al. (2018) note, for example, that:

> Knowledge production that reinforces Whiteness as its undisputed, unexamined frame is incapable of asking what we might learn from the experiences of those who have been, for decades if not centuries, dispossessed of their lands, policed, bombed, detained, indebted, and rendered illegal. (p. 262)

Reflexivity and scrutiny over privilege, including Whiteness, is an important facet to uncovering, in this case, experiences from Indigenous communities who have been, as noted above, "disposed of their lands." With Smith and Chakravartty et al. in mind, I reread the failed diversity moment below.

In rereading my failure, geography becomes central when grounding a community perspective that is reflexive and communicative. The lacrosse speech took place in Lawrence, Kansas. This may, on its face, seem like an irrelevant piece of historical information; however, Lawrence is significant when considering Indigenous histories. Before White settlement, Lawrence and the surrounding area were home to Indigenous communities with rich Native traditions. In fact, Lawrence is currently home to Haskell University—a tribal university that offers "quality education to Native American students" ("About Haskell"). I mention this history to underscore that the speech performed was delivered on land that was previously non-White. The very space-place was imbued with a non-White historicity and cultural disbursement that resulted from colonialism. The very land was material evidence of a Eurocentric narrative.

In addition to geographic location, a community-oriented pedagogical approach means a re(flexive) reading of the history of lacrosse. As I mentioned in the section above, the history shared by the student was a Eurocentric narrative whereby "friendly" relations between communities led to the adoption and "formalizing" of lacrosse as we know it today. A focus on broader audiences and community members would require students to ask: who are cultural groups that are being represented in this narrative? What are the implications of those narratives? Rather than prohibit the student from discussing the history of lacrosse, he would be challenged to look more critically at research that told the story from the perspective of White Europeans. White narratives are troubled as the correct and privileged historical telling.

The narrative absences—both geographically and historically—are placed in the forefront when rhetorical acts are understood as world-making, as creating reality, and as implicatory for subjects constituted in and through students' words. It would allow a framework for students and speakers to critically reflect and begin by acknowledging that "what I say matters." Using a reflexive and community-focused approach will not resolve any and all future failures, but it does ask that we shift curricular practices beyond the center, beyond the visible, and beyond who is present. It is a small shift born through failure.

CONCLUSION

Higher education, in our ongoing moment of diversity-talk, should undergo disciplinary reflection, including our oft-forsaken curricular traditions. I heed Wanzer-Serrano's (2019) reminder that, structurally, our institutions, policies, and norms privilege "white methods, white theories, white voices, and (at the end of the day) white able-bodied cisgender men" (p. 470). Without interrogation, we risk carrying on traditions that no longer serve us, that are based on a model of democracy that privileges the few, and that fail to account for implications rendered through our rhetoric. Without interrogation, neoliberalist logics of individualism will supersede community concerns. Without interrogation, Whiteness will continue, resulting in White-supremacist violence, the reduction of self-esteem for non-White students through racism (Boomer et al., 2011, p. 81), and knowledge that "is filtered through a racialized White tinted epistemological and ontological lens" (Smith, 2014).

Such interrogation requires failure—failure is innovation's prerequisite. After all, failure is a great teacher (Loscalzo, 2014). In the case of my failure, practiced reflexivity allowed for a deeper investigation of my own "business-as-usual" pedagogical practices, adopting curricular insights without consequence. It allowed a deeper reflection of my own Whiteness— of how my own White body always already inhabits the space of correct

106 MEGGIE MAPES

citizen-subject, the key demographic to a Eurocentric or colonialist narrative. I conclude with Giroux (2014) who reminds that:

> At the heart of this crisis of education are larger questions about the formative culture necessary for a democracy to survive, the nature of civic education and teaching in dark times, the role of educators as civic intellectuals, and what it means to understand the purpose and meaning of education as a site of individual and collective empowerment. (p. 34).

We will fail. But change may require that we lean in to that failure—to fail often and to learn often.

DISCUSSION QUESTIONS

1. What individual and cultural barriers have you experienced around diversity in a classroom setting?
2. How are student passions—on campus broadly, in specific classes, or in reference to a specific assignment—tied to their individual interests rather than community concerns? How can one shift this focus to foster global citizenship in the classroom?
3. What resources might students obtain that can connect them to communities and cultural groups in their area of interest? How can faculty and universities at large help students acquire those resources?
4. How can reflexivity be integrated into and across campus activities to better situate students beyond their individual context?
5. How can faculty encourage students to "see" and challenge their own privileges?
6. How can faculty help students realize the impact of assumed centers in the classroom and beyond? How can faculty challenge assumed centers pedagogically?

REFERENCES

Boomer, P. M., Hopkins, C. A., & Spaulding, L. (2011). *Perceptions of high school minority students and high school teachers regarding racism: A phenomenological study, ProQuest Dissertations and Theses.*

Broeckelman-Post, M. A., & Ruiz-Mesa, K. (2018). Measuring college learning in public speaking. *Social Science Research Council*, highered.ssrc.org /wp-content/ uploads/2018.10-MCL-in-Public-Speaking-Report.pdf.

Chakravartty, P., Kuo, R., Grubbs, V., & McIlwain, C. (2018). #CommunicationSoWhite. *Journal of Communication*, 68(2), 254–266. https://doi-org.www2.lib.ku.edu/ 10.1093/joc/jqy003

Charland, M. (2016). Constitutive rhetoric. In *Contemporary rhetorical theory*, 2nd ed. Mark J. Porrovecchio & Celeste Michelle Condit, eds. Guilford Press, pp. 382–395.

Floyd, K. (2019). *Public speaking matters*. 2nd ed. New York, NY: McGraw-Hill Education.

Giroux, H. (2014). *Neoliberalism's war on higher education*. Chicago: Haymarket Books.

Giroux, H. (2015). Political frauds, Donald Trump, and the ghost of totalitarianism. *Knowledge Cultures*, 4(5), 95–108.

Goldhill, O. (2017). Rhetoric scholars pinpoint why Trump's inarticulate speaking style is so persuasive, *Quartz*. https://qz.com/965004/rhetoric-scholars-pinpoint-why-trumps-inarticulate-speaking-style-is-so-persuasive/

Haskell Indian Nations University (2019). *About Haskell Indian Nations University*. https://haskell.edu/about/

hooks, b. (1994). *Teaching to transgress: Education as the practice of freedom*. New York, NY: Routledge.

Kapoutsis, I., & Volkema, R. (2019). Hard-core toughie: Donald Trump's negotiations for the United States presidency. *Negotiation Journal*, 35(1), 47–63.

Lemaster, B. (2015). Discontents of being and becoming fabulous on Rupaul's drag U: Queer criticism in neoliberal times. *Women's Studies in Communication*, 38(2), 1–20.

Loscalzo, J. (2014). A celebration of failure. *Circulation*, 129(9), 953–955.

Mapes, M. (2019). *Speak out, call in: Public speaking as advocacy*. Lawrence, KS: KU Libraries.

Morreale, S. P., Myers, S. A., Backlund, P. M., & Simonds, C. J. (2016). Study IX of the basic communication course at two- and four-year U.S. Colleges and Universities: A re-examination of our discipline's "front porch". *Communication Education*, 65(3), 338–355. doi:10.1080/03634523.2015.1073339

Nakayama, T., & Krizek, R. (1995). Whiteness: A strategic rhetoric. *Quarterly Journal of Speech*, 81(3), 291–309.

Root, C. P. (2016). An examination in the evolution of Iroquois lacrosse. Dissertation. *SUNY Buffalo State*, http://digitalcommons.buffalostate.edu/cgi/viewcontent.cgi?article=1041&context=history_theses

Smith, B. (2014). Confronting race and colonialism: Experiences and lessons learned from teaching social studies. *In Education*, 20(1).

Troup, C. L. (2002). Common sense in the basic public speaking course. *Basic Communication Course Annual*, 14(7). http://ecommons.udayton.edu/bcca/vol14/iss1/7

Wanzer-Serrano, D. (2019). Rhetoric's rac(e/ist) problems. *Quarterly Journal of Speech*, 105(4), 465–476. Doi: 10.1080/00335630.2019.1669068

Chapter 7

Envisioning Equity and Inclusion Through Art

Audra Buck-Coleman and Rashawn Ray

CONTEXTUAL BACKGROUND

When the 2015 University of Maryland, College Park (UMD) freshman cohort members began their studies, many were full of excitement and eager to call themselves "Terps," the nickname for the school's mascot. Most were optimistic about the site of their education and the people joining them in their academic endeavors. This large, public, urban university had one of the most diverse student bodies for a flagship in the country (Loh, 2018). This diversity included differences in race and ethnicity, religious beliefs, political ideologies, lifestyles, and culture. Racial minorities comprised more than one-third of its 40,000 student population (Richman, 2018).

UMD's structural diversity, the variation of different populations on campus, was a source of pride for administrators and a reason many students said they chose to attend this university instead of less-diverse ones. Many members of the 2015 cohort anticipated that this multifaceted campus would be a diversity utopia, as it was hyped by its Asian-American president, portrayed in promotional materials, and touted by student tour guides. The campus seemingly represented a microcosm of the United States' different racial, ethnic, political, and religious identities (Anderson, 2019), and it was viewed by some as a model for a pro-diversity environment.

Reaffirming this positive outlook was the notion that the nation was well into what some called a post-racial era (Goldman, 2012; Goldman & Hopkins, 2019; Ikuenobe, 2013).[1] When this cohort began their undergraduate career, Barack Obama, the first Black U.S. president, was ending his second term, and a candidate with another new identity for the position—female—was predicted to succeed him. In their sophomore year,

ENVISIONING EQUITY AND INCLUSION THROUGH ART **109**

these students had their first official opportunity to participate in this political process via the 2016 U.S. presidential election. With less than 10 miles separating their campus from the White House, they had a front-row view of the national political action. Some said this added to the significance of choosing a presidential candidate.

However, by the time these cohort members completed their undergraduate degrees, this utopian diversity "golden age" was in question. By their graduation, most had discovered some of the challenges of sharing the same space with diverse communities: the friction of competing ideologies, feelings of isolation stemming from belonging to minority identity groups—racial, religious, political, or otherwise—on a predominantly White campus, and the unease of having taken-for-granted opinions and beliefs questioned. Additionally, these students' undergraduate careers were shaped by on-campus, local, national, and international hate crimes and racial discrimination incidents, and divisive discourse about race, particularly regarding the treatment of Blacks and other people of color by police. The anticipated utopia was not the reality.

"PREPARING" STUDENTS FOR A DIVERSE CAMPUS AND WORLD

In Fall 2015, we employed an experimental research design to find out what influence, if any, artistic activities might have on students' acclimation to a structurally diverse campus, with specific attention given to opinions about racial and ethnic diversity and identity development. This research used a distinct set of diversity-training activities that were part of a larger project called Sticks + Stones, of which the first author was an original co-author. We employed these activities in a campus-wide, multi-section freshman course aimed at orientating students to college. The course included units about campus resources, developing effective study skills, navigating college life, and learning about diversity. Although most students anticipated the diverse campus population, many were unfamiliar with interacting with and being proximate to the differences they had sought. Our activities were intended to destigmatize and reduce the perceived gaps between these differences.

Fifty-one instructors agreed to participate, 37 of which led treatment sections using the Sticks + Stones component as their diversity unit. The authors conducted pre-course training with these instructors, who then implemented these activities in their courses. The other 14 instructors' courses served as control sections. These instructors used diversity units of their choosing. More than 1,000 students participated.

The Sticks + Stones activities had six components. The first was an abstract self-portrait assignment that prompted students to visualize

110 AUDRA BUCK-COLEMAN AND RASHAWN RAY

salient aspects of their past, present, and future identities, including lived locations, hobbies, future plans, pop culture references, and ideas about their possible future selves (Markus & Nurius, 1986). Students created imagery that represented both how they saw themselves and how they wanted others to see them through their most salient identities. This component was central to this investigation. Artistic objects play a significant role in society. Art has been used to reflect norms and behavior, offer a reconsideration of those norms, serve as provocation for new possibilities, and represent ideas about the self. Further, art and visual imagery's capacity to surprise and communicate in unexpected, less-confrontational ways suited this project. Art can create a greater level of openness and receptiveness than other direct means of communication, such as lectures and writing (Polletta & Lee, 2006). The process of creating visual imagery calls upon the maker to consider what they want to communicate, the understanding audiences have about different signs and symbols, and how best to relate the two. To create their abstract self-portraits, students would grapple with how to represent who they are rather than what they look like.

The process of viewing this imagery calls upon individuals to decode and synthesize the different signs and symbols represented to create an interpretation of another's work. These visual communication and interpretation processes create a distinctive form of diversity-training engagement that can disrupt stereotypical ideas about diverse others and reshape opinions of others' identities as well as one's own.

Next, the self-portraits were exchanged with those from other classes. Students were assigned to anonymously label and stereotype the people depicted in those portraits, revealing backstage thoughts (Goffman, 1959) about ingroup and outgroup member identities (Tajfel & Turner, 1979). A central philosophical assumption in this activity is the notion that categories or labels students consciously and subconsciously use for themselves and others influence their choice of preferred communication partners in social and personal contexts, and their behaviors within those interactions (Callero, 2014). Notably, this labeling and stereotyping process made overt identity categorization practices that are often covert. Identifying and deconstructing the negative aspects of these categorization processes offered an opportunity to disarm those terms (Jung, 2015).

Students then participated in the third component, the Privilege Walk, a physical performance activity. Participants took steps forward for advantages and backward for hardships or disadvantages. By the end of the activity, the more privileged students stood towards the front and disadvantaged students toward the back. The Privilege Walk proved to be an impressionable activity because, once completed, some understood, at a deeper level, the extent of their privilege. That they come to understand this in juxtaposition to their peers can clarify the notion of privilege and its functions (Tajfel & Turner, 1979). We directed instructors to emphasize the students' shared identities (Crisp & Hewstone, 2007; Hogg, 2016), including being a Terp, to minimize the negative effects of seeing differences (Tajfel & Turner, 1979) and to maximize the positive effects of seeing similarities. Course instructors facilitated a brief discussion addressing the students' positions at the conclusion of the Privilege Walk. Students were also invited to interrogate their levels of privilege during the larger peer-to-peer discussion.

For the fourth component, instructors presented students with empirical information about how stereotypes operate in our daily lives and the different ways they can be detrimental to minority groups. Preceding activities and this information became the foundation for the fifth component: peer-to-peer diversity dialogue. Students addressed the positive and negative stereotypes mobilized in the process of completing these activities, how those categories applied (or not) to themselves and their peers, and why they exist. Importantly, students were invited to critically reflect on and discuss why they stereotyped and what they could do to reduce their propensity to stereotype in the future. We provided instructors with discussion prompts related to each component of this unit, as well as general questions about students' lives and diversity issues. Students were prompted to consider the multifaceted aspects of their and their peers' identities in an effort to find commonalities rather than categorize one another on a majority-minority spectrum. Previous research suggests that peer-to-peer interaction is potentially the most effective way of prompting change during college (Astin, 1993; Feldman & Newcomb, 1969; Pascarella et al., 2005).

The final component was a written assignment that prompted students to describe their thoughts about and takeaways from these activities. This presented an opportunity for introverted students to express their otherwise-undisclosed input and opinions, allowed consideration of insights that formed after the activities concluded, and offered students a sense of closure about any lingering thoughts or impressions from these activities. Collectively, these activities were multimodal, offering a variety of ways—class discussion, visual expression, written expression, and didactic information—for students to (re)consider their identities and the presumptions they make of others.

Our goal was to investigate what impact, if any, these activities might have upon college students' views of their senses of self and diverse others. Research suggests that cross-racial interactions have the potential to reduce prejudice (Allport, 1954; Pettigrew & Tropp, 2006, 2011) increase comfort with people from other races (Engberg, 2007; Engberg & Hurtado, 2011); foster more racial and cultural understanding and engagement (Astin,

112 AUDRA BUCK-COLEMAN AND RASHAWN RAY

1993; Chang, 1999; Denson, 2009; Denson & Chang, 2015; Denson & Zhang, 2010); increase college satisfaction and sense of belonging on campus, leading to increased retention (Astin, 1993; Bowman, 2013; Bowman & Denson, 2012; Chang, 1999); and shape students' overall success in college (Pascarella, Whitt, Nora, & Edison, 1996). If we could propagate ways for students to understand the identities and perspectives of their diverse peers and reduce perceived differences at the beginning of their college career, we expected those effects would only magnify as the students progressed. Importantly, we projected that by graduation, their receptiveness to racially, ethnically, religiously, and culturally diverse others would increase through additional informal interactions.

DIFFERENTIAL IMPACT OF DIVERSITY COURSEWORK

To capture the impact of the Sticks + Stones activities, we conducted individual in-depth interviews with this cohort during their freshman and senior years ($n = 62$), administered an online survey in their first semester and last semesters ($n = 170$) and a three-item questionnaire ($n = 537$) at the end of this freshman course. We included students from both control and treatment courses and asked them to self-identify gender, race, and political identity for the interviews and online survey.

The questionnaire asked what part, if any, of this course's content had (1) been most useful to them, (2) made the deepest impression upon their behavior and social choices, and (3) they shared with others including friends, coworkers, and family members. Responses addressed different aspects of these courses. Following are a few question-one response exemplars that mentioned our activities:

> Comment 1: I found the Privilege Walk most useful to see where I stood in comparison to others, and it allowed me to understand the diversity in my class.
> Comment 2: The self-portraits and the essay questions after the self-portrait were the most useful to me because it helped me understand how I view myself and how I wanted to view myself.
> Comment 3: I was used to diversity and different cultures prior to the class. However, I learned that this is not the case for everyone. It has made me more open about my culture....

Overall, students mentioned that they now had a better understanding of the inherent tension between self-perception and the labels placed on us by others. They also had a deeper understanding of their unique standpoint in relation to their peers.

ENVISIONING EQUITY AND INCLUSION THROUGH ART **113**

The second question asked how the course's content shaped students' behavior and social choices. This question received the most diversity mentions:

> Comment 1: The lesson we did on stereotypes probably had the most direct impact on my behavior and social choices. It made me more aware of how common certain stereotypes are in my daily life, so I try to avoid jumping to conclusions when meeting new people.
> Comment 2: Definitely the labeling. ... There were so many different pictures and yet we always associated an image with a stereotype we had.
> Comment 3: The time we discussed racial differences made me realize how diverse this place really is. It made me feel less alone.

These responses showed how students were applying lessons learned from the Sticks + Stones activities. Through them, students realized how their identities were similar and different from others. Critically, students remarked how their opinions and behaviors have been reshaped.

The third question asked how the diversity components might be influencing others. Following are a few responses:

> Comment 1: The one thing I remember sharing was the stereotype activity where we wrote down typical stereotypes for different ethnic groups and read them off anonymously. I just thought it was a unique and memorable activity that illustrated how implicit biases form.
> Comment 2: Outside of class, I have had conversations regarding stereotypes with my friends and peers.
> Comment 3: I have shared my abstract self-portrait with most of my friends and family. I liked this activity because it allowed me to notice all aspects of my life and portray them in one single image.

Relating these activities to others revealed their salience to students and their audiences. It also called upon students to articulate the content in their own way, indicating a higher order of learning and cognitive processing.

Overall, the questionnaire responses showed that the Sticks + Stones activities had a positive impact on the way students viewed themselves and their UMD peers. Whereas almost half (47%) of the answers from treatment sections mentioned one of the Sticks + Stones diversity activities as something that was either useful to them, made a deep impression, or that they had shared with others, only 20% of control section respondents mentioned their course's diversity component. By the end of this course, the Sticks + Stones diversity activities had more salience and resonance than diversity units offered in control sections.

114 AUDRA BUCK-COLEMAN AND RASHAWN RAY

We also interviewed students ($n = 62$) at the end of their freshman (2016) and senior (2019) years. At the end of their freshman year, a little more than one-third (37%) of the control-section interviewees said they could not recall any diversity content from the course. Approximately six months after it had concluded, they remembered other aspects, but not the diversity unit. Other students had only a vague recollection of the diversity component. In contrast, all treatment-section students could recall these exercises at the end of their freshman year, and 75% could recall the activities and their peers' reactions to them when we interviewed them in their senior year. Three-and-a-half years after they had completed these activities, they were able to describe some, if not all, of the components in detail. This indicates the higher degree of resonance of the Sticks + Stones activities versus those used in control-section courses.

IMPLICATIONS AND LESSONS LEARNED

Almost half (47%) of our interviewees mentioned diversity as something they were expecting, if not looking forward to, as part of their undergraduate career. They talked about how tour guides and promotional materials boasted this diversity and that they expected good things from it. When these students began their time at UMD, they had a positive view overall of how diversity benefits their studies, their classroom discussions, their peers, and their campus. During their freshman year, students responded positively overall to our questions about diversity via the online survey. Using a zero to four scale, where zero indicates strongly disagree and four indicates strongly agree, they largely agreed that a diverse campus benefited them (3.13 average out of 4.0), that diversity was a good goal (3.29 average), that UMD was a diverse campus (3.13 average), that they felt comfortable on campus (3.19 average), and that they liked being a student at UMD (3.28 average). By their senior year, all of these response averages dropped except for responses to diversity being a good goal (see Table 7.1). Further, when we looked at responses based on racial identities, those from Black respondents were lower than those with other racial identities on average. In addition, these responses were on average lower with statistical significance as compared to non-Hispanic Whites (see Table 7.2).

What caused this decrease in opinions about diversity? What caused the Black respondents to respond less-positively on average with statistical significance? Allport's (1954) contact theory, supported by Pettigrew and Tropp's meta-analyses (2006, 2011), states that as individuals interact with outgroup members, their prejudice is reduced. We expected our results to support this theory, but we did not anticipate the local, national, and

ENVISIONING EQUITY AND INCLUSION THROUGH ART **115**

Table 7.1 Opinions about Campus Diversity

	Freshman Year	*Senior Year*
Average opinions about campus diversity		
A diverse campus benefits me	3.13 (1.0)	3.04 (0.88)
Diversity is a good goal	3.29 (1.05)	3.5 (0.71)
UMD is a diverse campus	3.13 (1.04)	3.06 (0.87)
I feel comfortable on campus	3.19 (0.92)	3.08 (0.88)
I like being a student at UMD	3.28 (0.94)	3.06 (0.93)
Averages by race and political views		
Comfortable on campus		
Non-Hispanic White	3.32 (0.83)	3.22 (0.81)
Black	2.64 (0.76)	2.12 (0.97)
Hispanic	3.143 (1.46)	3.571 (0.79)
Asian or Asian-American	3.21 (1.11)	3.29 (0.63)
Multiracial or foreign	3.33 (0.5)	3.0 (0.5)
Like being a student on campus		
Non-Hispanic White	3.35 (0.87)	3.2 (0.88)
Black	3.04 (0.98)	2.32 (1.14)
Hispanic	3.29 (1.5)	3.571 (0.79)
Asian or Asian-American	3.24 (1.03)	3.09 (0.75)
Multiracial	3.44 (0.53)	3.11 (0.60)
UMD is a diverse campus		
Non-Hispanic White	3.3 (0.94)	3.27 (0.61)
Black	2.56 (1.08)	1.96 (1.17)
Hispanic	2.71 (1.60)	3.29 (0.76)
Asian or Asian-American	3.06 (1.09)	3.21 (0.73)
Multiracial	3.56 (0.53)	3.22 (0.67)

Notes: Standard deviation in parentheses. Overall, there were 165 respondents for the freshman-year survey and 170 for the senior-year survey. Racial response numbers were the following: 91 in freshman year and 95 in senior year for non-Hispanic Whites, 25 for both years for Blacks, 7 for both years for Hispanics, 33 and 34, respectively, for Asians, and 9 for both years for multiracial.

international incidents of identity-based violence and discrimination that would occur during this cohort's undergraduate career.

For example, as they were making decisions about which school to attend, Freddie Gray died as a result of alleged violent treatment by police in nearby Baltimore City (Ruiz, 2017). At the end of their freshman year, campus police used unnecessary force to break up a graduation party attended mostly by Black students (Thomas, 2016). During their sophomore year, a noose was found hanging in the kitchen of an on-campus fraternity house, White-supremacist flyers were posted on campus (Brown, 2017; Campisi & Richman, 2017), and a Black visiting student, Lt. Richard Collins III, was stabbed to death on campus by a UMD student with alleged White-supremacist ties (Massimo, 2017). At the start of their sophomore year, NFL football star Colin Kaepernick began protesting the treatment of people of color during the national anthem. Others followed suit.

Table 7.2 Regression of Opinions about Campus Diversity

	Freshman year		Senior year	
	P value	*Coefficient*	*P value*	*Coefficient*
UMD is a diverse campus				
Black	−0.88 (0.23)	0.000***	−1.42 (0.164)	0.000***
Hispanic	−0.67 (0.38)	0.080	0.08 (0.28)	0.776
Asian	−0.35 (0.21)	0.096	−0.107 (0.14)	0.459
Multiracial	0.38 (0.34)	0.267	−0.02 (0.24)	0.920
Comfortable on campus				
Black	−0.59 (0.22)	0.008**	−1.06 (0.18)	0.000***
Hispanic	−0.17 (0.36)	0.646	0.37 (0.32)	0.239
Asian	−0.153 (0.2)	0.441	0.07 (0.16)	0.678
Multiracial	0.19 (0.33)	0.558	−0.14 (0.27)	0.606
I like being a student at UMD				
Black	−0.16 (0.22)	0.481	−0.88 (0.20)	0.000***
Hispanic	−0.07 (0.37)	0.859	0.4 (0.35)	0.264
Asian	−0.15 (0.20)	0.448	−0.13 (0.18)	0.468
Multiracial	0.24 (0.33)	0.478	−0.02 (0.30)	0.953
A diverse campus benefits me				
Black	−0.004 (0.24)	0.985	−1.36 (0.16)	0.000***
Hispanic	−0.12 (0.4)	0.760	−0.002 (0.28)	0.994
Asian	−0.31 (0.22)	0.159	0.26 (0.14)	0.075
Multiracial	0.5 (0.36)	0.164	0.04 (0.24)	0.853

Diversity is a good goal				
Black	0.44 (0.25)	0.082	0.04 (0.15)	0.81
Hispanic	0.005 (0.41)	0.991	0.29 (0.26)	0.268
Asian	0.02 (0.23)	0.942	0.31 (0.13)	0.020*
Multiracial	0.46 (0.37)	0.221	−0.02 (0.22)	0.926

$*p < 0.05$, $**p < 0.01$, $***p < 0.001$

Notes: Standard error in parentheses under coefficient, 95% confidence intervals

Freshman diverse campus: $F(6, 140) = 4.93$, $P > F = 0.0001$, $R^2 = 0.1743$

Senior diverse campus: $F(6, 160) = 14.33$, $P > F = 0.0000$, $R^2 = 0.3496$

Freshman comfort on campus: $F(6, 140) = 4.93$, $P > F = 0.2330$, $R^2 = 0.0553$

Senior comfort on campus: $F(6, 160) = 6.57$, $P > F = 0.0000$, $R^2 = 0.1977$

Freshman like being a student: $F(6, 140) = 0.46$, $P > F = 0.9066$, $R^2 = 0.0149$

Senior like being a student: $F(6, 160) = 3.62$, $P > F = 0.0022$, $R^2 = 0.1195$

Freshman benefits me: $F(6, 140) = 1.87$, $P > F = 0.0905$, $R^2 = 0.0741$

Senior benefits me: $F(6, 160) = 15.78$, $P > F = 0.0000$, $R^2 = 0.3717$

Freshman good goal: $F(6, 140) = 2.76$, $P > F = 0.0144$, $R^2 = 0.1058$

Senior good goal: $F(6, 160) = 5.56$, $P > F = 0.0000$, $R^2 = 0.1724$

118 AUDRA BUCK-COLEMAN AND RASHAWN RAY

The following year, President Trump would lambast Kaepernick and the protests in general for being un-American. By the end of this cohort's junior year, the campus administration had verified 15 of the 27 reported on-campus hate- and bias-motivated incidents that occurred since Fall 2017 (Brennan, 2018).

The summer before their senior year, Jordan McNair, a Black student on the UMD football team, died due to alleged negligence by the coaching staff (Jenkins, 2018; Rittenberg & VanHaaren, 2018), and the university-level repercussions of his death continued to make headlines throughout their senior year. Meanwhile, 40 students contracted the Adenovirus, 15 of which were hospitalized, and one died from the illness (Abelson et al., 2019). Because the administration was so flummoxed as to how to handle the issues surrounding McNair's death, they were unable to respond adequately to this campus health crisis (Abelson et al., 2019). During the middle of their senior year, UMD's racist legacy was reaffirmed when a current student found old yearbook photos of Terps wearing blackface (Atelsek, 2019).

These students' undergraduate career was also marked by record-setting numbers of events tied to White supremacy (Schwartz, 2019). During their senior year alone, an anti-Semite killed 11 at a Pittsburgh synagogue (Robertson et al., 2018), a gunman in New Zealand killed at least 50 at two mosques (Harris & Sonmez, 2019), and an Alabama newspaper editor proclaimed it was time for the Ku Klux Klan to "ride again" (Brown, 2019; Farzan, 2019). All the while, a White man serving as U.S. President routinely made racially demeaning statements such as calling White supremacists "very fine people" and describing Africans as people hailing from "shit-hole countries" (Jamison, 2019; Kendi, 2019). The Southern Poverty Law Center, which tracks hate groups across the country, noted a 7% increase in the overall number of hate groups as well as the "firm foothold in the mainstream" they made since Trump came into office (Beirich, 2019).

Perhaps given the above, it should (Denson & Zhang, 2010) not have been surprising that our Tables 7.1 and 7.2 results revealed that some students with minority identities showed reduced value for diversity and reduced feelings of inclusion and belonging on campus. For example, on average, Blacks had the lowest averages for comfort on campus and least liked being on campus in both their freshman and senior years. Their responses were the lowest out of the racial categories and had the largest decreases from freshman to senior year. They were also, on average, significantly less likely to say UMD was a diverse campus, less likely to say they liked being a student on campus, and less likely to say UMD's diversity benefited them. In our interviews, Black students attributed this significant amount of distance and lack of fit on campus to the treatment they received from other students, the administration's lack of strong visible response to racial hate crimes and caring for students in general, and the racially unwelcoming and politically divisive campus climate. These negative feelings increased over the course of their undergraduate career.

A separate 2018 UMD campus climate survey revealed that minority populations, including faculty, staff, and students of color and gender non-binary, felt less welcome and unsafe on campus, and that Latinx and Black students felt a reduced sense of belonging to campus than Asian and White students (Brennan, 2018). Students complained that the university had done a "horrible" job at managing the racial crises, especially in regard to Collins' death, and at addressing the racially "toxic" campus environment (Atelsek, 2018).

Lessons learned from the Sticks + Stones activities were relevant within the context of their freshman course but lost impact within the context of students' college trajectory. Daily interactions, the events described above, the campus administration's slow response to hate crimes, and the divisive national political rhetoric diluted the positive impact of these activities for some students.

PROMISING PRACTICES FOR CHANGE

Our results point towards three recommendations for college and university campuses: nimble and rapid responses to hate crimes and other identity-based incidents, diversity education requirements throughout students' college careers, and strong and visual support for minority students from across all levels of campus.

Nimble and Rapid Responses to Hate Crimes and Other Identity-Based Incidents

Universities must be more agile and decisive when events that have a negative impact on diversity and inclusion occur. For example, when the photos of Terps in blackface came to light, then-UMD President, Wallace Loh, merely tweeted his condemnation of the images (de Silva, 2019). Neither he nor other campus administrators made other overt efforts to address the underlying issues of racism and oppression raised by the images. The students we interviewed said this low-level of response sent a signal that Loh and others were not ready to dismantle White privilege and oppression. In contrast, when similar photos were discovered at nearby George Washington University, the school held a "teach-in" about blackface and racism in response (Smith, 2019). The event demonstrated administration-level support for calling out this behavior.

120 AUDRA BUCK-COLEMAN AND RASHAWN RAY

Diversity Education Requirements Throughout Students' College Careers

Beyond swift responses to hate incidents, college campuses need to implement diversity and inclusion curricula units throughout students' college careers. One diversity unit in one course of one semester was not enough to counter the cumulative effects of everyday racism, the proliferation of hate crimes, and White-supremacy demonstrations. Although these events transpired on-campus, on the other side of the world, and places in between, students collapsed the distance by connecting similar events to each other, magnifying the impact. Within the context of the freshman course, the Sticks + Stones activities were salient, but against the larger social ecology of racial discrimination, hate crimes, and divisive political rhetoric occurring during their undergraduate career, they were not. We advocate that this does not negate the effectiveness of these activities, but rather supports an argument for more of such initiatives. Further, when the political climate also fosters divisiveness and further marginalizes and terrorizes minority groups, inclusion efforts become more vital. To this end, we recommend multiple curricular components that engage students on ongoing systemic and in-the-moment diversity issues.

Strong and Visual Support for Minority Students from All Levels of Campus

Finally, a university that touts its diversity needs to also visibly and strongly support the inclusion and retention of historically underrepresented and minority students who may experience greater feelings of disconnection (Sidanius et al., 2008). Students want and need to know that all levels and all populations—students, faculty, staff, and administrators—support inclusion and diversity. Anne, a Black female majoring in medicine, put it this way:

> I just feel like the racial and social climate on this campus isn't really great for learning. Since I've been here, three people have died ..., a majority of them being Black men, and that's not really the type of environment that I want to be in or around, especially when I feel like administration isn't doing their due diligence....

According to Anne and others, the upper-level administration was not reacting quickly enough nor with enough significance. Some talked about being misled by the diversity-promoting marketing materials: the support they thought they would receive did not materialize, especially when they needed it most, such as when White-supremacist posters were posted and after the murder of Lt. Richard Collins III.

CONCLUSION

These results show that the Sticks + Stones activities can be effective. However, one interaction cannot offset continued bias and prejudice. Further, lack of action by an administration only serves to burden the students they should be supporting. Kiara, a Black, first-generation college student described the toll of protesting against hate crimes and participating in demonstrations to seek more action from administrators in support of minority populations:

> They're exhausting, honestly. [While] some people ... don't have to worry about these issues .... I still have to go to class ... and do my homework.

Recommendations for future actions include conducting these activities in concert with other campus-wide diversity and inclusion efforts and clear, action-based, top-down support for minority populations.

DISCUSSION QUESTIONS

General

1. What do you feel is successful about diversity and inclusion efforts on your campus? What could be improved?
2. How welcoming have you and others been to minority populations? What welcoming efforts have you seen others make? What else might be done to make minority groups feel included?
3. What national social justice issues have impacted students on your campus in the last few years? Faculty and staff? How has your campus responded?
4. How do you feel about the diversity at your institution? How different or similar is it to what you have experienced in the past (e.g., other institutions, high school)?
5. In what ways have you noticed campus members—students, faculty, staff—defy your stereotypical expectations of them?

For Students

6. If you were to create an abstract self-portrait as described in this article, what content would you include? What aspects of your identity would you want others to know about first? Not know about at all? Why? Would your self-portrait be different if you were creating it for an audience other than this campus? Why?

122 AUDRA BUCK-COLEMAN AND RASHAWN RAY

7. Do you hang out with friends from high school, or do you have a new group of friends on campus? How, if at all, have your social circles changed? What are the shared interests or identities that connect you to friends?

ACKNOWLEDGEMENTS

This project would not have been possible without the financial support of the University of Maryland Office of Diversity and Inclusion and the National Science Foundation's ADVANCE program.

NOTE

1. Many scholars disagree with this assessment including Dawson & Bobo (2009); Hutchings (2009); and Shaw & Brown (2013).

REFERENCES

Abelson, J., Brittain, A., & Larimer, S. (2019, May 16). A dangerous delay. *The Washington Post.*

Allport, G. W. (1954). *The nature of prejudice.* Garden City, NY: Anchor Books.

Anderson, N. (2019, January 30). U-Md. President Loh to keep post until June 2020 as board searches for successor. *The Washington Post.*

Astin, A. W. (1993). *What matters in college?: Four critical years revisited.* San Francisco, CA: Jossey-Bass.

Atelsek, J. (2018). UMD group is creating a video series to combat school's "abysmal" diversity messaging. *The Diamondback.*

Atelsek, J. (2019, February 8). President Loh responds to photos of blackface in old UMD yearbooks. *The Diamondback.*

Beirich, H. (2019). *The year in hate: Rage against change.* Retrieved from https://www.splcenter.org/fighting-hate/intelligence-report/2019/year-hate-rage-against-change

Bowman, N. A. (2013). How much diversity is enough? The curvilinear relationship between college diversity interactions and first-year student outcomes. *Research in Higher Education*, 54(8), 874-894.

Bowman, N. A., & Denson, N. (2012). What's past is prologue: How precollege exposure to racial diversity shapes the impact of college interracial interactions. *Research in Higher Education*, 53(4), 406-425.

Brennan, L. (2018, May 3). UMD campus climate survey finds some minority respondents feel unsafe, unwelcome. *The Diamondback.*

Brown, M. (2019, February 18). Alabama newspaper editor calls for Klan return to 'clean out D.C.'. *The Montgomery Advertiser.*

Brown, S. (2017, November 28). Why the U. of Maryland is hiring a 'hate-bias response coordinator'. *The Chronicle of Higher Education.*

ENVISIONING EQUITY AND INCLUSION THROUGH ART **123**

Callero, P. L. (2014). Self, identity, and social inequality. In *Handbook of the social psychology of inequality* (pp. 273–294). Springer.

Campisi, J., & Richman, T. (2017, March 13). White nationalist posters found in at least 4 UMD locations Monday. *The Diamondback.*

Chang, M. J. (1999). Does racial diversity matter?: The educational impact of a racially diverse undergraduate population. *Journal of College Student Development,* 40, 377-395.

Crisp, R. J., & Hewstone, M. (2007). Multiple social categorization. *Advances in Experimental Social Psychology,* 39, 163–254.

Dawson, M. C., & Bobo, L. D. (2009). One year later and the myth of a post-racial society. *Du Bois Review,* 6(2), 247–249.

Denson, N. (2009). Do Curricular and Cocurricular Diversity Activities Influence Racial Bias? A Meta-Analysis. *Review of Educational Research,* 79(2), 805–838.

Denson, N., & Chang, M. J. (2015). Dynamic relationships: Identifying moderators that maximize benefits associated with diversity. *The Journal of Higher Education,* 86(1), 1-37.

Denson, N., & Zhang, S. (2010). The impact of student experiences with diversity on developing graduate attributes. *Studies in Higher Education,* 35(5), 529–543.

Engberg, M. E. (2007). Educating the workforce for the 21st century: A cross-disciplinary analysis of the impact of the undergraduate experience on students' development of a pluralistic orientation. *Research in Higher Education,* 48(3), 283–317.

Engberg, M. E., & Hurtado, S. (2011). Developing pluralistic skills and dispositions in college: Examining racial/ethnic group differences. *The Journal of Higher Education,* 82(4), 416–443.

Farzan, A. N. (2019, February 19). 'Time for the Ku Klux Klan to night ride again': An Alabama newspaper editor wants to bring back lynching. *The Washington Post.*

Feldman, K. A., & Newcomb, T. M. (1969). *The impact of college on students.* San Francisco, CA: Jossey-Bass.

Goffman, E. (1959). *The presentation of self in everyday life.* Garden City, NY: Anchor.

Goldman, S., & Hopkins, D. J. (2019). When can exemplars shape White racial attitudes? Evidence from the 2012 US presidential campaign. *International Journal of Public Opinion Research,* 31(4), 649–668.

Goldman, S. K. (2012). Effects of the 2008 Obama presidential campaign on White racial prejudice. *Public Opinion Quarterly,* 76(4), 663–687.

Harris, S., & Sonmez, F. (2019, March 17). Mulvaney says it's 'absurd' to link New Zealand mosque attacks to Trump's rhetoric. *The Washington Post.*

Hogg, M. A. (2016). Social identity theory. In S. McKeown, R. Haji, & N. Ferguson (Eds.), *Understanding peace and conflict through social identity theory: Contemporary global perspectives* (pp. 3–17). Switzerland: Springer.

Hutchings, V. L. (2009). Change or more of the same? Evaluating racial attitudes in the Obama era. *Public Opinion Quarterly,* 73(5), 917–942.

Ikuenobe, P. (2013). Conceptualizing and theorizing about the idea of a "post-racial" era. *Journal for the Theory of Social Behaviour,* 43(4), 446–468.

Jamison, P. (2019, March 16). HBCUs seeing resurgent appeal amid rising racial tensions. *The Washington Post.*

Jenkins, S. (2018, October 1). Culture didn't kill Jordan McNair. Negligence did. DJ Durkin is responsible for both. *The Washington Post.*

Jung, Y. (2015). Post stereotypes: Deconstructing racial assumptions and biases through visual culture and confrontational pedagogy. *Studies in Art Education,* 56(3), 214–227.

Kendi, I. X. (2019, January 13). The day 'shithole' entered the presidential lexicon. *The Atlantic.*

Loh, W. D. (2018, February 2). UMD: We're committed to Black student enrollment, success. *The Baltimore Sun.*

Markus, H., & Nurius, P. (1986). Possible selves. *American Psychologist,* 41(9), 954–969.

Massimo, R. (2017, October 17). Hate crime charge in death of Bowie State student. *The WTOP.*

Pascarella, E. T., Terenzini, P. T., & Feldman, K. A. (2005). *How college affects students* (Vol. 2). San Francisco, CA: Jossey-Bass.

Pascarella, E. T., Whitt, E. J., Nora, A., & Edison, M. (1996). What have we learned from the first year of the national study of student learning? *Journal of College Student Development.*

Pettigrew, T. F., & Tropp, L. R. (2006). A meta-analytic test of intergroup contact theory. *Journal of Personality and Social Psychology,* 90(5), 751–783. doi:10.1037/0022-3514.90.5.751

Pettigrew, T. F., & Tropp, L. R. (2008). How does intergroup contact reduce prejudice? Meta-analytic tests of three mediators. *European Journal of Social Psychology,* 38, 922–934.

Pettigrew, T. F., & Tropp, L. R. (2011). *When groups meet: The dynamics of intergroup contact.* New York, NY: Psychology Press.

Polletta, F., & Lee, J. (2006). Is telling stories good for democracy? Rhetoric in public deliberation after 9/11. *American Sociological Review,* 71(5), 699–721.

Richman, T. (2018, January 29). Black student enrollment lags at University of Maryland. *The Baltimore Sun.*

Rittenberg, A., & VanHaaren, T. (2018, November 1). Timeline: Everything that led to DJ Durkin's firing at Maryland. *The ESPN.*

Robertson, C., Mele, C., & Tavernise, S. (2018, October 27). 11 killed in synagogue massacre; suspect charged with 29 counts. *The New York Times.*

Ruiz, R. R. (2017, September 12). Baltimore officers will face no federal charges in death of freddie gray. *The New York Times.*

Schwartz, M. S. (2019, March 6). White supremacist propaganda at 'record-setting' levels, ADL report finds. *The NPR.*

Shaw, T. C., & Brown, R. A. (2013). *After Obama: African American politics in the post-Obama America.* Paper presented at the *2014 National Conference of Black Political Scientists (NCOBPS) annual meeting.*

Sidanius, J., Levin, S., Van Laar, C., & Sears, D. O. (2008). *The diversity challenge: Social identity and intergroup relations on the college campus.* New York, NY: Russell Sage Foundation.

Smith, M. (2019, Feb. 16, 2019). 'I'm not shocked': Students and professors react to blackface photos in old George Washington yearbooks. *Washington Post.*

Tajfel, H., & Turner, J. C. (1979). An integrative theory of intergroup conflict. *The social psychology of intergroup relations,* 33(47), 74.

Thomas, B. (2016, July 20). University of Maryland police wrongly used pepper spray to shut down a party in May. *The Washingtonian.*

PART IV

ORGANIZATIONAL CONTEXT: BECOMING A DIVERSITY WORKER, PLANNING FOR CHANGE, AND CRAFTING PATHWAYS FORWARD

Chapter **8**

Muslim Students Combatting Institutional Inertia with Participatory-Action Research

Saugher Nojan

INTRODUCTION

Despite almost two decades of increasing numbers of anti-Muslim hate crimes on college campuses (CAIR, 2017) in 2017–2018, Muslim students still were not provided with a dedicated prayer space on our campus. As a practicing Muslim and graduate student, I witnessed the exclusion and lack of accommodations for Muslim students firsthand. During my first years on campus, I found closets, mailrooms, or empty labs to pray in at social gatherings or in-between classes. I felt awkward and anxious that someone would misunderstand me if they were to see me. I was not the only one; I observed undergraduate Muslim students praying under staircases or discreetly on chairs in the library. The burden of concealment for these students was always present: "who are you, what are you, explain yourself" (Ahmed, 2017, p. 123). Each Friday, students reserved temporary rooms for group prayers in classroom and conference spaces not designed for worship. The misfit between Muslim students and the institution was stark.

This chapter examines how university conditions and institutional inertia prompted a group of Muslim womxn from diverse academic and racial/ethnic backgrounds to conduct a collaborative, participatory-action research project. I argue that participant-action research (PAR) can be a strategic tool to catalyze institutional agents to enact their promises. I also argue that this method holds limitations when enacted within liberal university spaces that espouse diversity, equity, and inclusion, but only as "performative non-performativity" (Ahmed, 2017; Sexton, 2010; Walcott, 2018)—when universities make commitments to value diversity and equity but fail to act on these values (Sexton, 2010; Walcott, 2018, p. 88). Our PAR photovoice project

128 SAUGHER NOJAN

created space for excluded perspectives and challenged the university's performative non-performativity by shifting the responsibility of supporting students' basic needs from students to the administration.

ANTI-MUSLIM RACISM IN HIGHER EDUCATION

A growing body of literature in higher education suggests that Islamophobia is a blatant form of racism, resulting in an increased likelihood of suspicion, vigilance, and mental and physical health problems for the Muslim Americans who experience it (Nadal et al., 2012). Among Muslims, women who wear the hijab (veil) are at increased risk of experiencing harassment, such as minor instances of marginalization, prejudice, and discomfort (Seggie & Sanford, 2010). Non-visible Muslims also feel vulnerable due to stereotype threats (i.e., fears of being judged for their religious identity). Stereotypes include the labels "foreign," "terrorist," "oppressed," or "backward" (Ali, 2014, p. 1257). These stereotypes create anxiety and have negative implications for student success.

Although the academic performance of Muslim students is similar to other religious groups, Muslims are less satisfied with their educational experiences compared to other groups (Cole & Ahmadi, 2010; Nasir & Al-Amin, 2006). Muslim students' dissatisfaction may be due to the burden of representation they feel as a result of continually managing impressions with their professors and peers (Ali, 2014; Fine & Sirin, 2007; Nasir & Al-Amin, 2006). For this reason, Nasir and Al-Amin (2006) discuss the importance of creating "identity-safe spaces" on college campuses for Muslim-American students to mitigate feelings of being judged from external and internal sources regarding their religious identity (Ali & Bagheri, 2009). Studies on Muslim student success suggest universities are willing to support them by enacting their stated values of diversity, equity, and inclusion (DEI); yet, while DEI plans often mention religious inclusion, universities rarely offer material support for nondominant religious students (Cole & Ahmadi, 2010; Nasir-& Al-Amin, 2006).

DIVERSITY WORK AND INSTITUTIONAL INERTIA

For California higher-education institutions, *diversity* no longer signifies historical exclusion and systemic oppression; instead, the concept refers to inclusion and the positive goal of nondiscrimination (Mitchell, 2018). This definition is derived from California's history of court decisions and public referendums against affirmative action. When the Supreme Court argued in *UC Davis v. Bakke* that Davis could not legally "discriminate" against Bakke, a white man's claims of discrimination set the stage for *diversity* to take on new meaning (Mitchell, 2018). The Court's perspective reproduces anti-Blackness, even as it overlooks ongoing disparities impacting different racialized and marginalized communities (Mitchell, 2018; Walcott, 2018).

Amid the California higher-education context of espousing liberal multiculturalism while inequities persist, Ahmed (2017) suggests that institutional agents, such as diversity workers, can work within the university to combat institutional inaction. Diversity workers can challenge institutional inertia by functioning as "killjoys" (Ahmed, 2017)—agents of change that work *in* the university but are not *of* the university. Their killjoy-ness stems from their insistence on pointing to structures that remain racist and sexist (Ahmed, 2017). In this chapter, I share how an engaged group of students used PAR to work within one university system to expose inequities and make the university a safer, more affirming place for Muslim students.

THE SITE

Muslim students do not make up a large community on the California campus where our study took place. The university enrolls about 18,000 undergraduate students comprised of a number of racial groups: European Americans (30%), Asians (28%), and Chicanx/Latinx (27%), in addition to a small percentage of African American/Black and Caribbean students (4%) (ODEI, 2017). Middle Eastern, Southwest Asian, and North African (SWANA) students were conflated with White European students. The university's federal designation as a 'Hispanic Serving' institution often obscures the work that is still needed to foster the success of historically marginalized groups.

The town surrounding the campus is 84% white, with the rest being mostly Hispanic/Latinx (ACS, 2017). The high cost of living and lack of people of color make it difficult for non-white bodies to stay long-term; staff who cannot afford to live in the town leave or commute from neighboring cities. The town offers a variety of churches, but only one synagogue and one small mosque in a neighboring town. At the time of this project, the university provided no prayer space or designated reflection room for any religious faith.

THE SITUATION: LIBERAL TALK AND THE CHANCELLOR'S LISTENING TOUR

In the 2017–2018 academic year, Muslim students were still fighting for basic needs on our campus. Devout Muslims are obligated to pray five times a day, so, naturally, a safe space to pray is a priority. Muslim and

130 SAUGHER NOJAN

Arab students faced other obstacles as well. For example, a 2012 climate report suggested that Muslim and Arab students experienced the least respect for their religious identity compared to other groups (Turk et al., 2012). The report suggested that the University of California (UC) campuses were overall positive and welcoming environments for Muslim and Arab students; however, "for students who are visibly and apparently Muslim or Arab, as well as active participants or leaders of organized student groups, the daily experience on the campuses is notably negative and characterized by institutional insensitivity and daily harassment" (Turk et al., 2012, p. 4). The UC-wide study recommended providing students with access to halal foods, creating meditation or reflection spaces for all students, offering Islamic/Middle Eastern-related curricula, and recruiting faculty and staff of color to represent and support the SWANA/ Muslim community.

Our campus had yet to implement these recommendations. As a result, Muslim staff and students worked outside their primary responsibilities and roles to fill these resource gaps. For example, a Muslim residential coordinator or college advisor would create relevant programming for the entire Muslim community. Non-Muslim staff and faculty collaborated with students to host teach-ins about Islamophobia before the 2016 election. With every political tragedy, short-term programming would emerge to address Muslim students' needs; however, sustainable and long-term structural support was lacking.

The election of the 45th U.S. president was a pivotal moment for this campus. In January 2017, the Chancellor staged a meeting with the Muslim Student Association (MSA) in a gesture of support after the election (Ahmed, 2017). By this time, two staff members involved in advocating for the community had left the campus to pursue more fulfilling roles. The only staff present at the meeting were those the Chancellor brought with him: the Dean of Students, the Assistant Dean of Students, and the Diversity Officer for Staff and Students.[1]

The meeting began with the Dean stating that the Chancellor had to leave in an hour after having shown up late. The Dean went on to say that the Chancellor was meeting with "as many students as he could," including different student organizations, as part of his "listening tour." This opening proclamation made it clear that the administration was going to "listen" rather than take action. The act of listening appeared to be all the "work" that would be done in meeting the university's diversity and equity goals.

Repeatedly during the meeting, students mentioned a prayer space as the top item on their list of basic needs. The Chancellor responded with joking statements like, "Space is the ultimate problem on this campus—the final frontier!" or by judging the content of students' words with a, "That's a fair question," or "Those are sensible and reasonable requests." Notably,

MUSLIM STUDENTS COMBATTING INERTIA **131**

he did not answer our questions or address the requests, including: lack of halal food in the dining halls, the need for a safe place to pray on campus, and the troubling sociopolitical climate.

When we asked the Chancellor with whom we should follow up, he referred us to the Vice-Chancellor, claiming he "carries the weight of the Chancellor's office." At that moment, it became clear that the person who would enact change was not present at the meeting. And yet, in an eerie, cheery fashion, the Chancellor kept repeating how MSA was one of his "favorite" groups to meet with. *Why?* Perhaps, the Chancellor felt at ease with the students' nonconfrontational style of communication. Overall, this meeting was indicative of a larger pattern of institutional agents meeting with students to "listen" to their needs and challenges without actually doing anything.

Motivated by the Chancellor's expressed interest in supporting the Muslim students and the contradictions between institutional "listening" and action, I sought ways to use my training as a researcher to aid my community. As a Muslim graduate student and university employee, I had a unique positionality that gave me access to institutional resources and agents that were not available to my fellow undergraduate community members. After some community consultation, I proposed a collaborative, community-engaged research project that would involve Muslim students in the process of assessing how to serve the Muslim community best. I argued that the campus's overreliance on the MSA as "official" spokespeople for the entire Muslim community overlooked the racially and politically diverse community of Muslim-identifying students and their needs. I also knew that the university would perceive students' voices, concerns, and knowledge as more legitimate and actionable when "discovered" through research (Tuck & Yang, 2014).

THE PHOTOVOICE PROJECT

The year-long photovoice project emerged as a strategy to move the administration to act upon their promises of "diversity, equity, and inclusion" with regards to the Muslim community's needs. In the section below, I outline the purpose of PAR. Further, I share why we chose photovoice as our research mechanism.

What Is Participatory-Action Research?

PAR provides an alternative method to examine campus climate and school issues by collaborating with empowered research participants to improve

132 SAUGHER NOJAN

their well-being and to conduct effective research (Pope et al., 2009, p. 652). PAR values epistemic justice, to include those traditionally excluded from the process of knowledge production; and moral, ethical aims to advance the social justice agenda that we share with the community (Glass et al., 2018).

PAR can be adopted and enacted in different ways, as the community shapes it to serve their interests. It includes research participants in various aspects of the research process to make reform bottom-up and build skills among participants. This includes developing the research questions and collecting, coding, and analyzing data. Langhout and Fernandez (2014) suggest that PAR projects should strive to enact the following principles: (a) inclusion by creating student leadership opportunities, (b) capacity-building by teaching students about evidence-based strategies to work towards school improvement, and (c) social justice by promoting community action and ownership of data. The use of a PAR methodology enabled me to work with undergraduate students as co-researchers and co-builders of knowledge concerning the best ways to serve our community. In contrast to traditional research that extracts community knowledge without offering anything in return (Tuck, 2009), PAR enabled me to provide students with training and experience in research and a platform to reach critical administrators and stakeholders.

The Aims of Photovoice and the Steps We Took

We chose photovoice as our favored method of participatory-action research because of the power of photographs and narratives for communicating lasting stories. According to Wang & Burris (1997), photovoice is a participatory-research method based on grassroots social action that has three main goals: "(1) to enable people to record and reflect their community's strengths and concerns, (2) to promote critical dialogue and knowledge about important issues through large and small group discussion of photographs, and (3) to reach policymakers" (p. 369). We aimed to document the strengths and concerns of the community and to move away from the deficit-oriented methods and frameworks deployed by the university that left students feeling more marginalized. Following are the steps we took to complete the photovoice project (adapted from Agarwal et al., 2015).

Form an advisory committee. I spent two years getting to know the community, even before conceiving the project. I attended their events, supported their organizing efforts, and checked in on them periodically. A year before the project began, I formed a reading group; some would call it political education (Freire, 1970). We read and discussed literature on

Muslim student campus-climate experiences, and we related it to our own lives through discussion. The reading group consisted of four Muslim women, and together, we considered whether research would be the right intervention for our community (Tuck & Yang, 2014).

Recruit photovoice participants. Agarwal et al. (2015) suggest recruiting 8–10 participants that broadly reflect the participating community. Through snowball sampling, we intentionally recruited students not traditionally represented in the MSA. Together, our group of eight included undergraduate and graduate womxn from different backgrounds with various identities: Afghan, Iranian, Black/Sudanese, Palestinian, Pakistani/White, Indian, Filipina, Mexican, queer and heterosexual sexualities, and a variety of majors/disciplines. Three participants wore the hijab.

Conduct a participant orientation. During the orientation, I introduced students to the basics of PAR and photovoice. We discussed the power of photographs and looked at some examples of PAR projects and their outcomes to explore what might be possible. We also went over ethics and power dynamics within the research process and discussed the project's broader context on campus and in the general sociopolitical climate. I then offered students space to brainstorm the research questions they were interested in pursuing. We started with the guiding question: What are the joys and challenges you experience on campus related to your identity? We ended with: *How does the [city] community and campus affect your well-being as a Muslim student?*

Establish parameters. In our first full-group meeting, we engaged in relationship-building exercises and brainstormed research questions. We settled on "well-being" as a broad enough term to encompass the different aspects of our experiences as students. Next, we thought of different pictures we could take that captured our experiences. Finally, we discussed how to caption the photographs after they were taken (see de Heer et al., 2008; Wang, 1999).

Convene participant meetings for photograph discussion. At the meetings, students shared the photographs they took, why they took them, and the story behind each one. After the discussion, students posted the pictures on a private Google group so that we could all view and reference the photographs as they were collected. Participants did not always have captions prepared and would write them after discussions.

Repeat steps 4 and 5. We repeated this process five times. The final round was dedicated to photo analysis.

Analyze data. For this step, we printed all the photographs (about 100) and coded and categorized them into emerging themes. I began the meeting by conducting a workshop on ways to code. We also thought about how to come up with headlines for different emergent codes/themes to help get at the main point. We conducted two rounds of coding and

134 SAUGHER NOJAN

sharing. At this point, we began connecting ideas to our research question on Muslim students' well-being.

Prepare presentations to address policy- and decision-makers. Once our themes were gathered, we planned another meeting where each participant chose their favorite or most meaningful photos and action-items that they wanted to display to campus stakeholders. We started looking for venues and applied for funding for the photovoice exhibit. We planned a two-day exhibition on opposite sides of campus, culminating in a presentation and dinner during the Islamic holy month of Ramadan.

Disseminate findings through exhibitions and other outreach events. The exhibit guided people through the sociopolitical, local community, and university context, and ended with the ways the Muslim student community navigated these barriers and displayed resilience. We invited staff, administrators, faculty, and students to our exhibit. We also disseminated our findings and suggestions through a call-to-action list to make support and solidarity clear for different parties in attendance.

REFLECTIONS ON IMPACT

This essay argues that PAR is a useful strategy for spurring dialogue around organizational change. Reflective of this, the year-long project and the two-day exhibit impacted our campus in the following ways: by (a) uplifting marginalized student voices within the Muslim community and consolidating organizing efforts, (b) developing a visual and written trail of needs and demands, (c) changing the discourse from individualized student problems to university responsibilities, (d) building awareness and solidarity with the broader campus community, and (e) providing space for students to create community and organize.

Uplifting Voices

This project aimed to use university resources to draw attention to student voices and demands in a way that would hold administrators accountable for engendering change. We were successful because students participated in all phases of the project and made their demands through research. We purposefully recruited students who were not traditionally represented by the MSA and who were not typically "heard" by administrators, such as Palestinian, Latinx, and Black Muslim students who were not present at the critical meeting with the Chancellor. As the MSA preferred not to be overtly political, the organization's emphasis on spirituality rendered these student activists, with intersecting national, racial, and religious identities, silent

MUSLIM STUDENTS COMBATTING INERTIA **135**

and invisible. Importantly, while the administration gave the MSA a platform to share their concerns, they often dismissed these student activists. The photovoice project provided a space for marginalized Muslim students to create a platform to communicate their demands to key stakeholders by using the political force of the group and the legitimizing power of research.

Moving from Listening to Being Heard

We chose the photovoice method because photovoice requires that attendees do more than just listen. The Chancellor's "listening tour" made it clear that listening replaced any potential action to address our issues. It was common practice to place students on panels to speak about their marginality. I experienced this personally, as a panelist for the Chancellor's Diversity Advisory Committee to represent the "Muslim graduate-student voice." The "performance" of your trauma in a room filled with administrators makes you feel empty afterward, especially when the administration fails to follow up and address the problem.

In contrast, photovoice provided an opportunity to build students' research skills and amplify their voices. Attendees reflected on the rich information offered by the exhibit, stating that it was "powerful" and "moving." One administrator in attendance wrote, "I'm inspired by the resistance of folks who have to endure both the overt and covert forms of Islamophobia here, and I'll use what privileges I have to support folks. Thank you for modeling how we can do better." Another wrote, "This exhibit makes me grateful you are working to uplift this and voice your experiences, even if it makes us uncomfortable."

The exhibit inspired administrators to move beyond their feelings of discomfort, evoking a response in attendees that would last. It also provided a clear list of strategies for change that ranged from conducting cluster hires and providing mental health services, to establishing a cultural resource center.

Shifting the Narrative from Individuals to Structures

The content of the photovoice exhibit helped change the narrative from individual student "problems" to university responsibilities. Students wrote stories for each photo in ways that demonstrated institutional and administrator responsibilities. The photovoice project shifted the conversation to a broader organizational dialogue that included many voices. We shifted the narrative from individualized problems that would dissipate after particular students graduated to structural issues that required more systemic and long-term changes. For example, in a submission called "Institutional baby

136 SAUGHER NOJAN

steps," one student wrote, "We recognize the importance of making sure administrators are continuously held accountable. The fact that it took over 20 years & for Trump to get elected for the university to start taking Muslim students' needs seriously is unsettling." In this narrative, the student identifies the problem with the university and its failure to address Muslim student needs proactively. Another student wrote:

> This University, the Student Conduct office, campus administration, and some students on this campus have made my time here incredibly painful, scary, anxiety-producing, traumatic, and much more. On multiple occasions, when I have reached out to resources, they have made things worse. Such as the Title IX Office, they have said that they are 'sympathetic,' but then they don't push for any changes.

This student focuses on the university's resistance to change in serving the needs of its evolving student body. Many more posts like these captured the administration's attention, highlighting the role they play as institutional agents in perpetuating systemic bias against Muslims and other marginalized groups.

Building Consciousness and Solidarity

The photovoice project not only reached vital stakeholders but also served to raise awareness and build solidarity within the broader campus community. Students reflected that it helped them adjust their "Western gaze" and perceptions of Muslims; others related the project to their own experiences as people of color subject to the same systems of oppression. For example, the director of an ethnic center wrote: "It made me sad that other POC on campus who also feel alone and lonely don't have a way to come together to support you." Another student wrote, "It's sad to see that so many women of color don't feel safe living here. I hate being here, and I'm a light-skinned Latina. I can only imagine how it feels to be of darker skin." Communicating with students outside of our community and sharing our experiences was essential for coalescing around shared struggles and building a foundation for future solidarity.

IMPLICATIONS AND LESSONS LEARNED

This project taught me and others involved one vital lesson. One of the reasons for working *within* the university to advance social change is because of the financial, intellectual, and political resources available within its walls (Glass et al., 2018). The university entirely funded the photovoice facilitator, the project, and the exhibit. I strategically applied for funding from the Chancellor's office and the Student Success Division. This move provided an institutional platform for the project while building into the process a direct line of communication with funders on the outcomes and recommendations. It also enabled me, as a graduate student, to devote time and labor to facilitate this project and purchase food for every meeting and other resources that sustained undergraduate student involvement. Receiving departmental support to provide students with course credit also helped. I was also able to offer students community service or academic mentorship hours if they needed it.

Despite the many victories, this project was not without its challenges. Moving forward, I illuminate one key implication of diversity work that crystalized while completing this project.

Inadvertently Benefitting the University by Contributing to Its Performance of "Diversity"

At the same time, being entirely funded by the university made the project susceptible to its performative gestures that erased the history of struggle that the community endured to obtain such resources. For example, after the Spring 2019 tragic terrorist attack on Muslims attending prayer at the mosque in New Zealand, the university used the photovoice project in a campus-wide email to show that they were aware that they needed to support the Muslim student population better. On March 15, 2018, the Chancellor sent out the following:

> Our commitment is to create inclusive campus culture, and through the impact of our students, faculty, and staff, a world that values and supports every individual, no matter their religious beliefs. The recent Photovoice project about Muslim student experiences on our campus makes clear that our Muslim community does not always experience that support. Therefore, we must strive to improve the experience of our Muslim community. We plan to launch a broader conversation with our Muslim students next quarter, in which we will discuss the steps we have already taken and the work that still needs to be done.

The "broader conversation" never occurred. Here, the university used the photovoice project as an image-management tool (Ahmed, 2017). Thus, the university once again engaged in performative non-performativity by displaying the photovoice project as evidence of "doing" diversity work (Ahmed, 2017; Walcott, 2018). In this context, any critical work addressing institutional failure is "appropriated as evidence of institutional success" (Ahmed, 2017, p. 111). In this way, the photovoice project was co-opted and became about the university and its achievements (Ahmed, 2017). Even projects critical of the university may benefit the university by contributing to its performance of diversity (Ahmed, 2017; Walcott, 2018).

138 SAUGHER NOJAN

PROMISING PRACTICES FOR CHANGE

In the Midst of Struggle, Come Together and Build Communities of Support

The photovoice project had a positive impact on the students who participated. It provided us a community space to process events and feelings as they happened in real-time. It gave students space to voice their ideas about how the university could address their community needs better. It also enabled students to reflect on their resilience and agency; they created a community despite barriers to their success. The process of participating in the photovoice project fostered friendships, and some of the participants began organizing together to make sure the prayer space became a reality even after the project was over.

Work from the Grassroots to Share Knowledge and Build Capacity

After the project ended, students invited me to a workshop they organized with some local activists to teach other students how to plan a successful nonviolent protest. They wanted me to talk a little about the photovoice project. One of the goals of PAR is building the capacity of the community so they can continue the work without the researcher. It was apparent that the students, having realized their power, were ready to move to the next step of getting the administration to implement their promises.

CONCLUSION

The photovoice project played a role in moving the campus to take action in prioritizing the needs of Muslim students. The exhibit also created visibility for the multifaceted ways that this community is affected by anti-Muslim racism and lacks institutional resources to combat it. Our findings and presentation contributed to efforts to secure a prayer space and receive funding to hire a Southwest Asian and North African (SWANA) coordinator and student intern, while also highlighting the long-term vision for a SWANA cultural resource center. The administration is currently using the action-item flyer we distributed at the exhibit as a to-do list on how to support Muslim students.

While administrators may have otherwise dismissed student activists, the photovoice project provided an alternative outlet for amplifying those voices. Practitioners should consider using institutional funds and resources to create strategic audiences for change. They should also consider participant-action research as a viable method that builds skills among students, builds capacity within marginalized communities, reaches vital stakeholders, and moves institutional agents to prioritize action.

DISCUSSION QUESTIONS

1. What (if any) contradictions exist in your institution's rhetoric of diversity, equity, and inclusion and its implementation?
2. What key DEI challenges exist at your institution?
3. How do your institution's diversity issues reflect larger societal concerns?
4. How can you become an "institutional killjoy" to combat institutional inertia and spur action (Ahmed, 2017)?
5. How can you seek and harness institutional resources to address problematic diversity issues in your department/unit?
6. What communities are you a part of? What skills or access to resources do you have to offer your community or the communities you serve?

NOTE

1. Later, I learned that administrators did not inform the directors of the Ethnic Resource Centers, who supported Muslim students, about the meeting that was taking place. It is not clear whether it was intentional not to advertise these meetings with the Chancellor.

REFERENCES

ACS (American Community Survey). (2017). Quick facts, California. *United States Census Bureau.* Retrieved from https://www.census.gov/quickfacts/CA

Agarwal, N., Moya, E. M., Yasui, N. Y., & Seymour, C. (2015). Participatory action research with college students with disabilities: Photovoice for an inclusive campus. *Journal of Postsecondary Education and Disability,* 28(2), 243–250.

Ahmed, S. (2017). *Living a feminist life.* Durham: NC: Duke University Press.

Ali, A. I. (2014). A threat enfleshed: Muslim college students situate their identities amidst portrayals of Muslim violence and terror. *International Journal of Qualitative Studies in Education,* 27(10), 1243–1261. doi:10.1080/09518398.2013.820860

Ali, S. R., & Bagheri, E. (2009). Practical suggestions to accommodate the needs of Muslim students on campus. *New Directions for Student Services,* 47–54. doi:10.1002/ss.307

CAIR (Council on American-Islamic Relations). (2017). *CAIR-CA school bullying report 2017.* Retrieved from https://ca.cair.com/sfba/wp-content/uploads/sites/10/2018/04/2017_CAIR-CA_School_Bullying_Report.pdf?x69434

CCS (Campus Climate Survey). (2014, March). University California, Santa Cruz: Campus climate project final report. *Rankin & Associates, Consulting.* Full report here: http://campusclimate.ucop.edu/_common/files/pdf-climate/ucsc-full-report.pdf

Cole, D., & Ahmadi, S. (2010). Reconsidering campus diversity: An examination of Muslim students' experiences. *The Journal of Higher Education,* 81(2), 121–139.

de Heer, H., Moya, E. M., & Lacson, R. (2008). Voices and images: Tuberculosis Photovoice in a binational setting. *Cases in Public Health Communication & Marketing,* 2, 55–86. Retrieved from www.casesjournal.org/volume2

140 SAUGHER NOJAN

Freire, P. (1970). *Pedagogy of the oppressed* (M.B. Ramos, Trans.). New York: Continuum.

Fine, M., & Sirin, S. R. (2007). Theorizing hyphenated selves: Researching youth development in and across contentious political contexts. *Social and Personality Psychology Compass*, 1, 16–38. doi:10.1111/j.1751-9004.2007.00032.x

Glass, R. D., Morton, J. M., King, J. E., Krueger-Henney, P., Moses, M. S., Sabati, S., & Richardson, T. (2018). The ethical stakes of collaborative community-based social science research. *Urban Education*, 53(4), 503–531.

Langhout, R. D., & Fernández, J. S. (2014). Empowerment evaluation conducted by 4th and 5th-grade students. In D. Fetterman, S. Kaftarian, & A. Wandersman (Eds.), *Empowerment evaluation: Knowledge and tools for self-assessment, evaluation capacity building, and accountability* (pp. 193–232). Thousand Oakes, CA: Sage.

Mitchell, N. (2018). Diversity. In E. R. Edwards, R. A. Ferguson, and J. O. G. Ogbar (Eds.), *Keywords for African American studies*. New York, NY: NYU Press.

Nadal, K. L., Griffin, K. E., Hamit, S., Leon, J., Tobio, M., & Rivera, D. P. (2012). Subtle and overt forms of Islamophobia: Microaggressions toward Muslim Americans. *Journal of Muslim Mental Health*, 6(2). doi:10.3998/jmmh.10381607.0006.203

Nasir, N. S., & Al-Amin, J. (2006). Creating identity-safe spaces on college campuses for Muslim students. *Change: The Magazine of Higher Learning*, 38(2), 22–27. doi:10.3200/CHNG.38.2.22-27

ODEI. (2017). *Campus demographics AY 15–16*. Retrieved June 15, 2017, from https://diversity.ucsc.edu/diversity/campus_demographics/index.html

Pope, R. L., Mueller, J. A., & Reynolds, A. L. (2009). Looking back and moving forward: Future directions for diversity research in student affairs. *Journal of College Student Development*, 50(6), 640–658. The Johns Hopkins University Press.

Seggie, F. N., & Sanford, G. (2010). Perceptions of female Muslim students who veil: Campus religious climate. *Race, Ethnicity, and Education*, 13(1), 59–82. doi:10.1080/13613320903549701

Sexton, J. (2010). People-of-color-blindness: Notes on the afterlife of slavery. *Social Text*, 28(2), 31–35.

Tuck, E. (2009). Suspending damage: A letter to communities. *Harvard Educational Review*, 79(3), 409–428.

Tuck, E., & Yang, K. W. (2014). Unbecoming claims: Pedagogies of refusal in qualitative research. *Qualitative Inquiry*, 20(6), 811–818.

Turk, J., Senzaki, N., Howard, T., & Rowther, A. (2012). Muslim & Arab student campus climate at the University of California fact-finding team report & recommendations. *President's Advisory Council on Campus Climate, Culture, & Inclusion*, pp. 1–51. Retrieved from https://cascholars4academicfreedom.files.wordpress.com/2012/07/muslim-arab-student-climate-report-final.pdf

Walcott, R. (2018). Against social justice and the limits of diversity or Black people and freedom. In E. Tuck & K. W. Yang (Eds.). *Toward what justice?: Describing diverse dreams of justice in education*. New York, NY: Routledge.

Wang, C. (1999). Photovoice: A participatory action research strategy applied to women's health. *Journal of Women's Health*, 8, 185–192.

Wang, C., & Burris, M. A. (1997). Photovoice: Concept, methodology, and use for participatory need assessment. *Health Education & Behavior*. doi:10.1177/109019819702400309

Chapter 9

BIPOC Students Using Polyvocal Narratives, Co-Witnessing, and Spectral Engagement: "Seen" But Not Heard

Meshell Sturgis, Brian J. Evans, Anjuli Brekke, Andrea Delgado, and Erin Lee

INTRODUCTION

In this chapter, the five of us scholars of color, Andrea, Anjuli, Brian, Erin, and Meshell, come together to share the proceedings of a particular academic conference panel that aimed to think about institutional diversity during our time as graduate students at the University of Washington (UW) in Seattle. In reflecting on this roundtable discussion as a seemingly "failed" diversity, equity, and inclusion (DEI) moment, we have continued to think through the organizational context of DEI issues on university campuses. After setting the scene of the campus context in 2019, we then rescript the public conversation held that spring and conclude by sharing how we, as an organic collective, have proceeded to address this failed moment. Each of us experienced that particular day in ways unique to our social positions. Therefore, we have chosen to recapture that moment in hopes of preserving it as a case study to be included in the archive of critical equity and inclusion efforts on various campuses across the United States higher-education system.

As students of color with intersecting identities, we all have experienced incessant tokenization, invisibility and hypervisibility, and microaggressions unique to our social positions. Crenshaw (1994) notes how standpoints must be understood intersectionally and describes the politics of identity as "diverse structures" that intersect and are "implicated together" (pp. 94–95; see also Collins, 2009). As she explains, a "focus on the intersections of race and gender only highlights the need to account for multiple grounds of identity when considering how the social world is

142 MESHELL STURGIS ET AL.

constructed" (p. 94). Some of us have participated in student-led protests while others have had to confront campus climate issues within our volunteer organizations and committees, the centers and departments we work for, and the programs we attend and help to organize. Minoritized and underrepresented individuals in academia are expected to perform disproportionate unpaid and unacknowledged labor by their peers, students, faculty, and administrators who oversee internal organizations and programming. This additional labor, paired with tokenization and microaggressions, has profound mental, social, economic, and physical impacts on graduate students of color (see June, 2015; Lerma et al., 2019; Matthew, 2016; Padilla, 1994; Rideau, 2019; Rojas, 2017). In order to address and work towards changing this inequity within the University of Washington as it pertains to graduate students, we formed a roundtable entitled, "Graduate Students Interceding Institutional Diversity" in April of 2019 for the Graduate and Professional Student Senate's (GPSS) annual academic conference, themed "Inter(connected)."

Our goal was to intercede on behalf of the marginalized student populations to which we belong by staging a public conversation. Across our campus communities, some students express frustration with the university's enthusiasm for marketing its diversity while often silencing or devaluing our expressed needs and diverse perspectives. Even with the undergraduate student population being somewhat commensurate with the state's overall racial demographic, UW is still a predominantly White institution (PWI). Reflective of this, UW acknowledges that it sits on the unceded land of which the Coast Salish peoples are stewards, but refuses to uphold equitable and reparative commitment to Indigenous groups within the region (see Deerchild, 2019).

It is important to note that UW Seattle, founded in 1861, is the largest university campus in Washington state, with about 48,000 students, and is part of a tri-campus university system that also includes UW Bothell and UW Tacoma. Both of these smaller campuses, with student populations of about 6,000 and 5,000, respectively, are each about an hour away from Seattle and have twice the number of first-generation students and students eligible for Federal Pell Grants. Despite the graduate student-led conference's theme of "connection," all the GPSS conference panels were located solely on the Seattle campus. Though not exclusive to Seattle students, the student senate, which was founded in 1967, operates and supports the main campus primarily. Graduate students at Bothell and Tacoma are often required to trek to Seattle in order to participate. Furthermore, while the GPSS as a governing body is meant to serve all UW graduate students, the Bothell and Tacoma graduate students are without representation as the sister campuses do not have permanent seats in the senate. Clearly, the Seattle campus is privileged as the "primary" campus.

Less than a century after UW was founded, in 1988, voters in the state of Washington passed I-200, which placed a ban on affirmative action practices for employment, contracting, and college admissions. It wasn't until 2015 when the board of regents appointed Ana Mari Cauce as the university's 33rd president—the first woman, person of color, openly queer, immigrant to hold this position at UW. That same year, President Cauce launched the Race & Equity Initiative, a campus-wide campaign to "take personal responsibility for addressing our own biases and improving our university culture" ("Race and Equity," n.d.). Just two years later, a four-year diversity strategic plan for the whole tri-campus system was released. It seemed as though the institution was making great strides towards DEI. Yet, in January 2017, a registered student organization invited Milo Yiannopoulos—a noted violent provocateur—to give a speech that, despite massive student protests to prevent it, incited violence so extreme that one person was shot (Gilbert, 2017). Then, in 2019, the state of Washington passed I-1000, effectively lifting the ban on affirmative action. In response, the same conservative student group on campus held a controversial bake sale that assigned cookie prices to purchasers based on their race. Just a number of months later, this ban was quickly reinstated through a statewide vote on Referendum 88 (O'Sullivan, 2019).

Time and again at UW, as at many institutions of higher education, the guise of free speech is used to condone events that further target people already marginalized by the systemic inequities of state institutions. Such is the context that informed the organization of our panel and our collective understanding as we prepared to discuss diversity and equity at a PWI. Although the campus proclaims its commitments to minoritized and underrepresented students, faculty, staff, and administration, because of historical and contemporary failed DEI moments, the question remains: is anyone listening?

Resisting Ecologies of Constraint

UW's 2017–2021 Diversity Blueprint focuses on "shared responsibility" where "administrative units [sic] do their part." The school's president states in the opening letter of the document, "we must work together because it is not—and could never be—the sole responsibility of one person, one office, or one initiative to solve these systemic and complex issues. It will take ongoing and sustained effort from all of us." In contrast to the letter from the president, the Diversity Council chairs suggest it is individuals who should take responsibility, citing the president's initiative as an exemplar for how this work is done. Following this, a "Message from Diversity Council Chairs" applauded the president's work on the Race and

144 MESHELL STURGIS ET AL.

Equity Initiative, describing how it seeks "new ways to support and sustain diversity at the UW, centers on creating an inclusive experience for students, faculty, and staff, and directly addresses issues of institutional bias and structural racism" (UW 2017–2021 Diversity Blueprint). What is rhetorically amiss here is that the president as a sole actor is in fact part of larger relational networks that interact with and are folded into structural relations of power. The final goal of the university system's four-year plan is to "improve accountability and transparency."

Building on Bronfenbrenner's (1977) work, we suggest that when considering the challenges and potential for enacting DEI-centered change within higher education, it is crucial to consider the imbricated relationship between individuals and various overlapping layers of influence. Using Bronfenbrenner's social–ecological framework provides a means of conceptualizing the complex web of interactions between individual actors and social structures that led to and shaped the roundtable discussion. Building from this framework, we aim to account for the influential layers of relation impacting how we intercede on behalf of our communities, ranging from interpersonal interactions to political, historical, and economic systems. Rather than analyze individual interactions and larger structures independently, the ecological model emphasizes the ways in which the unique experiences of individuals are interwoven into larger social systems, creating a web of reciprocal causation. Put another way, just as we are shaped by our environments, we simultaneously work to shape our environments. Our relationships with other people have the power to impact how we experience structural constraints. If our work as graduate students necessitates a sustained effort of speaking back to power, the five of us ask, in conversation, whose sustained effort is it, then, to listen to what we have to say, and to act?

In the edited collection, *Racial Ecologies*, Nishime and Hester Williams (2018) address how "dispossessed communities preserve memories, share knowledge, and enact ways of being that reflect an awareness of and resistance to the detrimental consequences of enduring structures of colonialism, imperialism, and neoliberal capital accumulation" (p. 6). Although graduate students who push institutions to center equity and value difference will inevitably be constrained by power relations within their own departments, the larger university, and national and international neoliberal systems, these larger structures can be similarly constrained by us.

As students, faculty, and staff have modeled through various teach-ins, coming together as counter-networks contrary to formally organized groups within institutions offers educational ways of resistance[1] (see also Jones & Reddick, 2017). The effort we put into the academic conference panel went mostly unnoticed. It could be perceived as a failure in that it did not incite macrolevel change. Yet, the research and writing group that has formed since the five of us came together that day has had a positive impact on us,

"SEEN" BUT NOT HEARD **145**

providing a place to continue thinking through the precariousness of our positions on campus and to cross-strategize tactics for inciting change. Though the roundtable was neither a campus-wide protest or sit-in, nor an online social media campaign or "un-conference," it demonstrates the more subtle forms of resistance that occur from within the university.

In an institution where graduate students are primarily seen as inexpensive teaching and research labor, and where the intellectual innovations of students of color are often dismissed, it is powerful to share a space where we can polyvocally narrate and interrogate our experiences. As Moraga and Anzaldúa (2015) state in the introduction to *This Bridge Called My Back: Writings by Radical Women of Color*, "the very act of writing then, conjuring/ coming to 'see', what has yet to be recorded in history is to bring into consciousness what only the body knows to be true" (p. xxiv). In writing about our individual and shared experiences as racialized bodies in academia, we recognize the complicated networks of relation between our lived experiences and engaging in a critical social practice.

What follows is a series of fragmented accounts of what took place during our roundtable at the GPSS academic conference. Following the description of each speaker is an abbreviated script that includes italicized personal thoughts that the speaker originally withheld. By presenting each person's statement separately, we seek to foreground the contradictions and differences that make up our unique social positions and collective narrative. Each person spoke about personal DEI-related experiences that have impacted them while on campus. This initial event, seemingly a failure, becomes the foundation of our pathway forward. Using Moraga and Anzaldúa's theory in the flesh, we then trace the three central themes running through all five of our presentations. Finally, we conclude by considering how anticipating institutional failure creates space for possibility and resistance.

THE SCENE: "TALKING" DIVERSITY

The setting is a roundtable discussion at the 2019 Graduate Student and Professional Student Senate Academic Conference. It is early afternoon on a slightly sunny day as individuals begin trickling in. Several rows of tables parted by one walkway through the middle face two conjoined tables at the front of the room, stage right of a podium. Presenter 4, already at the front of the room, looks around after a group of people settle into seats in the back row and suggests that the room be rearranged to resemble an actual roundtable. The panel chair and respondent arrive separately, and everyone takes a seat. After a few short, light-hearted exchanges and an introduction from the chair, the first presenter and organizer of the panel begins.

146 MESHELL STURGIS ET AL.

Presenter One

A 28-year-old, first-generation, queer, Black-mixed, cis-woman graduate student from Olympia, Washington.

This year, I have found myself constantly tormented with the postracial, seemingly neutral 'diversity' language of our university. The Diversity Committee of the GPSS struggles to maintain the relationships that it seeks to celebrate and underutilizes the skills of its members, exploiting their labor. With a focus on "getting results," "creating direct impact," "doing it right," and "appeasing constituents," the committee's sense of self is predicated on the notion that the university is and can be a force for change. Upon joining the leadership team of the committee, I advocated for a redrafting of the mission statement. Since the bureaucratic work we do within the university is not always inherently educational, I rallied together three other committee members and organized a small study group for drafting an equitable mission statement over the 2018–2019 winter break.[2]

> Why aren't members from the GPSS Diversity Committee and leadership board here? Should I have worked harder to invite more people? I feel spent for time to contribute. But, I really do wish we had more people in attendance. Even though we are a diverse panel, there are many folks who are missing. I am honored to have such conscientious colleagues and friends show up in support, but I wonder, how could I have made it more inclusive?[3]

The newly written mission statement reads:

> The GPSS Diversity Committee is a community of resistance undertaking strategic actions to eradicate the historical inequities inherent in institutionalized academic structures and settings. We recognize the inequities existing along lines of difference including racism, homophobia, sexism, ableism, bigotry, xenophobia, and other -isms resulting from systems of oppression that perpetuate disempowerment. Rather than celebrate a neutral 'diversity,' 'tolerance,' or 'multiculturalism,' the committee instead acknowledges the lived experiences of various groups of underrepresented minoritized (URM) graduate and professional students on campus by combating injustices and empowering students through university resources. (GPSS Diversity Committee, n.d.)

After sharing this work with the larger committee, a white committee member calling in over the phone asked if we thought the mission might be 'too aggressive.' She might as well have said, "Don't you think it's a little angry?" My response was and still is, yes, as it should be, as I am, as we are, as we all should be.

> *The group acknowledges this last statement. Despite a mostly empty room, I feel a bit heard, more than I had during that encounter in the committee meeting.*

Kelley (2018) describes a "subversive way of being in but not of the university" as a sort of "fugitive planning" that gets at the root of institutionalized inequity. It interrupts, it upends, it interjects, it intercedes, and it participates in the university, but is not part of it (p. 158). I am still a firm believer that the GPSS Diversity Committee must evolve into a source of sustenance for our underrepresented students and serve as a check and balance for the larger GPSS organization before we can really celebrate anything, but I also believe that what we did with the mission statement, though small, is a triumph. However, whether or not the committee will act on the mission is questionable.

> Is this even worth it if no one is here? I hope the other panelists aren't disappointed and feeling like this invitation was a waste of their time.

Presenter Two

A 30-year-old mixed-race second-generation South Asian-American, straight cis-woman from Madison, Wisconsin.

> I feel a dual sense of relief and disappointment. Relief that the group is small and intimate, thereby removing some of the pressure to perform. At the same time, my heart sinks that such few people have taken the time to attend this panel.

The work I'll be talking about today is the culmination of a messy process of community engagement, recording and editing stories, and encouraging and teaching a practice of radical listening. Presenter one brought up the important question, "How do we, as graduate students, create the change our communities desperately need?"

> As I look up from my notes, I wonder whether change is possible when no one in power even shows up to listen.

In my dissertation, I'm looking at tensions that arise when testimonials of personal trauma related to racial discrimination are made public. The politics of who hears these stories and how they use them remain central to the possibility of these stories doing some public good. These politics are intensely personal, as storytellers of suffering negotiate (mis)appropriation, ownership, and control of their representation. In my discussions with participants from an anti-racist digital storytelling project, the common thread throughout has been the simultaneous and contradictory pull of publicly sharing stories of pain and suffering, and the desire/need to control the way those stories are picked up and heard.

As I embarked on this project, I had to grapple with my positionality in relation to other participant storytellers. I felt a gnawing uncertainty as a

148 MESHELL STURGIS ET AL.

mixed-race South Asian-American woman about my role organizing and participating in a storytelling initiative archiving experiences of racism and resistance. Given my relative privilege as a racially ambiguous individual who is sometimes able to pass in hegemonic White spaces, should I be inserting my voice in this conversation? Can my stories of navigating the liminal spaces between racial and cultural identities add anything? I also wondered how my research praxis might impact participants, for better or worse. I attempted to check in with those who shared their stories, to circle back to them and keep them actively involved at each stage of the project. I held follow-up interviews with participants after the original recording session to discuss their hopes and concerns while making public these stories, which were often intensely personal.

As the sound editor for our digital storytelling project, I struggled to navigate the ways in which my editing of participants' words into short segments might simplify the complexity of their narratives and obscure the structures and histories behind their words. Ideally, these stories would have been edited by the participants themselves. The time commitment in terms of both learning the audio-editing software and constructing the stories, however, was too much of a burden to place on participants. I wanted the project to be accessible, but I also wanted storytellers to have control over how their stories were being represented. As a graduate student juggling multiple responsibilities and struggling to make deadlines, however, I worried about whether I was doing it 'right'; whether I was doing enough work to seek out and properly address storyteller concerns and silences. As I've noted, research through doing is a messy process. Listening can be painful and does not always end in a tidy resolution.

> As I am saying these words, I can't help but recall the contradictory pull participants expressed to me of wanting their stories of racism and resistance to be heard and their pain to be recognized, while also wanting to protect these experiences from the too-often hostile public gaze. Am I angry that no one with institutional power is listening to us, or am I relieved to be speaking/listening in this intimate yet powerful community of fellow graduate students of color? Perhaps both. The bodies absent from our circle speaks to the value (or more accurately, lack thereof) this institution places on listening to marginalized voices. Although we are expected to speak, to provide evidence that the university is making space for diverse perspectives, no one in power is expected to show up. We stand on the stage over and over again, performing the obligatory diversity speech to an empty room. But as I run through these familiar thoughts in my mind, I realize that this is not completely true. The room is not empty because we have each other, and we are listening. That means something.

There are endless examples of instances when voices from the margins have broken through boundaries of power, demanding to be heard, seen, and understood. Despite a persistent lack of listening, the marginalized, then, find new and innovative ways to be heard and understood.

Presenter Three

A 24-year-old, first-generation, Black cis-woman graduate student from Cleveland, Ohio.

The experiences, culture, and histories of minoritized populations are interwoven into our society; however, the contributions of our oppressed communities are often dismissed, hidden, or overlooked.

> In this moment, I reflect on how I was first approached to participate in this panel and was unsure of how I could truly contribute meaningful words and perspective to this discussion focused on graduate students who intercede where the university has insufficiently addressed DEI.

As a graduate student of color, I have the same workload, if not more, than other graduate students. Often times, I, like many others, am asked to sit on panels or in focus groups that involve the one word we sometimes use very loosely—diversity. I am expected to add on extra labor and time, on top of everything else, to discuss some of my own uncomfortable experiences as a Black woman—with there being little to no hope of things changing. As a first-year graduate student in the School of Public Health, I am one of three Black students out of a cohort of 45. In the classroom, we often discuss racial disparities or gaps in health outcomes for people in the United States. On a consistent basis, I hear many facts and encounter data depicting how much shorter my lifespan will be in comparison to my White counterparts. At the root of these disparities, many researchers state that experiencing racism and discrimination takes a tremendous toll on one's health among many other factors (see Gómez, 2015). Oftentimes in these moments, I feel unseen and not supported by faculty or my colleagues when sensitive and triggering moments like these occur. Despite all of this, in the classroom, one way I disrupt our conversations surrounding diversity or structural racism is by speaking up for communities that are continually silenced.

Because of this, I am extremely passionate about centering the various lived experiences of Black people and centering the academic work of scholars of color in my research, many of whom are not reflected in the "diverse" and supposedly well-rounded education I am receiving. As a graduate student of color, I often assume the role in many spaces here on campus (especially in the classroom) of the unpaid educator when microaggressions take place. These situations are seldom comfortable situations that I wish to have on a regular basis. While I believe it is important for graduate students of color to speak up and speak out when ignorant things are said and done, I don't believe that it should be our job. I do not believe that it is our job to make our lived racist/sexist/xenophobic experiences more "comfortable" for others to hear and hopefully learn from. I do not believe

150 MESHELL STURGIS ET AL.

it is our job to comfort others' guilt, and I do not believe it is our job to give faculty, staff, our departments, or this institution credit for infusing and embedding diversity, equity, and inclusion into our fabric and culture.

While I believe it is important for graduate students of color to speak up when ignorant things are said and done, again, I don't believe that it should be our job. It is the institution's sole responsibility to make this space more equitable and inclusive of marginalized communities. There is work being done. We have a long way to move forward.

Presenter Four

A 34-year-old, second-generation, mixed-race, straight, cis-man graduate student from rural Gaylord, Minnesota.

Are you the ideal? When you think of your academic career to date, or your life as a whole, have you been treated or considered to be the ideal by yourself, your peers, or the institutions within which you find yourself? Did those who drew up the blueprints that shape the infrastructure of your life have you in mind when they put pen to pad?

> The reality of my experience in an education system rooted in exclusion is that my answer to these questions tend to be mixed. Which makes sense, since I am mixed. My perspective is already positioned as polyvocal compared to competing monolithic narratives. This is why I find myself feeling, at once, thoughtfully considered and completely discarded within academia.

Institutional idealism has roots far more profound than most can remember, and those roots tend to draw nutrients from structures that never intended the "diversity" of scholarly pursuits. Candid talks about systemic issues of disenfranchisement have a hard time springing to life in academia when it comes to the structural overhaul of an academic system that has its foundation in a privileged majority determining the 'correct' way of being.

> I question my validity in discussions where the very nature of those discussions do not have a place for me to root myself. Also, how do we incite a conversation without ostracizing those who need to hear the message that "being a part of the problem positions you to play a crucial role in the solution?" How do we empower voices while maintaining authenticity so that they can advocate? As a champion of the voiceless, am I no longer a part of that group if I am the one being heard? Which begs a final question: Is anyone listening?

Presenter Five

A 29-year-old first-generation Chicana/Latina, queer, cis-woman graduate student from Los Angeles, California.

As students of color in a PWI, we often encounter moments that either offer us opportunities to name our identities or require us to identify in some specific way; usually, both happen at once. Faced with the opportunity and task to name my identity, I realize how difficult this is.

My parents are from small towns in Mexico, and I was born and grew up in Los Angeles, where I got huarache tan lines in the summer sun and heard past lore of the way life used to be. As a Chicana/Latina who is intimately bilingual in English and Spanish with a working-class background and an immigrant family, what was my role in this conversation?

I came to this panel unsure, knowing that any work we do to think through the implications of racial capitalism will not only be co-opted by the university, but also used as evidence of the university itself working towards racial equity, even though we bear the burden of that labor. Here at the end of my graduate career, it is difficult to prepare an argument about how the university excluded me; so much of what I thought on the matter did not fit into what the university, or academia, for that matter, deems empirical or intellectual. Ethnic studies is niche. My experience of organizing protests and teach-ins has taught me that the university will only support racial equity when it is convenient. After many campus-wide walkouts where people of color and marginalized people from different schools within the college wrote out specific demands for the university, college administrators only agreed to a few rhetorical changes, such as changing street names to reflect the Native groups of the area.

Those changes have yet to materialize.

Thus, I am wary of presenting my true thoughts on a panel in an event put on by the university itself.

I am participating by listening to my panelists and responding: a group of intellectuals getting together and building upon each other's ideas, and in turn, building each other up.

IMPLICATIONS AND LESSONS LEARNED: "SEEN," BUT NOT HEARD

The panel's respondent, a dean, offered remarks following each panelist. In hearing the dean's response to our presentations, we felt both seen and a bit placated by her sentiments. As a woman of color administrator working in higher education for over 27 years, the dean shared some of her experiences with us, offering encouragement and strategies for coping with the institutional oppressions we all face on a daily basis. She saw us— she saw a bit of herself in us, perhaps—but the question of whether she

152 MESHELL STURGIS ET AL.

heard us lingers. Her personal story and acknowledgement that she too faces institutional oppression, still, affirmed that our contributions, though seen by the few individuals in the room that day, remain largely unheard by the larger academic institution. After taking questions from the few audience members, the panel concluded. We were expected to return to our normal graduate student routines, as if the act of "talking" about diversity was enough. Yet what had just happened sat with us. This couldn't be it—nothing seemed to have changed.

The audience's questions receded, yet our personal narratives, woven into a collective narrative, remained. Instead of viewing this incident as another moment where our stories, emerging from the margins, were being "devalued precisely because" they are "feminized and racialized reproductive labor of the institution" (Desai & Murphy, 2018, p. 24), we chose to see ourselves differently. Our efforts mattered. We recognized that if any good would come from our labor, we would need to redirect our efforts. Instead of focusing our energy on the disappointment of yet another institutional waste of our labor, we focused our energies on pathways forward. This mindset led to our ongoing dialogue post-roundtable.

Our continued efforts post-roundtable has entailed both separating "the fibers of experience we have had as ... struggling people" (Moraga & Anzaldúa, 2015, p. 19) and piecing together our narratives to unravel the relations between individuals, and individuals and institutions. This is one medium by which theory in the flesh is enacted. Through such efforts, we seek to pursue a "society that uses flesh and blood experiences to concretize a vision that can begin to heal" (p. 19). From our location within the university, we "study up," critically examining the ecological factors that foster our place and interactions with and within the academic institution. As anthropologist Nader (1972) asserts, "studying up" is an ethnographic method that looks up the chain of influence mapped by Bronfenbrenner's framework—from the individual to larger systems of power that structure our experiences. Pairing a "theory in the flesh" with the method of "studying up" reveals "the complex confluence of identities—race, class, gender, and sexuality—systemic to ... oppression and liberation" (Moraga & Anzaldúa, 2015, p. xix).

PROMISING PRACTICES FOR CHANGE

Post-roundtable dialogues revealed three avenues by which the institution impacts us simultaneously: we embody and face the consequences of monolithic narratives daily, we experience direct instances of violence and oppression, and endure constant hypervisibility paired with silencing.

These issues are supported by an imbricated ecological system that spans human relationships and organizational structures that support the institution's colonial legacy. Using the idea of theory in the flesh and "studying up," we found ourselves navigating institutional constraints using three strategies: polyvocal narratives, spectral forms of resistance, and co-witnessing. Our group's presentation and analysis thereafter demonstrates how graduate students can intercede when institutional failure is anticipated in the area of diversity, equity, and inclusion.

Employing Polyvocal Narratives

Drawing solely on a single individual's experience reduces the nuance that we as humans are built to express. Adichie (2009) speaks from the TED stage about the danger of a single story:

> Power is the ability not just to tell the story of another person, but to make it the definitive story of that person ... a single story creates stereotypes, and the problem with stereotypes is not that they are untrue, but that they are incomplete. They make one story become the only story.

Furthermore, though experience itself can be the gateway to addressing personal bias, one person's story cannot change larger structures. By employing polyvocality, our group resisted monolithic representations of students of color and in doing so, illuminated the ways that institutional DEI language often fails to account for diverse student experiences.

Illustrative of this, presenter two emphasized the value of listening and how it requires centering the complexities of lived experience. When addressing DEI issues, we must resist the urge to simplify the complexity of people's experiences or "obscure the structures and histories" that shape those experiences in the name of finding neat solutions. Listening pluralistically means holding multiple stories and a polyvalent sense of narrative cohesion; a sort of creative compositional strategy that does not create the horizontal violence we see when stories are made to compete with one another to represent the "definitive" marginalized voice. Centering polyvocality reveals contradictions, differences, and complexity, and the ways the term "diversity" fails to sustain nuance.

Benhabib (1996) argues that we are in need of "a regulative principle of hope," without which "not only morality but also radical transformation is unthinkable" (p. 553). While it is necessary to be attuned to "the theoretical and political traps of why utopias and foundational thinking can go wrong," we cannot lose hope in the possibilities of ideals (p. 554). Therefore, even as we hold the ideal of diversity as a guiding principle of hope, institutions must make room for the complexities and possibilities

154 MESHELL STURGIS ET AL.

inherent in the uncertain process of working through differences. Single-mindedly seeking one path forward to attain the ideal can thwart efforts to work through the messiness of difference.

Spectral Modes of Engagement and Collective Co-Witnessing

While social movements require many forms of engagement, there is a counterproductive and often monolithic narrative of what successful social justice and "DEI work" looks, sounds, and feels like. Though it appeared as though no one was listening on the day of our roundtable, is it possible to still label our efforts "activism"? Beyond presenting polyvocal narratives, we argue that the roundtable, subsequent discussions, and this chapter, are a form of spectral engagement. Spectral engagement covers a wide array of tactics that often go unnoticed on larger structural levels and are underappreciated, but still chip away at injustice. Singular narratives of progress—often centering large-scale political action, primarily—hinder the potential of other forms of activism. In the words of cultural activist and public scholar Lee (2018a), "this way of relating to our communities' pain is broken" (p. 6). We must leave room for diverse forms of social action.

Too close a focus on "correct" actions, and, as Joseph (2017) notes, correct language, "can also be a silencing device that temporarily presses mute on racist, homophobic, transphobic, misogynistic, or generally prejudiced sentiments" (p. 3307). Instead, scholars like Lee (2018b) urge us to pause when we find ourselves "being shaken out" of our "familiar understandings of what justice means and how to move towards it..." (p. 6). Even though our panel did not have the intended outcome, through co-witnessing one another's efforts, we heard and saw each other—a form of activism that set the stage for future efforts.

The popular narrative that minoritized groups will inevitably be woven fully into higher education belies ongoing inequities. Consequently, scholars like Oliha-Donaldson (2018) note that most students "feel there is still work to be done in understanding and negotiating diversity issues—defining diversity (personally, organizationally, and socially), operationalizing it, and ensuring access, inclusion and equity for all" (p. 140). This work, by necessity, must take on many forms to address the interlocking nature of oppression and to remedy its effects at micro and macro levels (Bronfenbrenner, 1977).

Although our roundtable went unheard, the experience allowed us to consider the impact and possibilities of other modes of engagement. In this case, through co-witnessing one another's efforts, engaging in polyvocality,

"SEEN" BUT NOT HEARD **155**

and writing together, we are part of larger efforts to agitate for change and make "comprehensible and occupiable, intellectual, ethical, and political positions antagonistic to contemporaneous configurations of racial capitalism" (Melamed, 2011, p. 48). By co-witnessing our labor, we were empowered to continue our efforts, knowing we are not alone. Although our panel only helped the university check off their obligatory "diversity" box and was merely discussion without direct action, the network that has emerged since has proven to be a fortifying force in our efforts to advocate for students of color and the diverse challenges they face.

CONCLUSION: ANTICIPATE INSTITUTIONAL FAILURE

These pathways forward were developed from our conversations to reframe our experience when confronted with the unfortunate reality of yet another failure of the institution to recognize our collective efforts (Halberstam, 2011). Kelley (2018) writes about demands from student protesters across 90 university campuses in the fall of 2015 in response to campus racism (p. 153). Some of the core demands were for campuses to assume "greater diversity, inclusion, and cultural-competency training" (p. 157). While not necessarily winnable, Kelley notes that, "winning is not always the point. Unveiling the university's exploitative practices and its deeply embedded structures of racism, sexism, and class inequality can be profound acts of demystification on their own" (p. 157). Kelley continues, "certainly universities can and will become more diverse and marginally more welcoming … but, … they will never be engines of social transformation. Such a task is ultimately the work of political education and activism" (p. 157). Our efforts in this project are a direct response to this assertion.

Courage is sustained from a place of hope. For West (1997), hope "enacts the stance of the participant who actively struggles against" evidence of "unregulated global capitalism, racial balkanization, social breakdown, and individual depression" (p. xii). Counter-networks like the one this writing team formed in response to a failed DEI moment provide interpersonal sustenance while advancing our capacity for political education and other forms of activism. Such efforts, no matter how small or underappreciated, allow us to courageously and hopefully find ways to learn from moments of institutional disappointment and garner strength to continue our labor, even if only for our collective well-being. Such networks prompt us to return to the drawing board, finding strength in our stories, unity in our numbers, and value in our different experiences.

156 MESHELL STURGIS ET AL.

DISCUSSION QUESTIONS

1. Identify spaces that currently allow for co-witnessing and spectral modes of engagement at your institution. What makes these spaces successful in promoting co-witnessing and spectral modes of engagement?
2. Have you ever experienced co-witnessing (either as a participant or observer)? How did it impact you?
3. When and how is institutional failure determined? Who is asked to respond to these failures and how are they supported in this task?
4. Identify modes of engagement on the spectrum of activism. Are there modes that hold more or less value? Why?
5. In what ways could experiences and scholarly work by people of color be centered in academic spaces without those scholars feeling an additional burden of having to educate others? What does it mean to have their polyvocal narratives truly heard by the institution?
6. What systems, structures, and relationships are in place at your institution to support underrepresented graduate students and students of color?

NOTES

1. These include the "From Rodney King to Michael Brown; Media's Impact on the Portrayal of Black Males" on November 14, 2014; the "Ferguson and Beyond: Race, State Violence, and Activist Agendas for Social Justice in the 21st Century," which was held on January 23, 2015; and the "#BlackLivesMatter: The Imperative of Racial Justice Activism in Our Time," which was held on January 22, 2016.
2. The readings included works from Black feminist scholars, hooks (1989) and Joseph (2017).
3. The use of italics signals reflections and internal thoughts that surfaced but were withheld during the discussion.

REFERENCES

Adichie, C. N. (2009, July). *The danger of a single story* [Video file]. Retrieved from: https://www.ted.com/talks/chimamanda_adichie_the_danger_of_a_single_story?langu age=en

Benhabib, S. (1996). Feminism and the question of postmodernism. In J. O. Appleby (Ed.), *Knowledge and postmodernism in historical perspective* (pp. 539–554). New York, NY: Routledge.

Bronfenbrenner, U. (1977). Toward an experimental ecology of human development. *American Psychologist, 32*(7), 513–531.

Collins, P. H. (2009). *Black feminist thought: Knowledge, consciousness, and the politics of empowerment* (2nd ed.). New York, NY: Routledge.

Crenshaw, K. W. (1994). Mapping the margins: Intersectionality, identity politics, and violence against women of color. In M. A. Fineman & R. Mykitiuk (Eds.), *The public nature of private violence* (pp. 93–118). New York, NY: Routledge.

Deerchild, R. (Host). (2019, January 20). *'I regret it': Hayden King on writing Ryerson University's territorial acknowledgement* [Unreserved Radio program]. Guest speaker Hayden King. Toronto, Canada: CBC Radio. Retrieved from https://www.cbc.ca/radio/unreserved/redrawing-the-lines-1.4973363/i-regret-it-hayden-king-on-writing-ryerson-university-s-territorial-acknowledgement-1.4973371

Desai, J., & Murphy, K. P. (2018). Subjectively inhabiting the university. *Critical Ethnic Studies, 4*(1), 21–43.

Gilbert, D. (2017, March). Milo Yiannopoulos at UW: A speech, a shooting and $75,000 in police overtime. *The Seattle Times* [Online]. Retrieved from https://www.seattletimes.com/seattle-news/crime/milo-yiannopoulos-at-uw-a-speech-a-shooting-and-75000-in-police-overtime/

Gómez, J. M. (2015). Microaggressions and enduring mental health disparity: Black americans at risk for institutional betrayal. *Journal of Black Psychology, 41*(2), 121–143.

GPSS Diversity Committee. (n.d.). *Get involved*. Graduate & Professional Student Senate. Retrieved from http://depts.washington.edu/gpss/get-involved/

Halberstam, J. (2011). *The queer art of failure*. Durham, NC: Duke University Press.

hooks, b. (1989). Choosing the margin as a space of radical openness. *Framework: The Journal of Cinema and Media,* (36), 15–23.

Jones, V. A., & Reddick. R. J. (2017). The heterogeneity of resistance: How Black students utilize engagement and activism to challenge PWI inequalities. *The Journal of Negro Education,* 86(3), 204–219. doi:10.7709/jnegroeducation. 86.3.0204

Joseph, R. L. (2017). What's the difference with "difference"? Equity, communication, and the politics of difference. *International Journal of Communication,* 11, 3306–3326.

June, A. W. (2015). The invisible labor of minority professors. *The Chronicle of Higher Education,* 62(11), 25.

Kelley, R. D. G. (2018). Black study, Black struggle 1. *Ufahamu: Journal of the African Activist Association* [Online], 40(2), 153–168.

Lee, F. (2018a, December 10). Seeking change without the commodification of pain and suffering. *The Seattle Globalist.* Retrieved from https://www.seattleglobalist.com/2018/12/10/seeking-change-without-the-commodification-of-pain-and-suffering/79110

Lee, F. (2018b). Toward an ethics of activism: Introduction. In F. Lee (Ed.), *Toward An ethics of activism: A community investigation of humility, grace and compassion in movements for justice* (pp. 3–6). Printed by the author.

Lerma, V., Hamilton, L. T., & Nielsen, K. (2019). Racialized equity labor, university appropriation and student resistance. *Social Problems,* spz011. doi:10.1093/socpro/spz011

Matthew, P. A. (2016). What is faculty diversity worth to a university. *The Atlantic.*

Melamed, J. (2011). *Represent and destroy: Rationalizing violence in the new racial capitalism.* Minneapolis, MN: University of Minnesota Press.

Moraga, C., & Anzaldúa, G. (2015). *This bridge called my back: Writings by radical women of color* (4th ed.). Albany, NY: State University of New York Press.

158 MESHELL STURGIS ET AL.

Nader, L. (1972). Up the anthropologist: Perspectives gained from studying up. In D. Hymes (Ed.), *Reinventing anthropology* (pp. 284–311). New York, NY: Pantheon Books.

Nishime, L., & Hester Williams, K. D. (2018). Introduction: Why racial ecologies? In L. Nishime & K. D. Hester Williams (Eds.), *Racial ecologies* (pp. 3–16). Seattle, WA: University of Washington Press.

Oliha-Donaldson, H. (2018). Let's talk: An exploration into student discourse about diversity and the implications for intercultural competence. *Howard Journal of Communications, 29*(2), 126–143.

O'Sullivan, J. (2019, December). With the loss of Referendum 88, affirmative-action advocates wonder what's next. Inslee offers some answers. *The Seattle Times* [Online]. Retrieved from https://www.seattletimes.com/seattle-news/politics/with-the-loss-of-referendum-88-affirmative-action-advocates-wonder-whats-next/

Padilla, A. M. (1994). Ethnic Minority Scholars, Research, and Mentoring: Current and Future Issues. *Educational Researcher, 23*(4), 24–27.

Race & Equity at the UW. (n.d.). Retrieved from https://www.washington.edu/raceequity/

Rideau, R. (2019). "We're just not acknowledged": An examination of the identity taxation of full-time non-tenure-track Women of Color faculty members. *Journal of Diversity in Higher Education.*

Rojas, P. M. (2017, December 12). Emotional labor from students of color ain't free, Cornell. *The HuffPost.* Retrieved from https://www.huffpost.com/entry/retension-at-cornell-yo-n-b_9760532

UW Diversity Blueprint 2017–2021. (n.d.). *Diversity at the UW.* Retrieved February 4, 2020 from https://s3-us-west-2.amazonaws.com/uw-s3-cdn/wp-content/uploads/sites/48/2018/07/24025214/17_DiversityBlueprint-010917.pdf

West, C. (1997). *Restoring hope: Conversations on the future of Black America.* Boston, MA: Beacon Press.

Chapter 10

Becoming Professors of Equity at San Diego State University: Reflecting on Professional Seminars on Implicit Biases and Microaggressions

Yea-Wen Chen, Feion Villodas, Felicia Black, Sureshi Jayawardene, Roberto Hernández, Daniel L. Reinholz, and Thierry Devos

FEION: As an African-American female, I have served as a representative of diversity for most of my life. From grade school to graduate school, it was typical that I was the only African American in the room, and unfortunately this is still often the case. My decision to engage in diversity work is driven by a hope that others will be invited to a seat at the table and will not be faced with the heavy burden of being the sole representative of diversity. My hope is that others will be meaningfully engaged and empowered to contribute to the important conversations happening around us and about us, and that our voices will no longer be silenced.

FELICIA: As a Black female, I have been engaged in diversity, equity, and inclusion work since I began my career as a teacher/caregiver and teacher-educator in early-childhood education classrooms in both suburban and urban contexts. For me, the work of social justice and advocacy has been inextricably linked to my care for other people's children and partnerships with parents and communities.

SURESHI: I have engaged in "diversity work" as a woman of color since I was a college student, and at every stage of my academic career, I have grown increasingly frustrated by the surface-level approach that tends to dominate this work. Seeing SDSU undertake a multiscalar evidence-based approach that engages the entire university community at every level renewed my perspective and prompted me to dive in and invest more deeply.

YEA-WEN: As an Asian/immigrant/woman/Other, doing equity work is simultaneously personal and political to me. I jumped at the opportunity to work with a team who would demonstrate "willingness to engage in ongoing professional learning around issues of diversity, equity, and inclusion."

ROBERTO: I have long avoided doing "diversity work" because of the cultural tax placed on faculty of color and women, yet seeing the broader, substantial campus-wide efforts, beyond simply having one nominal Chief Diversity Officer, made me, as a man of color, finally feel invested in this work.

DANIEL: As a White, cisgender man, I am committed to dismantling the systems that oppress women and people of color. It has always been the people most oppressed by these systems who have also had the responsibility for changing them. My commitment is to use my privilege not to advance my own status, but rather to make space so that the stories of others can be heard.

THIERRY: I have studied implicit biases while holding privileged positions being a White straight man and a tenured faculty. Joining this team was an opportunity to step outside of my comfort zone, switch my lenses, and work collaboratively towards more equity on our campus.

As a team of diversity workers, we strive to align and/or put our own bodies on the line in solidarity with institutional members who always already struggle with being Othered, silenced, and erased by interlocking systems of oppression (e.g., racism, sexism, Islamophobia, etc.). Ahmed (2012) describes diversity workers as "institutional plumbers" who initiate, develop, and implement diversity strategies as "techniques for unblocking institutional blockages" against inclusion and equity (p. 32). Prior to becoming diversity workers under the institutional designation as "(Provost's) Professors of Equity (in Education),"[1] we were first and are still researchers who examine topics such as implicit intergroup biases, microaggressions, equity, and social justice across disciplines ranging from the life sciences to the humanities (e.g., Black, 2018; Chen, 2018; Hernández, 2018; Jayawardene & McDougal, 2019; Moses, Villodas, & Villodas, 2019; Reinholz & Shah, 2018; Yogeeswaran, Devos, & Nash, 2016). Collectively, we know/feel/understand the importance of embodying a (critical) praxis such as acknowledging our varying and differential levels of power, privilege, and agency as we work as a team of diversity practitioners. Keeping in mind what hooks (1991) calls the reality of "white supremacist capitalistic patriarchy," we will reflect in the space below how we, in our role as the Professors of Equity, have experienced and negotiated diversity work as filled with tensions, contradictions, and paradoxes. Based on our experiences, we will also offer suggestions and recommend promising practices for colleagues tasked with diversity programming.

CONTEXTUAL BACKGROUND

As an institution first conceived in 1897 and located along the U.S.-Mexico border, San Diego State University (SDSU) is a large-sized, four-year public university and also one of the 23 campuses of the California State University system. SDSU not only prides itself on having "a diverse campus,"[2] but also has been recognized for its commitments to diversity. In 2016, the Campus Pride Index ranked SDSU one of the top LGBTQ-friendly universities. In 2017, SDSU received the Higher Education Excellence in Diversity Award for the fifth consecutive year in recognition of its outstanding commitment to diversity and inclusion across campus. While SDSU strives to embrace an institutional climate that values and embraces cultural diversities broadly, at the same time, its commitments have been met with challenges. For instance, between 2015 and 2017, there have been at least two police reports of assaults and hate crimes against Muslim American students. On April 14, 2019, the Black Resource Center was found vandalized after being open for about one year. Since 2012, SDSU has been designated a Hispanic-Serving Institution (HSI) by the U.S. Department of Education; yet, conversations about how to embrace such status and what being HSI means did not begin until late 2018.

In June 2018, SDSU welcomed its ninth permanent president, Dr. Adela de la Torre, the first Latina and woman in this role. Under President de la Torre's leadership, the Professors of Equity is one of several initiatives that were launched in spring 2019 to promote diversity, equity, and inclusion. Institution-wide initiatives also include: Employee Resource Groups, the Equity Council, the Inclusion Council, HSI Task Force, Native Student Resource Center, Inclusive Faculty Recruitment and Retention, and more. Early 2019 also witnessed the start of an approximately two-year strategic planning process that would determine SDSU's institutional priorities for the next five years with important implications for resource allocations. In fall 2019, the Division of Diversity and Innovation (DDI) was named and established (based on one-time funding) as its own unit to house and bring together all the diversity initiatives, councils, and cultural centers, including the Professors of Equity.

As a team, the Professors of Equity are charged to "provide intensive, ongoing professional learning opportunities for SDSU faculty on diversity-related topics." So far, designing and leading interactive seminars on implicit biases and microaggressions has been the central focus. During the pilot semester of spring 2019, we as a team of five were led by Provost Chair of Faculty Diversity and Inclusion at the time, Dr. Cristina Alfaro. Collaboratively, we launched an inaugural Faculty Diversity and Inclusion Institute on March 4, 2019, and piloted several professional learning opportunities (e.g., Implicit Bias and Microaggression Awareness, and

162 YEA-WEN CHEN ET AL.

Implicit Bias in Hiring Practices) with eight departments/units by invitation/request, including the university's police department. In one semester, we served over 300 faculty and staff members. Due to various reasons, one Professor of Equity chose not to return. In the summer of 2019, we grew to be a team of seven with three new members. Since August 2019, the professional learning opportunities were rebranded as "professional learning seminars" (PLS) offered at set times for interested faculty and staff members to sign up and attend. Specifically, all members of search committees were strongly encouraged to attend the PLS throughout fall 2019. Between August 2019 and November 2019, we as a team of seven had facilitated 38 open-registration implicit bias seminars (21 of the Implicit Bias and Microaggressions foundational seminar and 17 of the Implicit Bias in Hiring seminar). Also, we facilitated three Implicit Bias seminars and two Bias in Hiring seminars by invitation for specific departments. In total, 655 individuals participated in at least one seminar (85 attended both), including 203 faculty members, 290 staff members, 77 administrators, and 21 students (as well as several individuals for whom we do not have their role/ position) from every college and division across the university.

Thus far, we as a team have developed and co-led/co-facilitated two main PLSs: (a) a general PLS on implicit bias and microaggressions; and (b) a context-specific PLS on implicit bias and microaggressions in hiring. Our approach to the PLS reflects some of our personal and scholarly commitments to equity and social justice. First, we are committed to the strategy of co-facilitation (in pairs). Even though each and every one of us is capable of delivering the PLS individually, we believe that the benefits of co-facilitation (e.g., reading the room and bringing multiple identities to the work) outweighs the push for efficiency. Second, reflecting our collaborative orientation, we strive to be as interactive and engaging as possible. For instance, we begin every PLS with the SDSU Kumeyaay land acknowledgement[3] followed by sharing our personal stories of how we come to this work and establishing communication agreements to set the tone for the seminar. In the spirit of decolonial consciousness-raising, a land acknowledgement recognizes the traditional territory and ancestral home of the Indigenous people(s) who (have) called the land home prior to colonization. In the case of SDSU, the university stands on the traditional territory of the Kumeyaay people. Starting each PLS with the land acknowledgement affirms a commitment to challenge ourselves to be inclusive of all minoritized groups. Third, we develop each PLS to reflect our collective belief in how implicit biases and microaggressions (re)produce social inequalities. In doing so, we take seriously the suggestions and recommendations of our participants alongside our own reflections and observations at the completion of a PLS to implement improvements, specific examples, and generally enhance the content of our materials to better reflect the experiences and processes germane to staff and faculty groups across our campus. Specifically, we come to see that implicit biases when uninterrupted can become manifested as microaggressions in everyday interactions. Further, microaggressions when uninterrupted contribute to (re) producing social inequities such as racism, sexism, and Islamophobia.

IMPLICATIONS AND LESSONS LEARNED: BIASES, MICROAGGRESSIONS, AND DIFFERENTIAL LABOR

"The most valuable portion of this presentation was the moment when we all got time to reflect on moments where these [biases and microaggressions] occur in our daily lives," commented one participant who attended a PLS with Feion and Daniel in spring 2019. This statement gets at the core of the kind of critical reflections that we strive to process with participants in our PLS. However, given the differential levels of awareness, lived experiences, and material conditions that both facilitators and participants bring into each PLS, we recognize that the same message can be heard, understood, and felt differently. We are also cognizant of both limited and potentially unintended impacts of one-time PLS. For instance, one participant this fall left this comment on a post-PLS evaluation form: "As a non-POC [person of color], I was slightly uncomfortable with the conversation but I learned how I can be thoughtful in my words and how to be an ally to my colleagues, students. I wish we had more time." As co-facilitators, we do not mean to trigger participants, but we recognize that conversations about implicit biases and microaggressions can be uncomfortable and triggering, especially for members of minoritized groups. Together, both comments in this paragraph signal the differential impacts of each PLS for participants as well as for ourselves as facilitators.

Rather than prematurely speculating the impacts on participants, we would like to take this opportunity to reflect on the differential labors and impacts across members on this team doing diversity work. Existing research has established that women and people of color are expected to and/or tend to shoulder a disproportionate amount of institutional services (e.g., Gutiérrez y Muhs, Niemann, González, & Harris, 2012). Consistent with that, this team is composed of more women and people of color as diversity workers, especially (pre-tenure) Black women (i.e., Felicia, Feion, and Sureshi). Also, most of the team members are pre-tenure faculty members. In addition, we vary in terms of our socioeconomic background, immigration status, prior experience with diversity work, marital status, and more. Mirroring the socially constructed racial hierarchy that persists in U.S. society, each of us feel, embody, and live with the stresses and labors of diversity work differentially. Yea-Wen recalls a

164 YEA-WEN CHEN ET AL.

troubling PLS incident in which one White male participant who seemed skeptical of biases and microaggressions kept looking at her while Felicia was speaking. Was his looking away from Felicia as a Black woman signaling his discomfort and/or unwillingness to believe and accept the reality of racism in higher education that Felicia was describing? Also, was his looking at Yea-Wen as a lighter-skin/Asian woman signalizing her to do something to help him feel more at ease? Daniel recalls multiple episodes in which members of the audience (typically White men) would question the words of a co-facilitator (typically a woman of color), and instead look to him as another White man for a more definitive answer, as though he was an authority on equity and inclusion. These troubling episodes highlighted the racism and sexism inherent even in diversity work and underscore the importance of building a team that can bring multiple intersecting identities to the work. Thierry reflects on how Feion seemed more deeply and personally affected than him after a challenging PLS with a group of faculty members who mostly did not believe the material impacts of implicit biases and microaggressions. During our debriefing about this PLS, Feion repeatedly commented on the expressions of sadness, frustration, and disturbance that she saw from the few women and people of color in the room. How long past the PLS had, or has, Feion carried with her the emotional burdens and labors of worrying about/for/with these participants? All of us are acutely aware of how diversity work weighs much more heavily on the browner, darker, and more deviant bodies among us. Recognizing that this critical issue deserves more attention and resources, we as a team make ourselves available to meet with participants after the PLS. In response, we have launched a biweekly reading circle in spring 2020 specifically with women faculty of color as a communal space for fellowship, support, and solidarity. Frankly, we struggle to address this issue directly within the constraints of the PLS.

In another example, during a PLS on bias in hiring that Daniel and Sureshi co-facilitated, when discussing an example of a certain college on campus lacking racial and gender diversity, a senior White woman faculty member, who serves on diversity committees in her own unit, ventured an explanation for this, declaring that there may not be enough Black women with Ph.D.'s to diversify that candidate pool and fulfill the tenure-stream needs of that college. Her comments were extremely triggering for Sureshi. What perceptions and evaluations does this faculty member have regarding Black women academics? Does she not have colleagues who are Black women with doctoral degrees? How is it that the stereotypes about an uneducated Black woman plague the mindset of a woman engaged in "diversity work?" Sureshi left that PLS not convinced that this faculty member fully understood the gravity of her comments or what it signaled about her understanding of bias. The irony of performing and representing

BECOMING PROFESSORS OF EQUITY 165

"diversity work" while mired by the very biases that impede equity highlights the paradox of what we do and the need for an ongoing investment in learning and unlearning in engaging with this work. In such situations, our team dynamics are not limited to the work of co-facilitation but also to ensuring advocacy for one another and self- and community-care practices among ourselves. Since we are institutionally designated "Professors of Equity," we want to be conscientious of what this team might represent or signal—whether intentionally or unintentionally—about diversity to various members and groups at SDSU in this moment. In particular, we refuse to fall into the trap of becoming a tool to check a box without doing our part to help transform the campus culture to be more inclusive of equity mindsets and practices that benefit all members of the institution.

At the institutional level, our experiences as team with differential impacts and labors of diversity underscore an underlying paradox in that there are unintended costs of inadvertently reproducing increased cultural taxations on darker and browner diversity workers. Our awareness of this has led us to demand large-scale assessment of the effectiveness and/or impacts of diversity initiatives, including our PLS, which is currently undergoing in spring 2020. We believe that institutions can benefit from attending to tensions, paradoxes, and struggles rather than shying away from them.

PROMISING PRACTICES FOR CHANGE

Practice 1: Co-facilitating Important Conversations Collaboratively

#1. "The discussion was the most valuable part of this."

#2. "The most valuable portion of this event is the discussion aspect throughout the presentation and hearing the perspectives of other faculty and staff at SDSU. It is empowering to know that there are people who are interested in creating a more equitable, diverse, and inclusive environment at SDSU."

#3. "The group discussion of implicit bias and microaggressions. It revealed to me how I am less aware of many of the microaggressions many others experience."

The participants' comments here evidence and affirm that we strive to design our PLS to be as interactive, collaborative, and cooperative as possible. Since we began these seminars in spring 2019, we have persisted to incorporate participant feedback through diligent debriefing after each PLS. In response, we have continually worked on tweaking, amending, and enhancing the seminar as a critical space for important conversations about

166 YEA-WEN CHEN ET AL.

implicit biases and microaggressions across race and ethnicity, sex and gender, immigration status, and more. Each PLS features various interactive activities such as reflective writing, think-pair-share, and small-group conversations with tablemates. Consistent with scholarship on critical communication pedagogy (Fassett & Rudick, 2018; Fassett & Warren, 2007), we recognize that how co-facilitators and participants relate to and engage with one another in the room plays an important role in informing, shaping, and influencing the conversations that take place within each PLS. That is, relationships with both the self and others stand to affect how we converse about implicit biases and microaggressions that involve difference, power, and privilege. In particular, our participants' feedback helps us to push against the pressure to make the PLS larger and draw the line in keeping the cap around 25 participants per PLS. Moreover, the interactive design of our PLS also indicates that we see participants as partners and collaborators in the process of making institutional change together. Ultimately, we believe that collaborative and cooperative practices are more likely to foster generative conversations and spaces for positive institutional change.

Practice 2: Utilizing Local Examples to Encourage Critical Self-Reflexivity

> #1. "The examples were very valuable because it gives you an idea of what bias is that you wouldn't think it was."
>
> #2. "I also appreciated that real examples from SDSU students, faculty, and staff were used."
>
> #3. "Most viable to me were the concrete examples from our campus (yikes!). And the time to talk through some of this with other attendees. Thank you! PS: more description of diversity on campus would be useful."

As evidenced by the excerpts here, another lesson is that examples matter, especially local ones that hone in on the message. We utilize institutional data and personal narratives from students, staff, and faculty (of color) to process and illuminate concepts of implicit biases and microaggressions. In addition, our collaborative design of the PLS welcomes and encourages participants to share their own examples. One of the benefits of doing this is that we learn to identify and mitigate these issues not just through abstract and distant anecdotes, but through an understanding of how close to home these issues really are. Fundamentally, such an approach makes it clear that diverse campuses like SDSU are not exempt from racism, sexism, homophobia, and other interlocking oppressions. When a specific example resonates with participants' experiences, it can validate past experiences, provide a vocabulary for processing, and invite critical self-reflexivity such as how one might unintentionally and/or complacently participate in upholding social inequalities.

As much as local examples are powerful, we also have had some examples that did not work as well as we had hoped due to various factors. Through trial and error and learning from participant responses, we have refined our examples over time as well as learned to tailor examples to the audience more. In our very first seminar, we talked about the pictures of all past SDSU presidents (i.e., exclusively White men) hung in one of the conference rooms on campus as an example that could be read as environmental microaggressions felt by women and people of color walking into that room. One participant responded that(s) he heard and felt "the presentation and tone of the material" was implying that "if you are an older White male manager, you are bad for a diverse society." Since then, we have stopped using that example—at least for now. While it is a good example of environmental microaggression, we stopped using it primarily because the unintended message could be used by resisters as an excuse to disengage and/or as a weapon of White fragility. When this happened to us as a small and new team, we decided to pick our battles by prioritizing inclusivity, minimizing potential backlash, and choosing to go slow and steady for long-term change. While the resistance to this example could be interpreted as a mechanism of White supremacy, we did not think the PLS was the space for having that conversation. This team and our efforts were and are one of the diversity initiatives, not the only one. As a visible team on campus, we at this stage are more suited to promote buy-ins and acceptance from faculty members across identity positions. Based on our experiences, we recommend the practice of documenting and strategically utilizing local examples to engage in conversations about equity, inclusion, and social justice.

Practice 3: Addressing without Re-centering Voices of Resistance

#1. "Suggestion: Perhaps begin the workshop w/a [sic] discussion about power (how it manifests)."

#2. "What I struggled with is that through this workshop/training, you're placing the need to respond on the individual receiving this offense. As an individual who has been on the receiving end all my life, it gets exhausting to continually have these conversations. It's exhausting and it gets quite old. Beyond these workshops/training, what is SDSU doing to address this? Have you all considered an implicit bias report?"

#3. "Suggestion: I would be able to recognize and acknowledge the privilege in the statement 'give them a second chance'; some folks aren't able to give or get second chances (people of color). It seems as though part of the presentation is also biased towards the perpetrator (ex: unintentional, second chances, etc.). Maybe privilege the victims more and provide tangible ways to reduce harm systemically."

168 YEA-WEN CHEN ET AL.

Together, participants' suggestions highlight that our collaborative approach tends to play it safe and tread lightly on critical topics such as power and privilege without calling folks out unless necessary. In our seminars, we have experienced on multiple occasions dominant and already-privileged voices challenging the very premise that implicit biases and microaggressions are real and impact members of minoritized groups differentially and materially. We have spent a great deal of time, energy, and labor debriefing about this issue and processing how we could address without re-centering voices of resistance in the moment. One strategy that we have talked about is for each of us as the facilitator to feel comfortable within a seminar naming and calling out, "I feel microaggressed by what you just said." At the same time, this strategy can work for some bodies more than others. For instance, pre-tenure folks run a greater risk deploying this strategy. This will continue to be a critical issue as we move forward.

We all recognize that one-time seminars with limited, short-term impact cannot be the answer to institutional changes. The three lessons are practices that we as a team find promising and enduring in facilitating collaborative and effective seminars. At the same time, we recognize that these practices are limited on their own and should be accompanied by other initiatives towards institutional change. For instance, we are apprehensive about not following up with participants, especially individuals from minoritized groups who have been waiting for awareness, reflexivity, and accountability. Moreover, how can we assess and understand the true impacts of the PLSs without pre-planned, systematic, large-scale assessments and evaluations? Without becoming informed of the impacts of the PLSs, how can we best strategize the next steps? In the context of diversity work, how could we as diversity workers ensure that we do not potentially and unknowingly do more harm than good, despite good intentions?

CONCLUSION

Returning to Ahmed's (2012) perspective on diversity workers as "institutional plumbers" developing diversity strategies as "techniques for unblocking institutional blockages" against inclusion and equity (p. 32), in our case, what are the benefits and limitations of treating the Professors of Equity as diversity workers and/or "institutional plumbers"? What role do and can researchers play in all of this work? Can the equity workers simultaneously be the researchers? As the Professors of Equity, we aim for long-term impacts for our institution in terms of inculcating a more welcoming culture and climate for all faculty, staff, and students across intersecting

BECOMING PROFESSORS OF EQUITY **169**

and differing identity positions. At the same time, we know that the path to long-term institutional change/impact is not linear but most likely filled with potholes and speed bumps, if not roadblocks, along the way. We urge more honest conversations and needed attention to systematic evaluations on if/how diversity work leads to long-term institutional changes towards equity and inclusion, particularly attentions paid to paradoxes, tensions, and contradictions.

DISCUSSION QUESTIONS

1. What is the best diversity training you have experienced? Also, what is the worst diversity training you have undergone? More importantly, what makes the training that comes to mind the best or the worst, and what lessons can be gained from both?

2. The short-term and limited impact of one-time diversity training has been documented. In light of this, how does your institution approach the goal(s) and anticipated outcome(s) of diversity training?

3. To what extent might diversity needs at minority-serving institutions (e.g., HSIs [Hispanic-Serving Institutions] and HBCUs [Historically Black Colleges and Universities]) be similar to and/or different from those at historically and/or predominantly white institutions (PWIs)? In other words, how might institutional contexts and histories affect, shape, or inform conversations about diversity, inclusion, and equity?

4. One challenge of diversity initiatives in general is a critical need to move beyond "preaching to the choir" in order to mobilize and sustain wider support. At your institution, how have you experienced this challenge being addressed or not?

5. Based on your experiences, should sensitive topics such as "power" and "privilege" be an integral part of diversity trainings, and why or why not? Also, what factors inform your decision about whether or not sensitive topics should be addressed?

6. Why do you think that Ahmed (2012) likens diversity trainers/workers to "institutional plumbers"? What might this analogy suggest about the nature of diversity work?

7. To what extent do, or should, diversity trainers' identity positions (e.g., race, gender, class, sexuality, immigration status, etc.) impact the work that they do? In this chapter, we have discussed the differential labors and impacts among us as an interracial team; to what extent do you agree or disagree with our argument, and why?

NOTES

1. Further information about the initiative concerning Professors of Equity in Education is described on this webpage: https://diversity.sdsu.edu/inclusion/professors.
2. "We have a diverse campus" is considered one of SDSU's achievements and distinctions. More details are provided on this webpage: https://stratcomm.sdsu.edu/achievements-and-distinctions.
3. Approved by the SDSU Senate on September 3, 2019, the university has passed a resolution to establish an official Kumeyaay land acknowledgement. A full and an abbreviated version of the SDSU Kumeyaay land acknowledgement is available at https://ais.sdsu.edu/articles/Land-Acknowledgement.htm.

REFERENCES

Ahmed, S. (2012). *On being included: Racism and diversity in institutional life*. Durham and London: Duke University Press.

Black, F. V. (2018). Providing quality early childhood professional development at the intersections of power, race, gender, and dis/ability. *Contemporary Issues in Early Childhood*, 19(2), 206–211.

Chen, Y.-W. (2018). "Why don't you speak (up), Asian/immigrant/woman?": Rethink silence and voice through family oral history. *Departures in Critical Qualitative Research*, 7(2), 29–48. doi:10.1525/dcqr.2018.7.2.29

Fassett, D. L., & Rudick, C. K. (2018). Critical communication pedagogy: Toward "hope in action." In D. Could (Ed.), *Oxford encyclopedia of communication and critical studies*. New York, NY: Oxford University Press.

Fassett, D. L., & Warren, J. T. (2007). *Critical communication pedagogy*. Thousand Oaks, CA: Sage.

Gutiérrez y Muhs, G., Niemann, Y. F., González, C. G., & Harris, A. P. (Eds.). (2012). *Presumed incompetent: The intersections of race and class for women in academia*. Boulder, CO: University Press of Colorado.

Hernández, R. D. (2018). *Coloniality of the US/Mexico border: Power, violence, and the decolonial imperative*. Tuscon, AZ: The University of Arizona Press.

hooks, b. (1991). Theory as liberatory practice. *Yale Journal of Law & Feminism*, 4(1), 1–12.

Jayawardene, S. M., & McDougal, I. S. (2019). Black student mothers: A culturally relevant exploratory study. In M. M. Gammage & A. Alameen-Shavers (Eds.), *Challenging misrepresentations of black womanhood: Media, literature, and theory* (pp. 9–26). New York, NY: Anthem Press.

Moses, J. O., Villodas, M. T., & Villodas, F. (2019). Black and proud: The role of ethnic-racial identity in the development of future expectations among at-risk adolescents. *Cultural Diversity and Ethnic*, Advance online publication. doi:10.1037/cdp0000273

Reinholz, D. L., & Shah, N. (2018). Equity analytics: A methodological approach for quantifying Participation patterns in mathematics classroom discourse. *Journal for Research in Mathematics Education*, 49(2), 140–177.

Yogeeswaran, K., Devos, T., & Nash, K. (2016). *Understanding the nature, measurement, and utility of implicit intergroup biases*. In C. G. Sibley & F. K. Barlow (Eds.), *Cambridge handbook of the psychology of prejudice* (pp. 241–266). Cambridge, UK: Cambridge University Press.

PART V

ORGANIZATIONAL CONTEXT: DEALING WITH ORGANIZATIONAL CULTURE AND CLIMATE

Chapter 11

Experiencing Symbolic and Linguistic Violence at Predominately White Institutions as Student and Professor

Angela N. Gist-Mackey

The University of Missouri, colloquially known as Mizzou, made national headlines in the fall semester of 2015 due to their racially tense culture. I was a doctoral student at Mizzou from 2009 to 2014 and experienced a series of racial incidents that set the foundation for Mizzou's public crisis. Upon my graduation in 2014, I accepted a position as a tenure-track assistant professor at the University of Kansas (KU). I have also encountered a number of racial incidents in my role as faculty. This chapter analyzes three racial incidents across two institutions by comparing two vantage points, that of a Black woman doctoral student and that of a faculty member, at Predominately White Instions (PWIs). It is my hope that comparing and contrasting these two different positionalities (i.e., student and faculty) across institutions will shed light on patterns of racism across institutions and the ways such incidents are experienced personally and professionally.

This essay offers insight into the way offensive symbolism and language manifest as racial violence in higher education. I close by discussing promising practices that foster resilience for individuals, departmental units, and institutions of higher education.

SYMBOLIC VIOLENCE: COTTON BALLS AND GRAFFITI WALLS

On February 26, 2010, during Black History Month, two White male students scattered cotton balls outside the Gaines/Oldham Black Culture Center on the Mizzou campus between 1:30–2:00 a.m. (Richardson, 2010; Obaro, 2019). According to Richardson (2010), those cotton balls stayed in front of the cultural center nearly 12 hours until 2:30 p.m. later that day.

174 ANGELA N. GIST-MACKEY

The Black undergraduate student group, Legion of Black Collegians, held a town hall (Richardson, 2010). I was one of three Black graduate students in my department at the time. Another Black graduate student, Jada (pseudonym), and I were upset. We were angry that this was happening, upset our department had not formally acknowledged the incident, and needed community. I was granted permission to miss class and attend the town hall. Personally, I attended to better understand how students felt and how the administration was going to respond, and I needed to be with my people.

I should share a bit of my previous exposure to the racial dynamics at Mizzou. My mother attended Mizzou for two years in the 1970s and had a difficult experience in regard to racism. When I wanted to apply to their School of Journalism for undergraduate studies (the third highest-ranked journalism program in the country in 1999), my mother forbad me to apply, blatantly stating that Mizzou was racist. Her resistance seemed illogical to me at the time for many reasons. First, I had grown up in a city that had racial tensions, metropolitan St. Louis, and had experienced the way racial segregation, colorism, and inequity thrived in the metro area. In fact, in 2018, the NAACP announced a travel warning for Black people for the entire state of Missouri (Hafner, 2017), where I grew up. I attended a predominately White high school that bussed in students from urban areas through the district's desegregation program because urban schools had lost accreditation (Strauss, 2017). In short, I was no stranger to racism and inequity, and felt equipped to attend school in a racially charged environment. Going to Mizzou for my bachelor's degree would have given me an opportunity to attend one of the best programs in the nation for my intended major, journalism, with in-state tuition. In my mind, it was a win-win for a prospective student from a financially strapped single-parent home. My mother won that debate. She was protecting me. I never applied to Mizzou for undergraduate studies. Instead, I graduated from another top journalism program at the time, Ohio University's E.W. Scripps School of Journalism. My mother knew what I would painfully be reminded of more than ten years later when I attended Mizzou for my Ph.D. Dr. William Robertson, Professor Emeritus of Urban Planning (the second Black faculty hired by the University of Missouri in 1970) put it succinctly: "Missouri has a history of racism, discrimination, and frankly resentment toward blacks," (Obaro, 2019, para. 35). This had been the case since before my mother attended the university in the 1970s.

Jada and I attended the town hall meeting in 2010. When I entered, I saw a room of students, faculty, and staff of color who were seeking answers and trying to hold university leaders accountable. At the end of the town hall, the room was promised by the head of campus police that the investigation would be carried out as a hate crime. The symbolism of cotton balls dropped in front of the Black Culture Center during Black History Month was symbolically violent. Cotton was one of the largest slave-supported

SYMBOLIC AND LINGUISTIC VIOLENCE 175

industries in the United States in the early to mid-1800s and greatly supported the growth of American economy (Gates, 2013). The connection to me was obvious, but I would learn that this part of our nation's history was lost on many Mizzou undergraduate students at the time.

As a Graduate Teaching Assistant (GTA), I taught public speaking that year. I walked in to teach my course and I knew I had to mention this incident, but did not quite have the words for what I would say or how I would approach the topic. I had no formal training in engaging difficult dialogues in the classroom at that point. So, I started talking honestly, beginning class with a conversation about the cotton ball incident. I shared the information I learned from the town hall. I told the students there were communities of people on our campus who were scared and did not feel safe. I had referred to the incident as symbolically violent. My students asked me what was symbolic about this incident, which gave me pause. I realized they had no context for the connection between cotton and slavery; it then became clear to me why there had been perceptions of hypersensitivity of the Black community on campus. So, I spent approximately half the class period explaining the connection to slavery, cotton plantations, the space of the Black Cultural Center, and the added salience that this happened during Black History Month—a time when Black heritage should be honored, not disparaged. The room grew quiet, there were nods, eyes dropped to the floor, and sighs. Several students told me they were sad such incidents were *still* happening. My students began to understand and realized why people were upset. There were no Black students in that class. At the end of class, one Latinx student thanked me for talking about this issue. She said I was the only instructor who mentioned it in her classes and asked why this issue was not openly addressed in all classes. I did not have an answer for her. Her experience was disheartening, yet similar to my experience as a graduate student. Not one professor that semester addressed the incident as part of my coursework; this silence spoke loudly to me.

I followed the investigation. The perpetrators were identified as two White male students. They were identified through a series of retail receipts because they purchased large amounts of cotton balls from local retailers and that was triangulated with their student ID card access to a residence hall that night. In the end, they were not charged with a hate crime. They were sanctioned with a littering violation and required to do community service. In an analysis of online responses to the littering conviction, Goldstein Hode and Meisenbach (2012, pp. 139–141) revealed divergent perceptions to this outcome:

> "Some saw the sentence as too lenient, others too harsh. The following blogged responses to a campus newspaper article reporting on the court case reveals the heated debate:
> [Response One] WHAT DO YOU MEAN "IF IT APPEARS TO BE RACIALLY MOTIVATED"!? HOW MUCH MORE RACIST CAN ONE GET? COTTON

176 ANGELA N. GIST-MACKEY

BALLS OUTSIDE OF THE BLACK CULTURE CENTER! (ASIM, Feb. 26, 2010) (emphasis in original)

[Response Two] Wow, since when is littering a racially motivated hate crime? (George, March 2, 2010)

[Response Three] ...So there are 1 or 2 idiots on campus who are bigots and joked around with cotton. Big whoop. If they were serious racists, they would've gone much farther than this, believe me. (Brandon, March 3, 2010)

[Response Four] Obviously you are not Black. If you were, you would understand that as a Black man you don't need to be "overly sensitive" or "liberal" to be offended by this egregious affront to our race and culture. (L'Darius, March 3, 2010)

The online debate brought these racial tensions to the surface. It also highlights the differing interpretations of the incident..." (Goldstein Hode & Meisenbach, 2012, pp. 139–141)

After the conviction was made, the Chancellor's response never mentioned a hate crime and did not call the incident racist (Goldstein Hode & Meisenbach, 2012). From my perspective, a littering conviction was a metaphorical slap on the wrist. I felt defeated, dismissed, and unsafe both psychologically and physically. While the rhetoric of the institution claimed diversity was a value, the misdemeanor for littering in lieu of a hate crime conviction communicated to me that Mizzou was only paying lip service to diversity. Little did I know, feelings of being dismissed, defeated, and unsafe would resurface.

Less than one year after the cotton ball incident of 2010, another racist act was perpetrated by another White male student on Mizzou's campus during Black History Month on February 12, 2011. This time, the perpetrator spray painted the N-word on a statue outside of Hatch Hall on campus (Associated Press, 2012). That same day, the local police found anti-Jewish language spray-painted on a car near campus. It was eerie. These racist acts were becoming an annual reminder during Black History Month that people like me did not belong at Mizzou.

This student was arrested and allegedly charged with a hate crime felony, but as the investigation unfolded, the perpetrator's charge ended up being a misdemeanor of property damage. The student pled guilty and was sentenced with 100 hours of community service (Associated Press, 2012). The demotion of the charges from a felony hate crime to a misdemeanor of property damage communicated that I was not welcome nor was I safe. Students who perpetuated symbolic violence towards my community were permitted to do so with little consequences. A flurry of politically correct responses ensued, including but not limited to another town hall, statements from administrators, and promises to change. I was remembering my mother's words more than ten years prior: the culture of Mizzou was infused with racism.

SYMBOLIC AND LINGUISTIC VIOLENCE 177

Goldstein Hode (2010) wrote an editorial in the University of Missouri's student newspaper, *The Maneater,* highlighting some ways the University of Missouri had been linked to a racist historical presence:

> Yesterday, I attended the Difficult Dialogues session about hate crimes held at the law school. I want to share some insights from that informative session that highlights why this crime is "a big deal."... Professor Frank Bowman gave a brief history of slavery in Missouri and Boone County. For those of us (like me) who didn't know, it was quite a shock to learn that the names we see every day in the place where we learn–Rollins, Switzler, Hickman–were the names of prominent slave owners. In other words, the history of racism is woven into the fabric of our daily lives and many of us don't even know it. History and present day are inextricably linked; what happens today is connected to everything that has come before us.

Reading this troubled me and created a deep sense of dissonance. I worked in Switzler Hall. Learning it was the name of a slave owner made me reconsider the work I did as a graduate student. I toiled countless hours for years in a building named after a slave owner. Was I a slave in some twisted contemporary sense? Bringing value to someone who stripped my people of dignity?

The cotton balls, the easily mobilized N-word, the names of slave owners used as common vernacular on our campus, and the failed discourses promising change were all symbolically violent to me. As a student of communication, I knew that words and symbols mattered. They directly affected me. I promised myself that as faculty, I would be part of the change that would better higher education through teaching, research, and service.

LINGUISTIC VIOLENCE: THE N-WORD AND TOKEN SERVICE

In 2014, I graduated with my Ph.D. in Communication with a perfect 4.0 GPA and was hired as a tenure-track Assistant Professor in the Department of Communication Studies at the University of Kansas (KU). I was a direct hire, which is an affirmative action hire. I knew that I was a solid candidate, but was privy to the fact that many people doubted my competence and capabilities throughout the hiring process. Having a second job offer at a prestigious peer institution helped my negotiation and curbed skeptics until I could prove my worth. Unfortunately, proving my worth came in direct relation to my marginalized identities as a Black woman.

In the fall 2015 semester, Mizzou's new student group, Concerned Student 1950 (Izadi, 2015) was in full force. They were marching at homecoming, engaging in a hunger strike, and the football team was protesting. Mizzou made national headlines garnering attention that had not happened during my years as a doctoral student. I was unprepared for the way

178 ANGELA N. GIST-MACKEY

the protests at Mizzou would spark social justice activism at KU. KU was experiencing what Martin and Van Stee (2020) dubbed the "trickle-down effect" from Mizzou's crisis. Our students developed a group called Rock Chalk Invisible Hawk, made up of a diverse group of underrepresented students, and began protests and made a list of demands of our administration (Shepherd, 2015). KU held a town hall. I was waxing nostalgic.

The auditorium was filled and I sat in the overflow space. I was happy to see others from my department. We listened to stories of those who were hurting, ostracized, and struggling in KU's campus climate. It was reminiscent of my time at Mizzou with a few differences. First, a Black woman chancellor, Dr. Bernadette Grey-Little, Ph.D., was leading this conversation. Second, many members of my department were present. Third, there were explicit complaints about microaggressions students experienced in our department.

Within the week, our department scheduled a town hall in order to address the departmental climate and our students' experiences. A few days before our departmental town hall meeting, there was an incident in our department. One afternoon while working in my office, I saw a parade of graduate students walk into the Director of Graduate Studies' office.

Within the hour, I was asked if I could speak to the graduate students. This request was peculiar because at this point, I had very little interaction with our graduate students. I was only in the beginning of my second year as faculty and had not taught a graduate seminar. I had no idea what happened but felt blindsided when I went into the large, open graduate student office. I was taken back by the nonverbals: tears, hanging heads, and pacing.

In sum, graduate students were in a pedagogy class and asked their professor how they could address racial issues that were present at KU in their public-speaking classrooms (with curriculum designed around civic engagement). The faculty member told students that they should not address racial issues, denied that KU's campus had issues with discrimination, and said the N-word referencing the 2011 graffiti vandalism at Mizzou as an example of 'real' racism. From her vantage point 'real racism' did not appear to be happening at KU. I do not have the space to analyze those comments, but they were wrong, uninformed, inappropriate, and offensive. Our students called out this injustice and demanded change. I am moved by their leadership.

It then became obvious why I was asked to speak to the graduate students; my racial identity as a Black faculty member and my gender identity as a woman seemed to connect with the needs of the moment. Historically, Black women have been saddled or charged with the responsibility to construct "spaces of care and nurturance in the face of the brutal harsh reality of racist oppression, of sexist domination" (hooks, 1990, p. 384). I believe I was being asked to play that role.

SYMBOLIC AND LINGUISTIC VIOLENCE **179**

This incident was racially charged and students needed comforting and mentoring, which is socially constructed as "women's work." For these reasons, I was tokenized. I submitted to that tokenism, offering words of comfort to our hurting students and recommending they document what happened in the class. One student suggested writing letters to this professor to communicate the pain she caused. One such letter was publically posted (Byrd et al., 2015). In my designated role as comforter, ally, and witness, I supported the students. I was both exhausted and motivated to deal with these issues at our upcoming departmental town hall. As faculty, I wanted to convey to the students that I understood and wanted to make our department more diverse and inclusive. I wanted to make good on my promise to be part of the change higher education needed.

Approximately one hour before the departmental town hall, I was asked to lead the discussion. I did not know how to respond to that request from my department chair. I felt entirely unprepared for this task. I was junior faculty and had only been in the department for approximately one year and four months at that time. I did not feel I was in a position to lead a discussion about departmental climate and culture because I was still trying to figure it out. I suggested maybe a senior faculty would be more appropriate but was told that senior faculty thought I was the best choice. I gave into being tokenized again.

I remember being on the student side of a town hall meeting, but felt unprepared to sit on the faculty side of this conversation at such an early point in my career. Yet, I was in a position of power, despite my vulnerability being untenured. The departmental town hall was intense, there were tears, painful stories, departmental demands, and threats of a GTA strike. I was remembering Mizzou. That discussion led to an investigation and ultimately, the faculty member was put on administrative leave.

IMPLICATIONS AND LESSONS LEARNED

Many people came together to organize departmental change at KU. I found myself central to this service. I led a microaggressions training, which at the time was not my area of expertise. I helped coordinate two third-party facilitators for workshops on diversity. I counseled, comforted, and coached countless students who wanted change. I distributed literature on fostering inclusive classrooms and curriculum. I helped our graduate student organization find speakers to address conscious conversations in classrooms. I spent countless hours talking with administrators, investigators, colleagues, and students about the incidents on campus. I was eventually tasked with leading diversity recruitment efforts. I traveled to multiple Historically Black Colleges and Universities (HBCUs) over the course of three consecutive years to diversify our application pipeline (two of these trips occurred on my research leave). These were *some* of my service commitments. I could go on. My point here is not to diminish the collective contributions of many faculty, staff, and students to make the departmental culture more diverse and inclusive. This was a collective effort. However, I do want to highlight that my involvement was not only disproportionate, but also directly tied to my identity as a Black woman academic.

All of this took a toll on me, and I stopped the most central component to my own professional success: researching and writing. I worked for a research-intensive institution, yet I did not have the mental or emotional capacity to do anything but survive this season, holding tight to the promise I made to myself: be part of the change.

The Dean of Diversity, Equity, & Inclusion (DEI) saw fliers posted about the microaggressions training I hosted and asked to have a conversation about my service-load. She advocated on my behalf and coached me through a process that would result in an additional year on my tenure clock. My extension was supported and approved. A victory, but also a loss.

While I did gain an additional year to publish research so that I could be more fairly considered for promotion and tenure, I lost significant funds that would have been put into retirement, ultimately affecting the well-being of my family for which I am currently the breadwinner. I lost a year (possibly more) of productivity on my research that I deeply love and am committed to, which seeks to understand struggles of social mobility and inequity, advocating for change through engaged community scholarship. My psychological and physical health declined due to the stress. My relational health suffered as I did not have the capacity to be a supportive partner, stepmother, daughter, sister, or friend. The students I taught that semester did not receive my best instruction because I was distracted and distressed. I can never regain the time with those students again. Notably, such experiences with tokenism are common.

Guarino and Borden (2017) found that women take on significantly higher service-loads than their male counterparts and that this is especially pronounced at doctoral degree-granting institutions, such as mine. Similar findings have been found in a number of studies (e.g. Bird et al., 2004; Porter, 2007), positing disproportionate service-loads are more pronounced for women faculty of color, especially when racial incidents occur (Butner et al., 2000; Gregory, 2001). Baez (2000) maintains that faculty of color who engage in race-related service make contributions that extend beyond their institutions, constituting larger social justice efforts that influence society, yet despite widespread impact (Baez, 2000; Gregory, 2001; Guarino & Borden, 2017), tokenized service is not fully accounted for the way it should be, because academics work in a system that privileges research over service and teaching.

Tokenism is a concept that emerged from the theory of proportional representation (Kanter, 1977), which defines tokens as people who have underrepresented identities making up less than or equal to 15% of organizational membership. When someone is a token, or a visible representative of their marginalized identity, they feel pressure to:

(1) participate and be seen...; (2) represent a social identity group's point of view...; (3) assimilate to dominant group norms; (4) resist stereotypes of the non-dominant groups in which they represent; (5) and succeed while representing their social identity group, typically without mentorship from senior-level organizational members (Gist & Goldstein Hode, 2017, p. 14).

All of these pressures I experienced throughout my years in various educational institutions, from kindergarten to the professoriate. Experiences of tokenism often lead to anxiety, depression, isolation, and lower levels of opportunity and power. In the midst of negotiating the impact of my own experiences with being tokenized, I received two noteworthy acknowledgments of my efforts.

First, the graduate student organization for our department awarded me Mentor of the Year. I was deeply honored. They had seen my service and dedication and recognized it formally in front of the entire department. Second, towards the end of the investigation, I was called into the Dean's office. The Dean led with an apology. He apologized that I had been thrust into the middle of a racially charged situation, tokenized, and overserviced in the early years of my tenure when my time should have been protected. He thanked me for all I did. Admittedly, I was surprised and grateful for this response. I never anticipated that level of honesty. Ultimately, this Dean decided to fire the faculty member who was investigated, despite the investigative report, which recommended otherwise (Flaherty, 2016; Shepherd, 2016). While I have mixed feelings about the decision to terminate this faculty, the decision communicated something different to me. In many ways, it was a substantive commitment to diversity, something I had not yet experienced from the administration at a PWI. I felt safer, supported, and valued. I felt my tokenism was not in vain. Employees who become tokenized often work towards becoming resilient. This is something I have tried to cultivate personally. Yet, resilience can be employed from micro to macro levels. The next section highlights promising practices for individuals, departments, and institutions of higher education to cultivate resilience when faced with such adversity.

182 ANGELA N. GIST-MACKEY

PROMISING PRACTICES FOR CHANGE: FOSTERING RESILIENCE FROM THE INDIVIDUAL TO THE INSTITUTION

Resilience has been widely theorized. Buzzanell et al. (2009) explain that resilience can be viewed as "a trait that only certain people or families possess, a quality that emerges over time, a process of sustaining hardship, and the human capacity to recover from tragedy in personal and professional lives" (p. 293). In Richardson's (2002) metatheory of resilience, he defines resilience as the process of reintegration after disruptions in life. Richardson (2002) argues that resilience incorporates varying levels of motivation, pursuit of wisdom, and altruism, among other aspects. The three racial incidents illustrate (a lack of) resilience in various ways that carry important implications. However, some resilience scholarship maintains that true resilience is manifest across a "whole-system," requiring individuals, groups, organizations, and institutions to respond to crisis "without engaging in an extended period of regressive behavior" (Horne & Orr, 1998, p. 31). This implies that while one or two resilient parties can make a difference, system-wide resilience is ultimately desirable because it suggests long-term, sustainable change. The remainder of this essay focuses on resilience at the individual, departmental, and institutional levels.

At the microlevel, self-care contributes to resilience. Taking care of one's self holistically (e.g. spiritually, emotionally, psychologically, socially, physically) can facilitate positive adaptation amid adversity. In other words, when stressors occur, individuals are able to better respond when they are in a healthy place rather than when they have neglected self-care. In addition, Garmezy's (1991) and collaborators (Garmezy et al., 1984) identified support systems as one factor contributing to individual resiliency. Personal support systems could take the form of friends, family, or even informal affinity groups (Friedman & Craig, 2004) that organize around social identies (e.g., gender, race, ethnicity, age, sexuality, disability, rank). Cultivating support systems can facilitate compassion during times of adversity where individuals can seek out informational, emotional, instrumental, and appraisal support (House, 1981). The creation and engagement with a homeplace (hooks, 1990) is another way underrepresented individuals may engage in resistance and self-preservation. A homeplace is a place of refuge, a private haven free from racism, a safe place where people are affirmed and affirming to others in order to heal and build community (hooks, 1990). Self-care, personal social support systems, and homeplaces are ways individuals can foster resilience in spite of racism (Oliha-Donaldson, 2018). Yet, the onus of resilience should not solely reside with individuals.

The cultures, practices, and structures of particular offices, departments, and programs can foster resilience as well. For instance, the

SYMBOLIC AND LINGUISTIC VIOLENCE **183**

creation and maintenance of developmental networks is one way to support underrepresented students, faculty, and staff. Developmental networks are sets of "people a protégé names as taking an active interest in and action to advance the protégé's career by providing developmental assistance" (Higgins & Kram, 2001, p. 268). Racial incidents have a tendency to disrupt career development, hindering one's ability to thrive in their role(s). Developmental networks provide a combination of both psychosocial support (e.g., emotional support, consolation, compassion, encouragement) and career support (e.g., sponsorship, networking, guidance, protection), ranging from personal to professional (Higgins & Kram, 2001). Leaders should formally structure such opportunities into their units. Ibarra (1995) found that racial minorities benefit most when their networks were diverse, incorporating people in a wide range of racial and ethnic groups, as well as from diverse ranks and experience levels. Departments should have mechanisms to closely monitor the service-load of underrepresented staff, faculty, and students in three ways: (1) requiring all members of the unit to be equitably involved in service, (2) ensuring engagement in service by people with underrepresented identities is both desired and voluntary, and (3) by providing appropriate accommodations and support for organizational members who choose to disproportionately engage in service (i.e., course releases, decreased expectations for publication, equitable rotation for demanding service roles).

Resilience can also occur at macro levels. Chewning et al. (2012, p. 3) describe organizational resilience as "the ability of affected parties to communicate and reorganize across periods of rapid change or chaos. It involves the ability to respond to situations as well as to adapt in terms of creating new solutions." At the institutional level, scholars such as Frangopol and Soliman (2016) have discussed resilience in relation to the life cycle, structure, and decision-making practices of an entity. At the level of institutional governance, schools, colleges, and provost's/chancellor's offices should work towards becoming more resilient in their systems and structures so they can better navigate and respond to racial incidents. Higher-education leaders should radically re-prioritize and positively evaluate service and teaching, particularly at research-intensive universities. It also means dedicating considerable resources (i.e., finances, personnel, time, expertise, authority) to diversity, inclusion, and equity programs, initiatives, offices, etc. This may mean un-rooting deeply seated ideological beliefs. There should be various ways to thrive and work in institutions of higher education where all types of labor and contributions are valued. Efforts to recruit, retain, and promote employees and students from underrepresented identities should be institutionalized, with an eye towards fostering resilience from individual to institutional levels.

CONCLUSION

I share these three personal experiences with you to illustrate the impact of such incidents. Systems and structures of racism and sexism lead to patterns of recurring incidents in institutions of higher education across the globe. Institutions of higher education are often tasked with advocating for diversity, yet such institutions have few who are willing and able to effectively lead the charge. I share these memorable experiences in the spirit of transparency, advocacy, and hope. I strongly believe that resiliency can be created and infused into structures of higher education from micro to macro levels. Over time, resiliency has the power to transform institutions of higher education for the better. My hope is that these words would continue to inspire change and progress for those who need it most. Instead of violence, I hope these words bring healing, hope, peace, reflection, resilience, and change.

DISCUSSION QUESTIONS

1. How have you been resilient when faced with adversity? Or how could you work to be more resilient in the future?
2. Who is part of your developmental network? Also, who could be added to your developmental network?
3. How have you inadvertently contributed to systems of racism, sexism, or oppression in your campus community? Or in greater society?
4. Are you aware of any homeplaces in your campus community? If so, describe them. If not, how could your campus create homeplaces for historically marginalized groups?
5. What are the risks of university leadership ignoring or downplaying racial incidents on collegiate campuses?
6. How could the University of Missouri have better addressed the 2010 and 2011 racial incidents described above?
7. What lessons can students, staff, faculty, and leaders learn from the University of Missouri's series of racial incidents?
8. How do you feel about the way the University of Kansas reacted to the racial incident described above? Did the Univesity of Kansas show resilience? If so, how? If not, why not?
9. How can universities avoid tokenism of underrepresented identities when faced with racial incidents?
10. What can universities to do to foster resilience for students, staff, faculty, and administrators who experience racial incidents on

campus? Similarly, what can universities to do foster resilience for programs, departments, schools, or colleges who experience racial incidents?

11. How could campuses across the nation and/or globe collaboratively work together to develop large-scale responses and initiatives to address racism in higher education?

REFERENCES

Associated Press. (2012, June 5). Student gets probation for racist graffiti at MU. *St. Louis Post-Dispatch.* https://www.stltoday.com/news/local/crime-and-courts/student-gets-probation-for-racist-graffiti-at-mu/article_33b8b072-af18-11e1-90d8-0019bb30f31a.html

Baez, B. (2000). Race-related service and faculty of color: Conceptualizing critical agency in academe. *Higher Education,* 39(3), 363–391. doi:10.1023/a:1003972214943

Bird, S., Litt, J., & Wang, Y. (2004). Creating status of women reports: Institutional housekeeping as "women's work". *NWSA Journal,* 16(1), 194–206. doi:10.2979/nws.2004.16.1.194

Butner, B. K., Burley, H., & Marbley, A. F. (2000). Coping with the unexpected: Black faculty at predominately white institutions. *Journal of Black Studies,* 30(3), 453–462. doi:10.1177/002193470003000309

Buzzanell, P. M., Shenoy, S., Remke, R. V., & Lucas, K. (2009). Responses to destructive organizational contexts: Intersubjectively creating resilience to foster human dignity and hope. In P. Lutgen-Sandvik & B. D. Sypher (Eds.), *Destructive Organizational Communication: Processes, Consequences, & Constructive Ways of Organizing* (pp. 293–315). New York, NY: Routeledge.

Byrd, G. A., Hampton, J. R., Bajorek, B. J., Beier, I., Compton, B. L., Kay, M. D., Kingsford, A. N., Raimond, A. R., Schumacker, A. L., Slaw, T. P., & Smith, J. (2015, November 17). An Open Letter calling for the termination of Dr. Andrea Quenette for racial discrimination. https://medium.com/@schumaal/what-follows-is-a-letter-collectively-written-by-the-students-currently-enrolled-in-coms-930-at-the-8f4914d4bbd5#.liulaej76

Chewning, L. V., Lai, C. H., & Doerfel, M. (2012). Organizational resilience following disaster: A longitudinal view of information and communication technologies use to rebuild communication structure. *Management Communication Quarterly,* 27(2), 237–263. https://doi.org/10.1177/0893318912465815

Flaherty, C. (2016, May 18). Professor cleared and still out of a job. *Inside Higher Ed.* https://www.insidehighered.com/news/2016/05/18/professor-says-she-was-fired-over-well-intentioned-ill-received-class-discussion

Frangopol, D. M. & Soliman, M. (2016). Life-cycle of structural systems: Recent achievements and future directions. *Structure and Infrastructure Engineering,* 12(1), 1–20. doi:10.1080/15732479.2014.999794

Friedman, R. A. & Craig, K. M. (2004). Predicting joining and participating in minority employee network groups. *Industrial Relations,* 43, 793–816. doi:10.1111/j.0019–8676.2004.00362.x

186 ANGELA N. GIST-MACKEY

Garmezy, N. (1991). Resiliency and vulnerability to adverse developmental outcomes associated with poverty. *American Behavioral Scientist*, 34, 416–430. doi:10.1177/0002764291034004003

Garmezy, N., Masten, A. S., & Tellegen, A. (1984). The study of stress and competence in children: A building block for developmental psychopathology. *Child Development*, 55, 97–111. doi:10.2307/1129837

Gates, H. L. (2013). 100 amazing facts about the negro: Why was cotton '*king*'? https://www.pbs.org/wnet/african-americans-many-rivers-to-cross/history/why-was-cotton-king/

Gist, A. N. & Goldstein Hode, M. (2017). Race and organizing. In C. R. Scott, J. R. Barker, T. Kuhn, J. Keyton, P. K. Turner, & L. K. Lewis (Eds.), *The International Encyclopedia of Organizational Communication* (pp. 1–13). doi:10.1002/9781118955567.wbieoc175

Goldstein Hode, M. (2010). Letter to the Editor: Contextualizing racist acts shows that we are all victims. *The Maneater*. https://www.themaneater.com/stories/opinion/contextualizing-racist-acts-shows-we-are-all-victi

Goldstein Hode, M. & Meisenbach, R. (2012). Higher learning: Rethinking crisis communication in response to racial incidents on campus. In D. Waymer (Ed.), *Culture, Social Class, and Race in Public Relations: Perspectives and Applications* (pp. 131–148). Lanham, MD: Lexington Books.

Gregory, S. T. (2001). Black faculty women in the academy: History, status, and future. *Journal of Negro Education*, 124–138. doi:10.2307/3211205

Guarino, C. M., & Borden, V. M. (2017). Faculty service loads and gender: Are women taking care of the academic family? *Research in Higher Education*, 58(6), 672–694. doi:10.1007/s11162-017-9454-2

Hafner, J. (2017, October 26). The NAACP never issued travel advisories. Until August. *USA Today*. https://www.usatoday.com/story/travel/nation-now/2017/10/26/naacps-american-airlines-travel-advisory-groups-president-sees-more-warnings-going-forward/801699001/

Higgins, M. C., & Kram, K. K. (2001). Reconceptualizing mentoring at work: A developmental network perspective. *Academy of Management Review*, 26, 264–288. doi:10.5465/amr.2001.4378023

hooks, b. (1990). Homeplace (a site of resistance). In J. Ritchie & K. Ronald (Eds.), *Available Means: An Anthology Of Women'S Rhetoric(s)* (pp. 383–390). Pittsburgh, PA: University of Pittsburgh Press. doi:10.2307/j.ctt5hjqnj.60

Horne, J. & Orr, J. (1998). Assessing behaviors that create resilient organizations. *Employment Relations Today*, 24, 29–39. doi:10.1002/ert.3910240405

House, J. S. (1981). *Work stress and social support.* Reading, MA: Addison-Wesley.

Ibarra, H. (1995). Race, opportunity, and diversity of social circles in managerial networks. *Academy of Management Journal*, 38, 673–703. doi:10.5465/256742

Izadi, E. (2015). The incidents that led to the University of Missouri president's resignation. *The Washington Post*. https://www.washingtonpost.com/news/grade-point/wp/2015/11/09/the-incidents-that-led-to-theuniversity-of-missouri-presidents-resignation/

Kanter, R. M. (1977). *Men and women of the corporation.* New York, NY: Basic Books.

Martin, J. M., & Van Stee, S. K. (2019). Racism Lives Here: The University of Missouri's Response to a Campus Crisis. *Atlantic Journal of Communication*, 28(4), 1–17. https://doi.org/10.1080/15456870.2020.1680554

Obaro, T. (2019, November 28). Before syracuse, there was Mizzou. *Buzz Feed News*. https://www.buzzfeednews.com/article/tomiobaro/mizzou-football-boycott-protests-2015-racism

Oliha-Donaldson, H. (2018). Journeying "home": Reflections on pedagogy, resistance, and possibility. *Women, Gender, and Families of Color*, 6(1), 3–11. doi:10.5406/womgenfamcol.6.1.0003

Porter, S. R. (2007). A closer look at faculty service: What affects participation on committees? *The Journal of Higher Education*, 78(5), 523–541. doi:10.1353/jhe.2007.0027

Richardson, B. (2010, March 1). Update: Cotton balls scattered in front of MU's black culture center. *Missourian*. https://www.columbiamissourian.com/news/update-cotton-balls-scattered-in-front-of-mu-s-black/article_d24e75f8-5832-5e1f-9996-a37d048cb950.html

Richardson, G. E. (2002). The metatheory of resilience and resiliency. *Journal of Clinical Psychology*, 58(3), 307–321. doi:10.1002/jclp.10020

Schumacher, A. (2015, November 17). An open letter calling for the termination of Dr. Andrea Quenette for racial discrimination. https://medium.com/@schumaal/what-follows-is-a-letter-collectively-written-by-the-students-currently-enrolled-in-coms-930-at-the-8f4914d4bbd5#.liulaej76

Shepherd, S. (2015, November 12). Student-led rock chalk invisible hawk group issues diversity-related demands for KU; here's some more context. https://www2.ljworld.com/weblogs/heard_hill/2015/nov/12/student-led-rockchalkinvisiblehawk-group/

Shepherd, S. (2016, March 18). KU investigation clears professor who used N-word in class. *Lawrence Journal World*. https://www2.ljworld.com/news/2016/mar/18/ku-exonerates-professor-who-used-n-word-class/

Strauss, V. (2017, September 7). The sad story of public education in St. Louis. *Washington Post*. https://www.washingtonpost.com/news/answer-sheet/wp/2017/09/07/the-sad-story-of-public-education-in-st-louis/

Chapter 12

Accented Others, Women, and Immigrants: A Conversation about Institutional Stalling and Dismissal

Anne C. Dotter and Cécile Accilien

ORGANIZATIONAL CONTEXT

Being foreign-born on the campus of a Midwestern public university is an othering experience regardless of one's intersectional identities. Despite our different geographical origins (Caribbean/European), race (Black/White), and class (faculty/staff), we share the alienation of those for whom the institution was not made, whose accents are tolerated so long as they keep to the script of the exotic other, and whose privileges get lost as their voices affirm otherness. Our exchange seeks to challenge the university to be a safe space for all, as it claims to be. We are particularly concerned with the institution's willingness and ability to be the inclusive space it claims to be, a space that allows individuals to hold all their intersected identities simultaneously—race, gender, sexuality, religion, and ability, but also nationality. This chapter is a case study of two foreign-national women educators in higher education in the U.S. and our experiences with discrimination. It is also our firsthand encounter with the limitations of the concept of diversity, equity, and inclusion (DEI). Our analysis draws from Sara Ahmed's (2015, 2019) extensive work on the shortcomings of DEI in the academic ivory tower.

The issue of discrimination in institutions like higher education is the object of rich scholarship; however, discrimination based on national origin or foreign accents are seldom included (Akomolafe, 2013). The history of how hyphenated Americans such as Italians or Irish became "White" is well-recorded (Ignatiev, 1995). In reviewing literature with the key theme "Foreign National" in *The Chronicle of Higher Education* over the last five years, the main articles focused primarily on foreign students' enrollment and visa issues, specifically in regions such as China, the Middle East, and Russia. There are very few articles related to discrimination and prejudice faced by foreign-born students and employees, or instances of cultural appropriation, harassment, or bias. Interestingly enough, research on the key word "Foreign National" produced a number of other themes related to DEI issues, such as discrimination against people based on ability, gender, and race. There are also several reports regarding diversity across U.S. campuses. Some focused on international education, including study-abroad, foreign language instruction, and experiences of U.S. faculty abroad. Overall, there are few articles that discuss the cultural negotiation at play for foreign nationals working in American higher education, whether faculty or staff.

Although international scholars are recruited to diversify institutions (Lee & Janda, 2006), once on U.S. soil, their national culture hardly qualifies as diversity. A growing body of scholarship focuses on academic migrants as a means to diversify U.S. institutions of higher education. However, only a small number of them focus on the unique challenges faced by this population. In their study, Bazemore et al. (2010) analyzed a sample of 162 foreign-born faculty members via an online questionnaire that addressed issues such as perceptions of rejection, loneliness, well-being, and self-perceived teaching effectiveness. The authors note:

> Despite the eagerness of U.S. colleges and universities to recruit foreign-born faculty, there is evidence that such faculty encounter a variety of hardships.... Foreign-born professors have also reported a lack [of, sic] collegiality with their American colleagues that may reduce job satisfaction and feeling of belongingness to the university. While there is clear evidence that, as a group, foreign-born faculty have difficulties adjusting to academic life in the U.S., there has been little, if any, research to explore individual differences in these adjustment problems. (pp. 85–86)

Although these adjustments can sometimes be experienced as discrimination and microaggressions, they are often hard to prove, legally or otherwise.

In her article, "The Invisible Minority: Revisiting the Debate on Foreign-Accented Speakers and Upward Mobility in the Workplace," Akomolafe (2013) argues that it is difficult to prove discrimination based on national origin or accent in a court of law because of bona fide occupational qualifications, which she defines as:

> A quality or an attribute (i.e. fluent English or effective oral communication in English) that employers are allowed to consider when making decisions on the hiring or retention of employees, [and are] qualities that when considered in other contexts would constitute discrimination. (p. 10)

190 ANNE C. DOTTER AND CÉCILE ACCILIEN

This is a way by which employers are protected from potential lawsuits. With no legal recourse and little scholarship focusing on discrimination against foreign-born staff or faculty, little has been done to support this diverse population, yet scholars like Spitzer and Zhou (2018) stress the key role that international faculty and staff play. Interestingly, it is well-documented that international faculty often fill the "diversity" vacuum at many institutions (Alberts & Hazens, 2013), yet, in our experience on a university campus located in the heartland, conversations about DEI are neither inclusive of foreign nationals, nor are individuals trained in DEI encouraged to think expansively about diversity. In this chapter, we argue that for diversity work to be truly effective, we must layer our understanding of diversity and invest in challenging the status quo. This is not to imply that colleagues currently doing diversity work are not genuinely concerned about foreign nationals; however, this chapter acknowledges that more must be done to provide institutional support to foreign-born faculty and staff who may experience particular forms of bias because of their identities. We close by offering strategies for understanding and responding to the experiences of foreign-born colleagues and others with "accented" identities.

We are women working at a predominantly White institution (PWI). Through informal conversations, we have found support and have created the safe spaces that the institution has failed to provide for us. Yet our experiences as both women and immigrants often prevent us from being fully accepted and finding a comfortable place in many circles within the academic ivory tower. These intersectional identities complicate our experiences in academia. Law professor and critical race theorist Kimberlé Crenshaw (1989) identified intersectionality as a way of explaining the oppression of African-American women. She notes:

> Intersectionality is a lens through which you can see where power comes and collides, where it interlocks and intersects. It's not simply that there's a race problem here, a gender problem here, and a class or LBGTQ problem there. Many times that framework erases what happens to people who are subject to all of these things. (para. 3)

In this chapter, we make a case for adding nationality to the list of other intersectional identities; we also contribute to the scholarship by offering an institutional analysis focused on the experiences of two foreign-born university employees.

As foreign-born academics, we have traded more than linguistic lexicons: in the same way that we bring a layered understanding of the English language (thanks to our Latin training or our knowledge of particular syntactic rules), our experience of intersectional identities was formed in places where they held different meanings. We are therefore keenly aware of the possibilities and promises for a brighter future held within a university

ACCENTED OTHERS, WOMEN, AND IMMIGRANTS **191**

where complex, diverse identities are seen as resources to be cherished. Ahmed (2017) affirms this when she states:

> But think of this: those of us who arrive in an academy that was not shaped by or for us bring knowledges, as well as worlds, that otherwise would not be here. Think of this: how we learn about worlds when they do not accommodate us. Think of the kinds of experiences you have when you are not expected to be here. These experiences are a resource to generate knowledge. (pp. 9–10)

Despite our confidence in our linguistic abilities and our awareness of the unique contributions we make, language has remained a challenge. Our foreign accents have often been used as a means of oppression and marginalization. Foreign accents represent a challenge to the happiness narrative of the institution, to the script of the exotic other we have always dutifully followed whether consciously or unconsciously. Ahmed (2019) understands happiness narratives within higher education as the steps required for a successful career. The script of the feminine foreign other assumes silent acquiescence and curiosity for the ways things are done at the local institution, with a polite recognition that these may not be the same elsewhere but with no effort to consider other ways. So, when one's accented speech interrogates the distribution of resources and questions preestablished pathways to success within the academy, we challenge this happiness narrative.

Speech acts are culturally prescribed, and the university setting comes rife with scripts individuals must follow knowingly or unknowingly. Institutional practices evolve to further obfuscate individual experiences behind a brick wall of procedures and practices that lead no further than the wall. Our failed diversity moments manifested in our experience with the office responsible for ensuring the respect of state and federal civil rights, a gatekeeper office devoted to all issues of discrimination. Instead of being the gateway to solutions, however, this office reinforced microaggressions by failing to understand the complexity of diversity and the concomitant need for equity and inclusion. Trained to prioritize binaries and to ignore any case that may not represent a legal threat to the institution, officers in charge of discrimination complaints at the university were unable to understand what falls outside of simple binaries and associated scripts, in our experiences.

FIRST NARRATIVE

As a 40-plus-year-old Black immigrant female who has lived in the U.S. for over 30 years, yet still has an accent and is still routinely asked, "Where are you from?", I am constantly aware of my positionality and of being labeled

192 ANNE C. DOTTER AND CÉCILE ACCILIEN

by colleagues as other. My "otherness" is often useful to the university because it allows people to ask me to serve on committees where they need a diverse body: Black, female, international, immigrant, etc.

In my own department, I served in some low-key administrative roles until I became acting department chair. During my time in those positions, there was no problem with my accent. Suddenly, when I became chair, the main person that had issues with my accent (I will call them Taylor) was someone I worked with for over two years prior. When the situation with Taylor escalated, I wrote a letter to an upper administrator in the dean's office requesting assistance, guidance, and some clear directives regarding administrative working relationships. In particular, I asked for help to interface with the Office of Human Resources (HR) because I felt my ability to effectively operate in my administrative capacity as chair was being severely undermined. I further noted that the various expectations regarding my duties and how to work with this particular colleague were becoming unrealistic and inefficient. For example, it was not efficient for me to have to write out every expectation followed by feedback on every duty I assigned to Taylor, whom I was supervising throughout the day. Furthermore, there was a pattern of undermining my position through repeated microaggressions as well as racialized and gendered behavior.

Following is an excerpt of the letter I sent to the representative in the dean's office:

> My .5FTE appointment as chair does not sufficiently allow me the time to document every incident and spend countless hours with HR on singular personnel issues.... I am not fluent in HR legalese. What is the recommendation for me to run the department with these increasing limitations? As you know from the various emails I have sent you over the past weeks, I am also receiving the anger and ire of some faculty from the department, as it appears as if I am not doing my work to adequately and effectively run the department. Also, I would like to request to have someone come and talk to the faculty and explain to them what is going on.
>
> Moreover, the time and energy required for dealing with the personnel issues has been very taxing. It is not appropriate for my administrative and academic responsibilities, nor for my health and well-being, to be spending so much time figuring out how to manage basic departmental tasks.
>
> I feel marginalized by HR and have received biased treatment. It is my observation and belief that HR is not dealing with the microaggressions that I have been a victim of, nor the racialized and gendered aspects of this situation. As a Black immigrant woman, I receive racialized responses from HR. The person's behavior towards me in many instances has also been racialized. As someone who speaks with an "accent," there have been at least two instances (including one in writing) in which I have been told by [Taylor] that they do not understand me when I speak to them. This started only after I became department chair. I sent them an email stating that in order to avoid misunderstanding and miscommunication, that we would communicate primarily via email. Recently, they stated in an email to me that: "Email is not the

best way to communicate and that they do not think that this 'solution' is working." While out of the office, they also stated to HR that when I send them too many emails, I am causing them anxiety. I cannot continue to work in this environment and constantly face these microaggressions every day. It is toxic and hostile.

After Taylor filed a complaint against me with the university's Office of Institutional Opportunity & Access (IOA) stating that I was not respecting their needs at work, I counter-filed my own complaint with the IOA. I did this not expecting any real result. I was not disappointed. Some colleagues had already warned me that IOA's main role was to protect the interests of the university. After two long meetings with IOA explaining the situation and various incidents of racial, gender, and national-origin bias, I received the following excerpted message from IOA:

You chose to file a formal complaint with the IOA because you believe that [Taylor] has created a hostile environment for you on the basis of race, gender, and national origin in violation of the Racial and Ethnic Harassment Policy and/or Nondiscrimination, Equal Opportunity, and Affirmative Action Policy.

In order to find that a hostile environment was created, the following must be met:

- The workplace is permeated with discriminatory intimidation, ridicule, and insult, that is sufficiently severe or pervasive to alter the conditions of your employment and create an abusive working environment; and
- The environment must be both subjectively and objectively hostile or abusive; and
- The environment must be a product of discriminatory animus.
- We appreciate this matter being brought to our attention. At this time, however, the IOA is administratively closing your complaint, because the conduct alleged does not rise to the level of a policy violation falling under the IOA's purview. Specifically, there is no evidence supporting a finding that Taylor's reported conduct is a product of discriminatory animus. You acknowledged during our conversation that you believe Taylor undermines you as a supervisor, though you did not provide a nexus to show that Taylor's behavior is due to your race. Additionally, both you and the former chair identify as African American, rendering it unlikely that Taylor's behavior is due to your race.
- Finally, with regard to gender, you provided no evidence to indicate Taylor's behavior is based on your gender aside from your statement that the former chair (a male-identifying employee) did not experience the same issues while supervising Taylor.

SECOND NARRATIVE

After six years of consistently exceptional annual evaluations and having received every available merit increase, an unexpected change in management practices led me, a White European woman working as a staff

194 ANNE C. DOTTER AND CÉCILE ACCILIEN

member in an academic unit, to be on the receiving end of unwarranted critiques. The justification for micromanagement, removal of job duties, and other pressures was the wording of my written work. Because two of my American colleagues had experienced similar pressures (though strictly centered on their behavior, not their writing), we decided to reach out to high-ranking administrators with whom we had worked and who we believed would see the absurdity of the situation and take necessary actions to redress it. To our surprise—and dismay—they all encouraged us to submit an official complaint for gender discrimination; we were told that no intervention would be possible without an official complaint.

Having worked with our director for three years, I never was convinced that the issue was gender-based; but since my colleagues experiencing similar pressures were women, we decided to submit individual complaints for gender discrimination, the one and only salient commonality. However, considering that most of the violence I experienced was directed at my use of the English language, I also filed for discrimination under Title VII, thinking that my being foreign-born was central to the case. To my surprise—and again, dismay—my title VII complaint was dismissed right away without further investigation because no jokes had been made in public either about my nationality, my accent, or my ability to communicate in English.

The investigator concluded against us. Our case, however, is a perfect illustration of the stalling, administrative detours and other obfuscations of the kind referred to as a "brick wall" by Ahmed (2017, 2019). The letter describing the investigator's findings epitomizes this process. Following are snapshots of the letter: "The IOA finds that you did not suffer an adverse action as the actions you outlined are not the type that are considered adverse employment actions. Adverse employment actions generally include hiring, firing, pay, discipline, demotions, and changes in benefits." The strict evidentiary standards by which the findings in my case were measured, and which undoubtedly led to the case being dismissed, minimized my experience and had an intimidating impact. The language made me feel inadequate (too sensitive) and reminded me that I was/am a guest on campus. Such statements as, "While [the director]'s tone regarding feedback may change from employee to employee, that is a management issue and does not rise to a level of discrimination," affirmed my sense of alienation. If my male colleagues indeed received feedback, it was in the form of encouraging and empowering emails, courteously worded, where I received bolded comments, red ink across my words, and text in capital letters. Affirming the right of supervisors to alter their mode of address, tone, and communication depending on gender and other protected identities is at best contrary to the goals and aspirations of this very office.

The investigator further went on to state: "While you certainly may feel that you are working in a hostile environment, a hostile environment under [our university] policy has not been created as the environment is not permeated with discriminatory conduct, is not ridiculing or insulting, and is not severe." This statement epitomizes the othering at work in this communication: though my feelings may be acknowledged, the sentence's intent is to demonstrate how invalid they are. There is, in such a policy, no place for the recognition of microaggressions and the recurrent and degrading effect of being repeatedly told that one's performance is not meeting a fleeting and incessantly fluctuating mark. The letter leads up to questioning the "discriminatory animus," which is a dubious process when all evidence of discrimination can be dismissed as discourteous behaviors. Needless to say, an appeal, or even the consideration of a complaint for retaliation were invalidated by the tone and content of the findings letter I received.

Nothing in my colleagues' and my conversations with upper-ranking administrators had led us to think this process would be belittling and othering. In fact, we filed our complaints because we were told that if our claim was dismissed, recommendations would be made for an HR intervention. No recommendations for further actions were made by the IOA investigator, therefore, no further action was taken.

The IOA states in their mission statement that they seek to encourage "a campus climate of respect and understanding of all aspects of the human experience." This experience revealed that their role is to prioritize "University compliance with state and federal civil rights laws." Not only did my complaint go unheard, the terse language in the findings letter intentionally obfuscated legitimate legal recourse. I felt unheard, belittled, and hurt by the inevitable conclusion in favor of the aggressor and in defense of the institution. It was clear that there were no institutional protections in place for me. I was expected to go along and get along.

IMPLICATIONS AND LESSONS LEARNED

Our experiences with the office in charge of protecting individuals' state and federal civil rights has been at odds with its mission. We question their claim to be "responsible for administering the [University's] equal opportunity and non-discrimination policies and procedures, as well as encouraging a campus climate of respect and understanding of all aspects of the human experience." Many informal conversations with friends and colleagues around the university affirm our experience. Just like us, their experience with discrimination was minimized and reformatted to fit within the institution's narrow understanding of difference and diversity. Our experiences epitomize failed DEI moments that echo Ahmed's analyses of the university's narrow understanding of discrimination. Our experiences align with what Ahmed describes as a dismissal: "a complaint [is] 'not

196 ANNE C. DOTTER AND CÉCILE ACCILIEN

a complaint' because it does not fulfill the technical requirements for being a complaint" (Ahmed, 2019, p. 161).

Because of institutional practices, we were negatively impacted by the absence of support and the systematic othering that led us to feel that we do not belong. Living through failed DEI moments has had real repercussions on our well-being, sense of safety, and purpose, as well as our respective thinking about our professional future. Though we followed this office's injunction to "speak up against discrimination," by doing so, we became the problem because we interrupted the university's happiness narrative. As we negotiated our intersectional identities—race, gender, class, and national origin—we experienced the ways in which these identities affect and influence power, privilege, and positionalities.

Beyond words, failed DEI moments have tangible consequences that further alienate those with marginalized identities. They include emotional stress, hyperconsciousness, and concern over inadvertently mobilizing the "angry Black woman" or aggressive urban-European stereotypes. Further, we had to moderate every word and action to ensure that we weren't perceived as the overly sensitive person of color who is playing the race card, or the unrealistic foreigner whose expectations are naïve. Scholars like Walley-Jean (2009) note that "negative stereotypes and specifically the angry black woman stereotype can have significant negative social and interpersonal consequences" (p. 73). In our case, we became scared to use the words we had so long cherished and hypersensitive of even the ways in which our appearances are perceived: while one of us was told that she looks young and would not be able to have certain responsibilities, the other was told that she scared a White person, caused them anxiety, and triggered experiences of abuse for them. This essay is an effort to grieve and reclaim our words. To colleagues dealing with failed DEI moments, we say: find your voice and affirm your identity. Identify ways to assert the strength stemming from difference in order to move away from the deficit logic imposed by exclusionary university practices.

PROMISING PRACTICES FOR CHANGE

We have highlighted incidents that demonstrate that the Title IX/VII complaints office at this university did not adequately deal with issues of diversity, equity, and inclusion. The position of this office as singular recourse in cases of discrimination of any kind on campus is the first and most important problem, as it illuminates the systemic preservation of the institution's happiness over individual cases of discrimination. This could easily be resolved. If a singular office were to remain, diversifying its staff as well as their areas of specialty and training would help. On this campus, it is very recent that this office hired a person of color after sustained criticism. Until gatekeeper officers understand that DEI issues are intrinsically linked to discriminatory practices, biases, and microaggressions, the failed diversity moments will continue. Following are a few other strategies:

- The Human Resources Industrial Complex is a multilayered machine whose main purpose is to protect the university from being sued and losing money or its reputation. Paradoxically, this office is the ultimate gatekeeper for any form of complaint and intervention. We urge institutions to place complaint tasks under the leadership of the office in charge of diversity and equity.
- Institutions are eager to document people's "concerns" in order to come to the non-messy conclusion that "the parties have to find better ways to communicate and come up with a consensus." Oh, how we hate that word "consensus" sometimes. It speaks to the culture of not being able to acknowledge and accept that we can disagree respectfully. It also speaks to the idea that we all have to play nice and be polite and not have real, hard, open, and challenging conversations. We suggest that any form of DEI training equip participants to engage in difficult dialogues.
- Unfortunately, we also have to acknowledge that for many people, diversity is only a buzzword. We know of colleagues who participate in semester-long social justice workshops and come out of them still very unaware of their privileges and positionalities. We urge administrators in higher education to expect all employees to recognize their privileges and positionalities, especially those working in direct contact with students.
- Scholar bell hooks affirms, "the classroom remains the most radical space of possibility in the academy" (hooks, 1994, p. 12). For there to be true transformation in the classroom, there must be engaged and radical pedagogy. This is also true for DEI training spaces. There must be a "holistic model of learning...where teachers [and facilitators] grow, and are empowered by the process" (hooks, 1994, p. 21). As educators and trainers "our capacity to generate excitement is deeply affected by our interest in one another, in hearing one another's voices, in recognizing one another's presence" (hooks, 1994, p. 8). DEI trainers should work on creating transformative spaces to probe intersectionality and varying identities, and to move beyond simple binaries.
- Prioritize yourself and your people. Create your own support system outside of the university. We had to reach out to our inner circles and figure out our true allies and trusted companions. We both drew from diverse outer circles that consisted of people outside of the

academic ivory tower who could help us stay connected to the real world. We relied on one another. We recommend that universities foster the community of foreign-born employees to help create these critical support networks.

While it may be more comfortable to reduce DEI issues to binaries such as Black versus White and men versus women, by doing so, however, we simplify the notion of diversity such that the comprehension of individuals not fitting in the predetermined boxes cannot be achieved, and the gray lines cannot be taken into account. Consequently, well-meaning colleagues are unable to understand the diversity of experiences people who work alongside us are having.

CONCLUSION

Diversity happiness narratives do not promote solidarity with those who have different identities, whether cultural, class, linguistic, racial, religious, sexual orientation, and national origin. Yet as Ahmed (2018) states:

> Solidarity does not assume that our struggles are the same struggles, or that our pain is the same pain, or that our hope is for the same future. Solidarity involves commitment, and work, as well as the recognition that even if we do not have the same feelings, or the same lives, or the same bodies, we do live on common ground. (p. 189)

We believe that institutions need to use the practices highlighted in Teaching to Transgress to transgress and transcend the binary spaces of DEI in order to create a space to have real, honest, hard, and respectful dialogues. DEI trainers should work on creating transformative spaces to probe intersectionality and identities from all perspectives and move beyond the simple binaries. Ultimately, the struggle continues.

In spite of our failed DEI moments, we are committed to working with others to create spaces where our voices can be heard in spite of our "foreign" accents, even if they tremble.

DISCUSSION QUESTIONS

1. What is needed for higher-education institutions to embrace intersectionality?
2. Considering the increase in academic migrants on U.S. campuses, what practices should be implemented to ensure that these individuals are supported?

3. People don't all communicate the same way. What do universities currently do to recognize this fact and ensure that all individuals, regardless of intersecting identities, can hear and be heard?

4. How would you describe the alignment of various campus units' mission statements with the actual work that they do? What systems could be implemented to ensure that units are consistent in policy an practice? How can your university's diversity mission statement truly align with the performance of offices like IOA?

5. What are some ways in which administrators can be trained to understand the implications of various microaggressions and how they keep the university from progressing and becoming a truly diverse intellectual space where all are welcome?

6. How can universities create a culture of sustainable care that truly embodies diversity from various perspectives?

7. DEI trainings on many campuses are rich and diverse. How would you enhance what is already offered at your institution so that offices like IOA can make their understanding of DEI more expansive? For example, the labels Black and African American are often conflated. Can and should trainings respond to such nuance? Why?

8. Knowing that most universities position the Title IX/VII offices as gatekeepers, how can the actual process for reporting discrimination be more supportive of victims? How do we create safe pathways for individuals experiencing discrimination to be heard, understood, and guided through the proper channels for seeking restitution?

9. How can institutions encourage employees to do the hard work of recognizing their privileges and understanding the diversity of experiences and identities held by many of their colleagues and students?

10. With increased social awareness of the value of diversity and equity, in what ways do you foresee efforts to make campuses safer spaces for all becoming a necessary feature that new students and their families expect?

REFERENCES

Ahmed, S. (2015). *The cultural politics of emotion*. New York: Routledge.

Ahmed, S. (2017). *Living a feminist life*. Durham, NC: Duke University Press.

Ahmed, S. (2018). Rocking the boat: Women of colour as diversity workers. *Dismantling Race in Higher Education*, 331–348. doi: 10.1007/978-3-319-60261-5_19

Ahmed, S. (2019). *Whats the use?: On the uses of use*. Durham: Duke University Press.

Akomolafe, S. (2013). The invisible minority: Revisiting the debate on foreign-accented speakers and upward mobility in the workplace. *Journal of Cultural Diversity*, 20(1), 7–14.

200 ANNE C. DOTTER AND CÉCILE ACCILIEN

Alberts, H. C., & Hazens H. D. (2013). *International students and scholars in the United States*. Palgrave Macmillan U.S.

Bazemore, S. D., Janda, L. H., Derlega, V. J., & Paulson, J. F. (2010). The role of rejection in mediating the effects of stigma consciousness among foreign-born university professors. *Journal of Diversity in Higher Education*, 3(2), 85–96. doi: 10.1037/a0019159

Crenshaw, K. (1989). Demarginalizing the intersection of race and sex: A Black feminist critique of antidiscrimination doctrine, *feminist theory and antiracist politics. University of Chicago Legal Forum*. 139–168. Retrieved November 25, 2019 from https://www.law.columbia.edu/pt-br/news/2017/06/kimberle-crenshaw-intersectionality.

Ignatiev, N. (1995). *How The Irish Became White*. New York: Routlege.

hooks, b. (1994). *Teaching to transgress: Education as the practice of freedom*. New York: Routledge.

Lee, G. L., & Janda, L. (2006). Successful multicultural campus: Free from prejudice toward minority professors. *Multicultural Education*, 14(1), 27–30.

Spitzer, L., & Zhou, J. (2018). Retaining international faculty: Meeting the challenge. *Global Research in Higher Education*, 2(1), 46. doi: 10.22158/grhe.v2n1p46

Walley-Jean, J. C. (2009). Debunking the myth of the "angry black woman": An exploration of anger in young African American women. *Black Women, Gender & Families*, 3(2), 68–86. doi: 10.1353/bwg.0.0011

PART VI

COMMUNITY AND STRUCTURAL CHALLENGES: MANAGING THE EFFECTS OF SOCIAL TENSIONS

Chapter 13

'The Blackface Incident': Diversity, Equity, and Inclusion under Fire at a Southern Women's College

Jade C. Huell and Crystal U. Davis

Immediately after three White undergraduate women posted a photo of themselves donning charcoal masks and wearing shirts depicting the college's name on Snapchat, the community at our small liberal-arts women's college began referring to the posting of the blackface photograph as "the incident." If one were to pick up any dictionary, one would soon discover that the word "incident" is described as either a violent or otherwise surprising event or occurrence, and/or an instance or unintended single case of something occurring. While the blackface incident does constitute a hostile and shocking circumstance, and the episode has not yet repeated on the campus, "the incident" was hardly accidental or unusual. In fact, similar incidents have been happening with some frequency in the U.S. over the past five years and have larger sociocultural implications that intersect with and exacerbate the racialized experiences on the campus at the center of this study and beyond (Neville et al., 2010; Jaschik, 2016). In this chapter, we, as Black professors at the college at the time of the aforementioned event, as scholar/artists dedicated to understanding the embodied reality of racism, and as pedagogues interested in examining the instructive tools that lie in examples where attempts to deal with racism fail, analyze "the incident," its fallout, and the response of the college administration. After contextualizing the inciting situation alongside the college's history and describing the effects on all parties involved, we close the chapter with strategies for change, with emphasis on resistance, practicality, and embodiment.

THE COLLEGE IN CONTEXT

...baptized by fire, over and over...

alumna describing the history of the college

The most cited "incidents" in the history of the college are its three separate brushes with fire, beginning with a near miss. Founded as one of the first women's colleges in the United States, the Southern institution was first under threat of fire during the Civil War. The story goes that a professor faced down Union soldiers and saved the college from the torch. Later in the college's history, in the 1800–1900s, three isolated fires ravished the campus, and three times the college was rebuilt. The stories of rebuilding after these fires are often drawn upon to garner support for the institution and inspire pride from those who are a part of it.

Indeed, fire is a part of the college's history and lore. The phrase "baptized by fire" also serves as a useful framework with which to understand the background of the institution more broadly. First, "baptism" alludes to the religious affiliation of the college. The private women's college was founded in 1854 by the United Methodist Church (UMC). This denomination is a large and powerful religious organization, one that believes deeply in sacraments such as holy communion and holy baptism. According to UMC doctrine, the sacrament of baptism serves to distinguish the Christian subject from other subjects and to signify the purity or rebirth of the Christian subject through ritual practice (The people of the United Methodist Church, 2019). Similarly, this particular college privileges ritual and distinguishes scholars affiliated with the college as different from those who attend other colleges. This symbolism will be explored further in upcoming sections.

Like most private colleges, the school at hand is run by a board of directors. The board of directors is more or less informed about diversity issues on campus at board meetings where administrators and faculty bring relevant topics up for discussion. In this context, decisions are often made under the watchful eye of the president, who is ultimately responsible for hiring and firing and who also likes to appear competent at putting the school in the strongest possible position to secure and maintain its donor base.

Further, the college has had a sweltering history when it comes to race relations. It is located in the center of a historically Black neighborhood, and though situated relatively close to the downtown area, it remains isolated—a lone, small campus with its own police department in the heart of a low-income community. As both a student and later a professor at the school, one of us has been continuously warned about venturing too far off campus. Perhaps one of the strongest contributing factors to the racial explosion at the heart of this study is the college's continuing problems with the lack of faculty diversity in comparison to the student population. According to Collegefactual.com, while the undergraduate African-American population is 32.9%, Black faculty make up only 16.5% of the total faculty (College Factual, 2019). At the time of the controversy, we were two of the six Black educators in a faculty of over 70. As a result of this imbalance, we were often informed by students that they had not had the opportunity to learn from a Black faculty member until they found themselves in our classes. Additionally, we were overburdened with requests for mentorship, complaints about discrimination against Black students by White faculty, and service obligations around the issue of race on campus.

Finally, the financial instability of the college only added fuel to the fires of injustice described above. At the time of the event in question, the college was under new consultation to address the college's financial crisis that included an inability to fund necessities such as employee payroll. This consultant was originally hired because of her expertise in stabilizing the finances of higher-education institutions and saving those institutions from closing. Within a year, this consultant had moved into the role of provost at the college. This student blackface complication exacerbated the financial situation because the negative public exposure might have potentially driven away important donors, especially Black alumni. Additionally, admitting the college's racial struggles might have opened the college up to expensive legal challenges that it could not have afforded at that time.

In sum, the history and living memory of the college, its sociocultural positionality, and its dire financial circumstances might be considered the smoldering ashes upon which the inflammatory blackface incident was built. The result? An inferno that finally forced the institution to reckon with the racial ghosts of its storied past, which demanded that the college explicitly address the ways in which racism continued to affect relations between students, faculty, and administration.

OUR APPROACH TO DIVERSITY, EQUITY, AND INCLUSION

> It is imperative that faculty of color feel empowered to share and implement their perspectives and ideas; that they feel they are valued...
>
> Marnel Niles Goins, PhD. and Leticia Williams, PhD. (2019, p. 24)

In "The Struggle of Being a Racial Minority in the Academy," Goins and Williams (2019) expound on the above quote, arguing that in order for diversity, equity, and inclusion to become a reality across the academy, the experiences and initiatives of faculty of color must be honored and acted upon. In the following sections, we, as Black scholars, take up Goins and Williams' call by telling our stories. In so doing, we foreground our voice and that of others like us by prescribing remedies for injustices in institutions of higher learning.

We, Crystal U. Davis and Jade C. Huell, came to the college two years apart from one another. Being the only two artists of color on the faculty and both having backgrounds in Performance Studies, Africana Studies, and critical cultural analysis, we quickly gravitated towards one another. What follows is our narrative analysis of "the blackface incident" as we experienced it. Here, we draw upon the various artifacts of our experience that extend and connect to the precipitating incident and its fallout, including meeting notes and recollections, conversations with colleagues, student responses from class activities post-incident, and our own visceral knowledge. We not only track the incident itself, but also the resulting effects and responses to the episode during our time at the college.

"THE BLACKFACE INCIDENT"

> ...Wise, good, and true eternally,
> No stain shall touch the purity of our [name of college]...
>
> Excerpt from school song

Three White students posted a photo to Snapchat with charcoal masks on their faces. Below the posted image was the caption, "drink the mf koolaid," apparently a crude reference to how African Americans consume the sugary beverage and/or to the Jonestown tragedy, where many people of color perished after drinking poison-laced Kool-Aid. The Snapchat posting was immediately picked up by the student body and circulated on multiple social media platforms. The morning after the posting, the entire 1,200-student campus was in chaos, and the diverse student population was awash in confusion, demands for immediate action, and spontaneous student activism. Here are our stories.

Jade's Story

I wore all black that morning because I was in a rush and I didn't have time to put together a matching outfit for my day of teaching. On the way to campus, I noticed that my cell phone notifications were particularly active, but I ignored them. When I arrived in my classroom to teach an African-American Communication class, the students were variously animated, upset, and whispering. When I asked them what the matter was, one student volunteered to bring the Snapchat image up on the large screen on her Facebook account. I was shocked, but

THE BLACKFACE INCIDENT **207**

this was not the kind of occurrence that I could very well move on from in a course about African-American communication and culture. I had to change my lesson plan on the spot. As a class, we discussed the history, impact, and emotion around the image. We discussed the context in light of the fact that 11 other universities had dealt with blackface imagery on social media in the same year. Some students cried, while others said that they did not feel safe on campus.

About halfway through the day, I learned that there was to be an open forum on campus so that the students could voice their concerns in a "safe space," with faculty and administration there to listen. Upon entering the venue, I noticed that a large, organized contingent of mostly African-American students were dressed in all black, some holding signs and some in black shirts displaying the words "Black Lives Matter." A former student, dressed in black, looked over at me, made a fist, and winked at me. I looked down at my outfit choice and realized I had unknowingly joined a student protest. As each student took the podium, I swelled with pride. They were passionate, strong, clear, and fearless. They voiced their disgust, not just at the blackface affair, but also at how the college had been ignoring their reports of racial discrimination in the classroom, in school policies, and in the curriculum. Two White male faculty members grumbled something about disrespect and walked out of the forum. I stayed. I was glad I chose to wear black that day.

Like a fire, the controversy spread uncontrollably. Students continued to agitate and petition the administration to have the students involved in the Snapchat posting expelled. The college released a statement promising that the students in the post would be held accountable. Then there was a meeting of the whole faculty, and there, again, the sparks began to fly.

Crystal's Story

In our next full-faculty meeting, the issue was addressed by the president of the college. She explained that there had been a racially insensitive incident, which some students on campus reported as offensive. The president went on to reveal that the students in question had been removed from campus while an investigation of the situation was pending. After the investigation, the college would determine the consequences, if any, for the students involved in posting the material.

While I did not experience the Snapchat post initially, the ripple effects of the post quickly caught up to me in this meeting. As a newly hired faculty member, I was still slowly becoming accustomed to the community and developing personal connections with the students. I had only heard mumblings of the incident through other colleagues and wondered whether I wanted or needed to know the details and see the actual inciting material or whether I would be able to trust the institution to inform me of all pertinent details of the matter.

After updating us on the situation, the president provided time for questions. One White male faculty (who I later learned had exited the student forum angrily) stood up to ask why the students had been removed and involved in an investigation if there is no way of determining what the operation of their mind was at the time of the incident. The professor went on to argue that if the students meant no harm or were unaware that they would potentially cause offense to other students on campus that they should not be faulted or penalized for such an oversight. This question ignited a long and heated debate between two White male faculty members and a number of Black female faculty members passionately attempting to explain the hurt and disregard inherent in the question. It was then clear to me that we would be dealing with the impact of this incident for a long time to come.

IMPLICATIONS AND LESSONS LEARNED

Hello white professor, I am your black student. I know you see me, but do you <u>see</u> me?

student at college just after "the blackface incident"

There are a number of aspects of the original incident that are offensive and hurtful. The painting of black charcoal masks on White faces is a performance that reconjures the toxic tropes of blackface. This act of minstrelsy disregards the insult and harm done to Black people and experienced by Black people as a part of the history and reification of racial oppression (Cole & Davis, 2013; see also Gura, 1999). Adding to the list of stereotypes this social media post engendered is the stereotype of Black people loving Kool-Aid. This stereotype is often a function of distorting the plight of Black people living in poverty (really a double stereotype that most Black people live in poverty) who lack access and financial ability to afford foods that are rich in nutritional value. Lastly, there is a lack of sensitivity and empathy surrounding the lives lost in the Jonestown

THE BLACKFACE INCIDENT **209**

massacre of 1978. This tragedy took place in Guyana where Jim Jones, a White male cult leader, caused the deaths of 918 of his followers, 69% of whom were Black people, by inspiring them to drink cyanide-laced Kool-Aid (Moore, 2017).

In addition to the sociocultural impact of the event and subsequent gatherings, the college was experiencing an economic firestorm. The incoming provost, originally hired as a consultant for her financial expertise, was asked to join for a portion of the meeting to speak to the incident and provide updates on the very urgent financial crisis facing the college. The provost sat in on the meeting, citing a need to better understand the community dynamics of the institution she was charged with saving.

After witnessing the fiery exchange between Black female faculty and the two White male faculty, we, Jade and Crystal, were called on to attend a meeting with the new provost. When we arrived at the meeting, the provost shared her intention to convene a meeting of the "faculty of color." In the course of the meeting, it became clear that she had not reached out to all of the faculty of color or even some of the Black faculty, including a Black male faculty member. The meeting resulted in an ask that we continue articulating needs and recommending action steps to improve the college environment for Black students on campus. This was an informal, unpaid ask for us to invest time and resources into improving the campus climate, a clear example of the additional work Black faculty are often charged with on college campuses (Baez, 2000; Duncan, 2014).

The administration seemed relatively unconcerned about the hurt, disrespect, and violation experienced by Black faculty and quickly turned to mitigating the unrest. The impact on faculty, however, is not isolated from the effects on students. After the events described above, we, as teaching faculty, had to find a way to conduct meaningful conversations around race on campus—our students expected it, and indeed, needed it. The following comments are taken from undergraduate students of all races responding to a prompt given by Jade Huell in the days following the disruption on campus. Students were simply asked what should be done to "fix" the problems on campus. The following are comments and fragments from their anonymously collected "fix it list":

> "There is a culture of willful ignorance and avoidance."
> "More recognition for Black History Month."
> "More support from faculty of the opposite race in regards to racial issues."
> "It's my fifth year, and Dr. Huell is my first Black professor."
> "All professors need to take a cultural-sensitivity class."
> "White men on campus need racial help."
> "Don't ignore racism!"
> "Stop excusing racist comments as if they are nothing."
> "Counselors on campus are all white."
> "My professors REFUSE to talk race."

210 JADE C. HUELL AND CRYSTAL U. DAVIS

One student employed a more narrative response to the prompt:

> Hello white professor, I am your Black student. I know you see me, but do you see me? Do you see my struggle? My pain? You probably don't, I try not to wear it on my shoulders, but it's there. And I am here. In your classroom, a whisper away from breaking down. Eyes full of pain, sorrow, and fear. But I can't talk to you about it for you don't understand this weight. For you don't understand that when you suck your teeth at my issues on race, you spit on my right to be in this class, this campus, this 'safe space.'

These student comments illuminate feelings of disregard and invisibility for their experiences on campus. They also reveal a clear call for faculty to do their due diligence in educating themselves about White supremacy, both its impact on the campus and how to disrupt its effects. There is also a clear sense of duration over time and pervasive scope that extends beyond a small group of White female students posting a toxic and hurtful message on a social media platform. It is apparent that this one incident is a symptom of a broader issue of racial insensitivity and ignorance felt across the campus. The impact on both faculty and students is difficult to fully comprehend. After these events, three of the six Black faculty members, including us, left the college and took jobs at other universities, no doubt further adding to the racial disparities blazing on the campus.

Lessons Learned

Imagine an ignorance that resists.

Charles W. Mills (Sullivan and Tuana, 2007, p. 13)

Reflecting on how the aforementioned events unfolded and moving forward to identify themes on which to act, we have isolated four major lessons: (1) do not underestimate the power and force of individuals' resistance to racial equity; (2) anticipate defensive reactions stemming from a need to escape feelings of blame or guilt about racial inequities; (3) do not underestimate the power and force of institutional resistance to racial equity, and its ability to marginalize and capitalize on that marginalization; and (4) understand that the fears of individuals and the institution can be mobilized to disrupt efforts for racial equity and change. To clearly illustrate these lessons while unpacking the general themes we isolated during the incident, the descriptions below focus primarily on the faculty meeting described earlier in the chapter, in which a White male faculty member took center stage in questioning the racial implications of the incident. We focus on the faculty member's comments, not to suggest that

THE BLACKFACE INCIDENT **211**

faculty like him are somehow singularly at fault, but to highlight the pervasiveness, ubiquity, and casualness with which the sentiments he expressed circulated as the events unfolded on campus.

Progress Interrupted

The first lesson we learned as a result of the above-described experience was the extent to which an embodied, willful ignorance performs as a function of identity privilege that serves to interrupt progress towards inclusion and equity. The assumed ignorance of the college students who created the offensive post reverberated beyond the students and echoed in sentiments expressed by faculty. Through the performance of White male privilege, there are a couple of inaccurate assumptions at best and attributes at worst that grew from the kindled fires of discord set by the students. For example, when the White male faculty member questioned the investigation of the offending students' behavior, he prefaced his statement by asserting ignorance about the entire subject. The performance of ignorance acted as a mechanism to interrupt and stymie further discussion. The next aspect of this performance of White male privilege was that it was acceptable for the faculty member to lack knowledge of matters and dynamics of race on the college campus. This professor did not invest resources in examining his identity privilege in ways that better support his teaching and his role as a professor in a community of college students and fellow academics.

The problematic issue of representation was also activated by this blackface incident. Not making the effort to understand the important role of representation, what Charles Taylor calls "a vital human need," for students of color is an egregious oversight that has serious repercussions for the learning environment of students of color (Taylor, 1994, p. 25). Had they done their due diligence, faculty members would know that assaults on the identities of students of color affect the viability of learning and educational experiences by relaying an often-internalized representation of inferiority. Misrepresentations of students of color fosters self-depreciation, self-hatred, and low self-esteem while fostering a debilitating inability to take advantage of opportunities as they are presented (Taylor, 1994, p. 25–26).

What was most significant in the faculty member's comment was the way they questioned the need for an investigation at all. The idea that the college was inappropriate in the mere search for a fuller understanding and evidence surrounding the incident runs counter to the idea of an institution of higher learning where seeking knowledge, accuracy of facts, optimal ways to promote student learning, and deeper understanding of contextual and nuanced elements of any event are paramount. Asserting a

212 JADE C. HUELL AND CRYSTAL U. DAVIS

lack of understanding along with a refusal to learn more is an effective diversion tactic that must be squelched when it redirects the energy that should be put towards student support and addressing injustices.

In Defense of…

Another issue present was the presumed innocent intent of the perpetrators of the social media post by some members of the community. An example of this is the question posed by the White male faculty member when he privileged the assumed innocence or "unknown intentions" of the White female students and, as a result, devalued the offence, hurt, and sense of peril it engendered in both students and faculty. The protection of the offending White students' innocence extended in the faculty meeting was an operation of the institution's investment in Whiteness both historically and in living memory (Macalpine & Marsh, 2005, p. 431). The silence and lack of ongoing discussion about race amongst faculty and administrators was punctuated by the lack of White faculty stepping in as allies to support the Black female faculty. At no time did any White faculty members step forward in defense of the arguments made by Black faculty. Instead, they shared their sadness, regret, and hurt privately; avoiding a public stance of support. The aggregate effect is that White faculty had a more difficult time speaking up on behalf of those Black students and faculty harmed than other members did in defending the White student perpetrators. The smoldering ashes of willful ignorance, disregard, and silence in the face of White supremacy that had haunted the institution for decades led to the tense breakdown in institutional response that was felt by both Black students and faculty.

The Structural and the Marginal

Structural obstacles, a function of the sociocultural positionality of the college, served as obstructions to decisive and efficient change. One instance of this was pulling the Black female faculty in to ask them to watch their tone and avoid outbursts during faculty meetings. Further, these faculty were asked to serve on committees with no power to institute change. In effect, they were being asked to be quiet and work on diversity and inclusivity initiatives and ideas that might make them "feel" good, but would do no institutional good. These actions reflect larger systemic issues in U.S. higher education where Black faculty carry a heavy burden in institutions where they are a small minority within the faculty ranks. They are both hyper-visible, in that they are often asked to speak for and represent the diverse perspectives of people of color, and are often invisible, disregarded as having little power and voice by being such a small number.

In addition, the Black faculty initially called in were female. The administration had to be reminded that they did not invite the one Black male to the table in this conversation. The cumulative disadvantage of Black female professors who experience marginalization, both as women and as Black faculty, results in difficulty attributing disregard to race or gender in any given instance. Furthermore, asking Black women faculty members to divert labor to non-tenurable service activities places these faculty at risk of not being promoted to long-term positions of power where they can enforce initiatives and truly enact change (Turner, 2002). This unpaid, unrecognized service to the college slows down progress, placates the community, and shifts the burden for change to those who often have the least institutional resources and influence.

Fear as a Disruptor

It is also important to note that the institution's choice in the selected solutions to the financial crisis subverted a number of student safety and inclusion considerations. The pattern of how financial fear is a common disrupter to progress made in inclusive and anti-racist initiatives and strategies is a function of White supremacy. Not only in the U.S., but abroad, we see places where the financial crisis of 2008 inspired and organized major political shifts towards xenophobia, racism, bigotry, and a general closing-off of boundaries between self and other, for example (Mughan et al., 2003). At this institution, where faculty were informed in the fall that the school didn't have enough funding for salaries for the spring semester, many initiatives were framed as being an urgent and necessary change to repair the institution's financial affairs with little consideration of the effects of the decisions on the racial climate at the college.

PROMISING PRACTICES FOR CHANGE

> Inclusion is not like Beetlejuice, saying it three times will not make it appear.
>
> Black faculty meeting notes

Embodied and Accountable Practices

Significant to the work we do as scholar-practitioners in our respective fields of Performance Studies and Dance is embodiment. This element of moving from language and visual representations of inclusion to an active, embodied practice of inclusion is critical for affecting change. Aristotelis

Santas (2000) notes the importance of this active practice in pedagogical anti-racism work, which is based on the accountability component of the People's Institute for Survival and Beyond's Undoing Racism™ Workshop and Paulo Friere's definition of praxis. Santas asserts that Friere's praxis of integrating reflection and action combined with an element of multifaceted organizational accountability (as described by the People's Institute) are critical for upending systems of oppression and inequity. Institutional training in the mechanisms and manifestations of White supremacy for incidents such as these could be addressed in a practical, proactive way that fosters an inclusive, anti-racist learning environment for all students. This should be done not only through institutional language, policies, and training, but also with the emphasis and training in how to move concepts into actionable behaviors for individuals, groups, and the institution. This nexus between doing and accountability, rather than stopping short of this with "showing" a knowledge and ability to apply the vocabulary of anti-racism and inclusivity, is a specialty of embodied performance practitioners. The attention to embodied action is often a challenge in communities, such as higher education, where intellect and facile use of language is valued over embodied practice and awareness of habitual behaviors.

Examples of embodied practices include the Embodied Anti-Racism Workshop (Davis & McCarthy-Brown, 2019) and Forum Theatre (Boal, 2013). The Embodied Anti-Racism Workshop is an immersive movement-based workshop that examines racial constructs. Through movement activities, participants respond to a series of prompts that address aspects of how racism operates in society and manifests in the behavior of individuals. Reflection after movement activities is a critical part of the learning process in this workshop. Forum Theatre is a theatre structure wherein the spectator engages with the actors to change the course of the performance. The content of Forum Theatre often reveals oppressive relationships and social structures, with actors and spectators engaged in reaching social justice aims.

With regard to this offensive post by students, prior institutional engagement with the praxis of both doing and accountability would have ensured that protocols were already in place for investigations of racial incidents on campus. Swift disclosure of accurate details surrounding the event, the position of the school, and investigative action steps should have happened immediately. Students should have had the opportunity to be involved in generating solutions for accountability and prevention of such incidents in the future.

Strategic Planning: Diversity as Visioning for Sustainability

Institutional policies that create safer spaces for students of color and marginalized students in general are a practical goal that serves the growing racial diversity in the U.S. (Vespa et al., 2018). This benefits recruitment, retention, academic performance, and positive experiences of current students and alumni. It is far more challenging to secure financial donations and support from alumni who had negative experiences, lacked a sense of belonging in the institution, and carry the burden of having graduated from an institution with unresolved racial baggage that continues to impact marginalized student populations on campus. There is a great need for institutional education regarding how racism negatively impacts the bottom line and the ongoing viability of institutions deemed as unsafe for emerging student populations.

Accountability and Critical Evaluation as Evolving Practice

Institutional change efforts require a mechanism to address the malleable, adaptive qualities of racism to resist its own undoing (Sexton, 2008). To combat the pull of the racial power structure to maintain its grip on institutions of learning, it is critical to routinely and methodically assess the impact of changes to the culture with respect to diversity and inclusion among students. This is an accountability measure geared to ensure that changes addressing diversity, equity, and inclusion challenges are actually leading to institutional progress in this area (Neville et al., 2010). Well-crafted assessments and diversity scorecards not only provide evidence that instituted changes are effective, but also provide valuable information on next steps for continued progress.

Radical Transparency as Educational Opportunity

The value of implementing anti-racist strategies on campus is directly related to the financial sustainability of the school. As such, institutional change should be communicated from the top down through radical and intentional transparency as progress is made. This transparency would be evident in the policies of the institution, the speedy and consistent application of those policies on campus, and the immediate public communication denouncing any future racist acts with reference to standing policies in place put forth by administration. This radical transparency would also include transparent dialogue between students and administration on how to develop effective and specific protocols and accountability for the unique institution and community. Embodying transparency in this way has the potential to alter the culture of the college and to inspire a new trajectory for the history, living memory, positionality, embodiment of student experiences, and sustainability of the college.

216 JADE C. HUELL AND CRYSTAL U. DAVIS

In a country projected to be more racially diverse than ever before, this radical transparency becomes more urgent to employ. For faculty and administration, integrating strategies of radical transparency into policies results in developing White allies with the tools, language, and lenses to support recruitment and retention of students of color and faculty of color. Anti-racist principles, tools, and protocols should be present and operating in a wholly integrated way, appearing in places, practices, and principles explicitly linked to anti-racist goals as well as where it may not explicitly reference such.

CONCLUSION

In "How We Fight White Supremacy," Akiba Solomon and Kenrya Rankin state unequivocally, "The fact is, White supremacy defines our current reality. It is not merely a belief that to be White is to be better. It is a political, cultural, and economic system premised on the subjugation of people who are not White" (vii). In this chapter, we document, critique, and offer strategies and practices for combating the White supremacy that Solomon and Rankin (2019) describe within in the context of one Southern women's liberal arts college. It is our sincere hope that by detailing the perils and possibilities at hand when looking at this particular "blackface incident," we ignite a blaze that will eventually lead to a true baptism by fire, a trial, a cleansing, a contract with the powers that be to fight fearlessly for educational and intellectual justice on every campus across the country.

DISCUSSION QUESTIONS

1. The history of the college in this case was a prominent part of the narrative. What are some ways that the history of your institution impacts diversity, equity, and inclusion at your institution?
2. What are some ways money or the economy of your institution supports or disrupts diversity, equity, and inclusion initiatives on campus? Can you think of ways that the financial structures of your institution can serve to improve diversity, equity, and inclusion initiatives on campus?
3. What are some solutions to the four problems illuminated in the "Lessons Learned" section of this chapter?
4. What are some embodied practices of action and accountability that already exist at your institution? Can you think of others that you can create, introduce, or integrate into the culture of your institution?

5. What are ways you would hold members of the institution accountable to the initiatives you established in Question Four?
6. In what ways might more radical transparency be integrated into your institution from the individual level, interpersonal level, and institutional level?
7. In what ways have social challenges at the national level impacted your campus?
8. In what ways have issues at other campuses created a "ripple effect" on your campus?

REFERENCES

Baez, B. (2000). Race-related service and faculty of color: Conceptualizing critical agency in academe. *Higher Education, 39*(3), 363–391.

Boal, A. (2013). *The rainbow of desire: The Boal method of theatre and therapy.* Routledge.

Cole, C. M., & Davis, T. C. (2013). Routes of Blackface. *TDR/The Drama Review, 57*(2), 7–12.

College Factual. (2019, June 28). https://www.collegefactual.com/.

Davis, C. U., & McCarthy-Brown, N. (2019). *Embodied anti-racism workshop.* Presented at Dance Studies Association. Evanston, IL.

Duncan, P. (2014). Hot commodities, cheap labor: Women of color in the academy. *Frontiers: A Journal of Women Studies, 35*(3), 39–63.

Goins, M. N., & Williams, L. (2019). The struggle of being a racial minority in the academy. *Spectra, 55*(2), 24.

Gura, P. F. (1999). America's minstrel daze. *The New England Quarterly, 72*(4), 602–616.

By water and the spirit. (2019). The people of the United Methodist Church. http://s3.amazonaws.com/Website_Properties/what-we-believe/documents/by-water-spirit-baptism.PDF.

Jaschik, S. (2016, September 26). Epidemic of racist incidents. *Inside Higher Ed.* https://www.insidehighered.com/news/2016/09/26/campuses-see-flurry-racist-incidents-and-protests-against-racism.

Macalpine, M., & Marsh, S. (2005). 'On being white: There's nothing I can say' exploring whiteness and power in Ooganizations. *Management Learning, 36*(4), 429–450.

Moore, R. (2017). An update on the demographics of Jonestown. Alternative considerations of Jonestown and people temple. https://jonestown.sdsu.edu/?page_id=70495.

Mughan, A., Bean, C., & McAllister, I. (2003). Economic globalization, job insecurity and the populist reaction. *Electoral Studies, 22*(4), 617–633.

Neville, H. A., Huntt, M. B., & Chapa, J. (2010). *Implementing diversity: Contemporary challenges and best practices at predominantly white universities.* Urbana: University of Illinois.

Santas, A. (2000). Teaching anti-racism. *Studies in Philosophy and Education* 19, 349–361.

Sexton, J. (2008). *Amalgamation schemes: Antiblackness and the critique of multiracialism.* Minneapolis, MN: University of Minnesota Press.

218 JADE C. HUELL AND CRYSTAL U. DAVIS

Solomon, A., & Rankin, K. (2019). *How we fight white supremacy: A field guide to black resistance.* New York, NY: Bold Type Books.

Sullivan, S., & Tuana, N. (Eds.). (2007). *Race and epistemologies of ignorance.* Albany: Suny Press.

Taylor, C. (1994). The politics of recognition. *New Contexts of Canadian Criticism.* Broadview Press. 98–131.

Turner, C. S. V. (2002). Women of color in academe: Living with multiple marginality. *The Journal of Higher Education,* 73(1), 74–93.

Vespa, J., Armstrong, D. M., & Medina, L. (2018). *Demographic turning points for the United States: Population projections for 2020 to 2060.* U.S. Department of Commerce, Economics and Statistics Administration, US Census Bureau.

Chapter 14

The Ripple Effect of Bias, Hate, and Activism: A Nation in Crisis, a Campus in Turmoil, and Pathways Forward

Cherese F. Fine, Kendra D. Stewart-Tillman, DeOnte T. Brown, and Jerad E. Green

"I have pain all over. I'm exhausted. Of course, I'm hungry. I've got an ongoing headache," said Jonathan Butler (as cited in Miller, 2015). Jonathan Butler was a graduate student at the University of Missouri (Mizzou) in the fall of 2015 when he undertook a seven-day hunger strike to protest racist and xenophobic incidents and lack of response from administration. Butler's resistance was part of the larger Concerned Student 1950 movement that occurred on Mizzou's campus at the time and illustrates the impact of student activism in higher education. Activism in higher education has a long-standing history that is often connected to institutional, structural, and societal oppression. Despite the exhaustion, burnout, and fatigue students experience as a result of activism, the long-term effects of unrest are substantial (Linder et al., 2019).

Examples of student activism date back to as early as 1766 with the Harvard Butter Rebellion, where students at the time challenged the food quality served in dining halls at Harvard University (Moore, 1976). The Settlement Movement of 1889 was initiated by collegiate women and paved the way for advanced social services and a general understanding of social work practice (Rousmaniere, 1970). Also, through the "Deaf President Now" protest at Gallaudet, students challenged the decision to hire the lone hearing president over other deaf candidates (Gallaudet University, 2019). Despite its 100 year existence, there had never been a deaf president. These examples are three of hundreds of cases of student activism leading to organizational change since 1636. To understand student activism today, it is important to note the historical context upon which contemporary movements build.

220 CHERESE F. FINE ET AL.

SOCIAL UNREST AND COLLEGE-STUDENT ACTIVISM

The roots of many current activism efforts date back to the 1960s and 1970s, when colleges and universities served as hotbeds of student activism (Weinberg, 1990). Movements of the time included the Free Speech Movement of 1964 (University of California, Berkeley, 2019), anti-Vietnam War protests in 1970 (Kindig, 2008), and the Anti-Apartheid Movement in 1978 (University of Michigan, 2019). During this time, a notable but often overlooked movement was taking place that would restructure diversity and inclusion for the next half-century. The Black Campus Student Movement at San Francisco State University is often noted as the beginning of this movement. Also, this campus is among the first to have an organized Black Student Union organization (Rogers, 2012). At the time, there was a significant push from Black students to address the racial tensions that persisted following the riots in Los Angeles in 1965. Furthermore, the first wave of the Civil Rights Acts, 1964 and 1968, brought an influx of students of color, particularly Black students, into higher education at historically White institutions (Rogers, 2012). Despite the increasing enrollment of Black and other racially minoritized students, services and support at universities rarely changed. Consequently, Black students and other groups on campus formed coalitions, began challenging campus administrations, and issued demands that included the creation of Black studies programs, an increase in Black faculty, and respite space to find community and support (Rogers, 2012). A movement of dozens of students at San Francisco State University prompted a nationwide push to reform higher education. The ripple effect of protesting from the movements in the 1960s and 1970s can be seen today with student responses to the Black Lives Matter movement and police brutality. To further understand these more contemporary movements, it is important to contextualize policing in the United States.

Policing in the United States

Policing in the United States has roots that link back to slave patrols of the 1700s and 1800s. The first known slave patrols emerged in 1704 in South Carolina and were initially created to prevent the Spanish invasion; however, they later became a mechanism to maintain social control over enslaved populations and manage race-based conflict that often arose on plantations (Turner et al., 2006). While practices related to controlling enslaved Africans was not new at that time, this was the first time publicly funded police agencies emerged in the South (p. 185).

The complex and historically rooted dynamics between the police and Black people in the U.S. evolved over time through numerous efforts, including the convict leasing system, the war on drugs and mass incarceration, and most recently, the Black Lives Matter movement. Through the system of convict leasing, states profited from free labor in the United States' railroads, mines, and plantations (Equal Justice Initiative, 2013). The Thirteenth Amendment abolished slavery; however, this amendment technically did not apply to those that had committed crimes. Through "Black Codes," miniscule acts were criminalized only for Black people, who were incarcerated and forced into free labor (Equal Justice Initiative, 2013). More recently, the War on Drugs and the Anti-Drug Abuse Act has been a contributing factor in the mass incarceration experienced by Black and Latino men in the U.S. Between 1980 and 2000 primarily. Incarceration for nonviolent drug offenses increased from 50,000 to more than 400,000 (History, 2018). This has further complicated the relationship between brown bodies and policing entities in the U.S. During this time period, an increase in racial profiling, time served, and convictions for a variety of offenses, including parole violations, contributed to a significant growth in mass incarceration (Schoenfeld, 2012). It is from this complicated past that the Black Lives Matter movement arose as the fourth major occurrence illustrating the complex relationship between racially minoritized groups and the police.

The Black Lives Matter movement grew to national prominence in 2012 following the murder of Trayvon Martin, a Florida teenager who was shot and killed by neighborhood watch man, George Zimmerman. In response to the acquittal of Zimmerman in Trayvon's murder, three Black women (Alicia Garza, Opal Tometi, and Patrisse Cullors) created a hashtag and sparked a national movement in support of Black lives (Garza et al., 2019). Widespread use of the #BlackLivesMatter hashtag united an activist community while illuminating the troubled relations between police and Black people—something that many people of color have known for a long time.

The "Ripple Effect" in Higher Education

Over the next two to three years, high-profile cases including Mike Brown, Tamir Rice, and Eric Garner sparked a national outcry. In response, college students protested in solidarity, which paralleled protests from the past, to increase awareness of police brutality and violence towards Black people. Notably, the ongoing national dialogue about police brutality against African-American people and the ensuing protests sparked the interrogation of problematic diversity, equity, and inclusion (DEI) issues taking place on campuses across the nation. Particularly after the death of Mike Brown in 2014, students began staging sit-ins and die-ins to occupy high traffic and/or notable spaces on campus such as administration buildings. These activism efforts raised important questions about climate issues while sparking debate about how institutions are addressing persistent inequities.

Students issued formal demands that outlined specific needs and outcomes they expected. Often, their demands included calls for recruiting and retaining students, faculty, and staff of color, as well as enhancing intercultural competence and increasing resources to support diversity-related initiatives. In recent years, an example of this phenomenon is the #NotAgainSU movement that took place at Syracuse University in 2019 (McMahon, 2019). This case perfectly articulates the reemergence of student activism, challenges between students and administration, and how these incidents can launch a protest that draws national attention.

THE SITE

The site of this case is Heritage University, a Research I institution located in the Southeast region of the U.S. Heritage University is a predominantly White institution (PWI), where students of color make up 17% of the student population. Black students comprise 6% of the campus, a number that has not significantly changed for years. The state in which the institution resides is approximately 27% Black, and 40% people of color.

Heritage University has experienced a number of racially based incidents in recent years. The university grounds are built upon indigenous land that was once occupied by eastern bands of the Cherokee nation. Additionally, the university sits atop a former working plantation and was largely built by convict laborers following emancipation. The university desegregated by court order in 1963, becoming the first PWI in the state to desegregate. Over the years, issues of campus climate and this racial legacy have been sources of contention for many students of color (e.g., some buildings on campus were named after publicly avowed White supremacists).

In response to student voices, the first Multicultural Center was opened in the late 1990s and underwent a few reorganizations and structural changes in response to economic and student needs. After a major blackface incident in the mid 2000s, Heritage University responded by hiring the first Chief Diversity Officer. The next major racially charged incident would occur approximately 10 years later, becoming a major watershed moment. This particular incident, and the national and institutional climate leading up to it, are described in the next section.

THE SITUATION

Just as protests and national events have been part of the history of higher education, students, particularly, students of color at Heritage University, utilized measures such as die-ins and marches to bring greater awareness to the injustices they perceived across the U.S. As students held demonstrations on campus in response to these national occurrences, their classmates began to respond negatively, with most of these negative interactions playing out on social media. Students instrumental in these demonstrations, most of whom were students of color, reached out to their classmates through social media groups and other platforms, asking them to show their support to these causes. Instead of support, the students of color were met with insensitivity or complacency, including racial epithets from their peers. Some of this backlash occurred anonymously through platforms such as YikYak, while others occurred through students' personally identifiable Facebook and Twitter accounts.

In response to these negative reactions, the student activists shifted their attention from national instances of injustice, to the lack of intercultural competence displayed by members of their campus community. Student activists wanted classmates hurling blatantly offensive remarks to face action through the university conduct process. They also pointed to the limited opportunities for campus constituents to grow in the area of intercultural competence.

Additionally in this time period, a long-standing tradition of a predominantly White fraternity hosting an event portraying culturally offensive stereotypes was unearthed publicly, both to the campus and on national news. Student activists saw this event, and the institution's perceived inability to directly reprimand this student group for violations related to bias incidents due to free speech, as further proof that the university needed more accountability to advance in the realm of DEI.

To make these desires known, the student activists issued a set of student grievances and demands to Heritage. This list referenced the university mission and highlighted ways in which they felt the institution was failing to uphold this mission. The grievances included a desire to have more direct language condemning instances of bias, a need for a safe space for students from marginalized backgrounds and their allies, a lack of racial/ethnic representation that more closely aligned with state demographics for both students and faculty, and incentivized diversity training opportunities for students, faculty, and staff.

The grievances and demands were presented early in the spring semester and by the end of the summer, the university administration responded partially to some of the demands by reconfiguring a standalone multicultural center on campus, since the previous multicultural center functions

224 CHERESE F. FINE ET AL.

had been absorbed into a larger unit during the recession. However, as a byproduct of this physical transition for the multicultural center, a popular area mainly used as a lounge for students of color had to be displaced to accommodate staff. The students expressed appreciation and dissatisfaction with this move.

The following year, minimal conversations regarding the grievances and demands occurred between the administration and students. As the academic year appeared primed to close, another bias incident occurred on campus and became a watershed moment. Student activists pointed to both the occurrence of this incident and the university's lack of public condemnation in response as a message that the university administration was not doing enough to address the issues they had been highlighting for the last couple of years. In response, student activists elevated their demonstrations to a sit-in at the main administrative building to call more public attention to these local issues. Initially, most students that participated in this sit-in were students of color, but as the weeks progressed, multiple marginalized communities and their allies joined in on the efforts as a form of coalition-building.

Additionally, students were not the only groups affected by these bias incidents and the narratives created around the campus-wide sit-in. Faculty and staff were also impacted by these situations. In particular, many faculty and staff of color directly empathized with the students' feelings and grievances, wanting to offer the students their support as well as needing support themselves. However, even if many (not all) faculty and staff were in support of students, they responded in disparate ways depending on varying factors. One of the main factors governing their response was the issue of employment protections. Tenured faculty were able to show support to the students in a more explicit manner, signing petitions printed in the university newspaper and/or actively marching in demonstrations. Many untenured faculty and staff experienced concern as they grappled with how they should and could show up in a way to effectively support students and not compromise their role and reputation at the institution. To complicate the situation for this particular group, there were also conflicting directives given by departmental/divisional supervisors on what was or was not allowed. Subsequently, each person had to make their own decisions by finding a balance between their personal convictions and the risks they were willing to take.

After many emotionally and mentally draining days for all parties involved, simultaneously, student organizers decided to suspend the sit-in and the administration issued a public statement promising a greater sense of urgency in addressing DEI challenges students had raised. Although the actual sit-in ended in 2016, the residue of such a large demonstration of student activism remains.

IMPLICATIONS AND LESSONS LEARNED

Bronfenbrenner's (1979) ecological framework offers guidance on the impact of the events at Heritage. Bronfenbrenner's framework states that there are a number of areas of influence and interaction, including direct interactions in the microsystem (regular interaction between an individual and others in their circle [e.g., classmates, family members, friends]) and mesosystem (interaction between groups in the microsystem [e.g., faculty–student interactions, family values to campus values]) and indirect interactions in the exosystem (people or processes that influence micro- and mesosystems [e.g., university policies, local community members, laws]) and macrosystem (larger cultural, societal, and historical factors that influence the prior systems [e.g., college access for marginalized groups, freedom of speech]). Through application of Bronfenbrenner's ecological framework to campus activism and related events, one begins to see the impact on student development and the campus.

Growth and Development at the Micro Level

At Heritage University, the microsystem impacts center students actively and passively engaging in activism. Interactions with students reveal that many of them gained new levels of social awareness and explored their racial identities. From a broad perspective, the impact on students at this level can be observed in the shifts noticed in students' knowledge, attitudes, and behaviors. Through activism and demonstrations, students began to gain awareness of inequitable practices within our criminal justice, economic, and education systems (Leath & Chavous, 2017). As it relates to Heritage University, both students with marginalized and privileged identities found themselves becoming more aware of issues and challenges within our society. Students with marginalized identities shared with their peers and faculty examples of how their educational experience has been negatively impacted through microaggressions, stereotyping, and bias. At the height of the demonstrations at Heritage, the campus sit-in was the first time many of our White-identifying students heard directly how they themselves or their peers created unnecessary barriers for Black students. Black students shared how they are ostracized in group projects or made to feel less-than by their White peers. As student-affairs professionals supporting students, we found ourselves in awe of the deep vulnerability students displayed to have these long overdue conversations.

As students became more aware of the challenges that existed for Black students on campus, there became a greater desire to act (White-Johnson, 2012; Hope et al., 2019). In order to act, students sought out opportunities

226 CHERESE F. FINE ET AL.

to understand their rights related to freedom of speech and the right to assemble in protest. Through an increased awareness of inequity, students found opportunities to engage for the greater benefit of their peers and the campus. Faculty and staff at Heritage remarked how the sit-in created the strongest, most authentic student community that the institution had seen.

Beyond raising awareness to social issues, activism can also serve as a factor in identity development (White-Johnson, 2012). Particularly for many of the Black students, the actions that led to demonstrations and subsequent engagement in activism served to move students through their Black identity development from the perspective of Cross' Theory of Nigrescence. Nigrescence is a developmental process that encompasses multiple levels to assist in understanding one's Blackness and also doubles as an explanation of Black identity development (Cross & Fhagen-Smith, 2001). Cross posits that in the pre-encounter stage, which is the first level of Nigrescence, individuals place less emphasis on their Black identity and often operate based on dominant White values until a relevant, meaningful experience serves as an encounter to push them to recognize racism's existence and impact on their life. Following this encounter experience, a Black individual enters immersion/emersion, which is a new or heightened desire to surround themselves with other Black individuals and Black culture to gain a deeper understanding of their Blackness while intentionally avoiding Whiteness. The recognition that pro-Black ideologies and ways of living can coexist in a space with respectful White individuals is representative of an individual's movement to internalization, as there is a sense of security in how the individual feels about their Black identity. In entering internalization-commitment, the final level of Nigrescence, an individual commits to protecting the value of Blackness while addressing challenges that impact the Black community. Achievement of internalization-commitment does not serve as an infinite status fulfilment given that contextual factors can shift, presenting new encounter experiences.

The encounter with racial discrimination served as the catalyst for exploration of what it means to be Black in the context of the campus and in the eyes of peers for some Heritage students (Szymanski, 2012). One student remarked to staff about their experience of walking on campus after a racist incident occurred, hoping that they would find other Black students. The desire to be in community with other Black students represented a need to feel a sense of safety during times of high campus tensions. Other Black students used this experience to identify ways that they can use their voice to create change.

Beyond identity development, for Black students experiencing racially charged encounters and demonstrations, the impact on their mental well-being and academic performance was a reality that most were unprepared to navigate. Students had little understanding that their quest to make their campus better would result in racial battle fatigue. The effects of

THE RIPPLE EFFECT OF BIAS, HATE, AND ACTIVISM **227**

racial battle fatigue are manifested through physical, emotional, or mental symptoms (Smith, 2008). Students experiencing racial battle fatigue or a general sense of being overwhelmed by activism have been known to experience tension headaches, elevated breathing and heartbeat, and anxiety; they may isolate themselves both socially and emotionally (Hope et al., 2018). The loss of the ability to think clearly during times of racial battle fatigue along with the previously mentioned symptoms can be detrimental to students' academic experiences.

The increased knowledge students gained about self and others led to common feelings and attitudes of frustration and hurt (Szymanski, 2012; White-Johnson, 2012). Students (in particular, Black students) grew increasingly frustrated by the consistent killing and mistreatment of Black people within society, impacting their on-campus experiences (Leath & Chavous, 2017). Specifically, students have been both frustrated and hurt by the disregard administration, faculty/staff, and their peers have exhibited with respect to the role culture and race has had on society and their campus experiences (Logue, 2016). The question "Do I belong?" is one that marginalized students agonize over constantly. During demonstrations, this question is amplified as students collectively support each other by listening to and sharing countless experiences of not feeling that they matter to the campus community.

When students question their sense of belonging, the impact is felt in their enrollment decisions. As students engage in demonstrations against their campus administration, they are highlighting the lack of support that exists for them to thrive. Many PWIs experienced decreased enrollment of Black students during this period of increased activism, while historically Black colleges and universities welcomed more Black students to an environment designed for them to be free of racial bias and discrimination (Straus, 2011; Williams, 2018; Tugend, 2019).

Campus and Peer Group Impact at the Meso Level

The mesosystem impacts at Heritage University focused on the interaction between a student's family and their campus "family." At Heritage, privilege and racism divided the campus "family," and students had to decide how they would navigate the tensions. Some students found themselves either at odds with the beliefs of their home family or their campus "family," which added to the frustrations and stress. The following played out in the minds of some: "My family said my main focus is getting an education and not demonstrating, but if I don't march or sit-in, my friends will be disappointed in me." This tension between home family and campus "family" caused some students to distance themselves from both groups.

228 CHERESE F. FINE ET AL.

The other, and equally important, impact in the mesosystem relates to the cross-peer group interactions that occurred between various student subpopulations (e.g. cultural identity-based peer groups, academic major peers, residential communities). Often students coexist within campus communities without taking time to understand the experiences of others. College administrators and faculty fall victim to the idea that the presence of a diverse student population will in essence create engagement across differences. Gurin et al. (2004) shared that benefits to a diverse campus include better student learning and students who are more prepared to be active citizens in our society. To realize these benefits, however, students need sustained cross-group interactions and dialogues, and cannot simply coexist within the campus community (Gurin et al., 2002; Oliha-Donaldson, 2018).

The sit-in created opportunities for intergroup dialogues—which many had not experienced since their first-semester required dialogue. Students holding privileged identities had an opportunity to visually understand the impact that racism can have on individuals by seeing their friends sleeping on the ground or marching in the streets to finally become visible to the administration. The sit-in provided space to discuss multiple topics (i.e., bias, discrimination, microaggressions) and coalesce around ways to move forward. The genuine dialogues and conversations that occurred between students, friends, peers, and others was one of the greatest impacts felt at this level, especially for our students.

The path to impact is littered with negative and positive experiences. Experiences at the individual and organizational levels worked to create change for this campus and many others. In recognizing that there was impact, we affirm to students that their actions mattered.

Lessons Learned

There were many lessons learned from the series of demonstrations that happened both nationally and at Heritage University during this time period. These lessons include monitoring current events, ensuring there are appropriate channels of direct and affirming communication, intentionally creating supportive spaces, and enhancing the institution's capacity to respond to bias beyond one or two offices on campus. Following, each lesson is discussed in-depth.

Staying Abreast of National and International Incidents

A major overarching lesson was the need to stay abreast of national and international incidents that may impact the local campus (Steil & Gibbons-Carr, 2005). Colleges and universities are a microcosm of the greater macro

THE RIPPLE EFFECT OF BIAS, HATE, AND ACTIVISM **229**

context, and students, faculty, and staff bring with them all of the backgrounds, perspectives, and identities present in the greater world. Therefore, they may be deeply impacted by an incident that happened hundreds of miles away. It is important for colleges to not only monitor what has occurred nationwide and/or worldwide, but to also anticipate what campus populations may be impacted and explore appropriate ways to support these communities (Carter, 2007).

Carefully Plan and Orchestrate Campus Forums and Dialogues

Another important lesson learned is the need to be strategic in addressing different incidents. Oftentimes, Heritage administrators would host forums immediately after an incident, where students had an opportunity to share how the incident impacted them (Gurin et al., 2002; Alimo, 2012). This strategy was used after a blackface incident many years before and had also been implemented on campus in more recent times after a string of police-related fatalities of unarmed Black men. The hopeful outcome of these dialogic forums are that the campus community will take a close look at the world around them and their place in it while simultaneously learning from others to create heightened understanding and engagement (Alimo, 2012; Hollis & Govan, 2015). While administrators may have good intentions in hosting a forum immediately after a bias incident, student emotions are still high. This can impact the conversation, leading to further trauma. As opposed to immediately jumping into forums, a helpful strategy may be an initial email from upper administration to the entire campus community. An email of this kind can acknowledge the incident, its impact on community members, and outline actions in progress to ensure that affected groups have their needs validated and met.

When the timing is right, it is also important to be mindful of the composition of the students brought into an intentionally created forum space (Alimo, 2012). Following a bias incident perpetrated by a predominantly White student fraternity, university administrators tried to get a small group of students from both sides to participate in a dialogue so that the students from the student organization could understand the impact of its actions on particular communities on campus. The predominantly White fraternity showed up with a great portion of their membership, outnumbering the small group of student leaders of color that were asked to share their feelings, causing a psychologically threatening environment. Administrators should have shown more intentionality in inviting a purposefully limited number of students to participate in this discussion.

As a result of this imbalance and discomfort, student leaders of color invited additional students of color to join the meeting and create more

230 CHERESE F. FINE ET AL.

balance through social media, leading to the predominantly White student organization members feeling overwhelmed and bum-rushed by an influx of angry students that they were not expecting. Unsurprisingly, the conversation did not produce many positive outcomes as emotions were still high from initial reactions to the incident, which occurred less than 18 hours prior. In fact, some students had not sobered up, literally, from the night's events, and others had not had ample time to process their shock and outrage at their peers' actions. More time was needed to ensure intentionality in both the form and execution of this forum.

Create Supportive Spaces for Impacted Communities to be Vulnerable and Process Issues

Another major lesson learned was the need for Heritage to provide intentional space for marginalized populations on campus. When many of the national incidents occurred with unarmed murders of Black people, impacted communities were searching for a place on campus to process these issues with people with similar reactions and feelings (Solorzano et al., 2000). This type of space provides a supportive and safe outlet for marginalized communities on campus, allowing them to be vulnerable in their processing of critical issues. Such spaces also offer a reprieve from others on campus that may not be equally impacted or may be blatantly insensitive or disrespectful. Finally, this type of space aids in community-building (Grier-Reed, 2010).

Campus Leaders Need DEI Education to Drive Institutional Change

Additionally, campus community members often look to DEI-related units on campus to take the lead in offering opportunities to build intercultural capacity. Student activists did not simply want punitive action for perpetrators, but also a greater understanding of cultural issues and histories in order to minimize bigotry and make the entire campus more inclusive (Solorzano et al., 2000). This need for greater intercultural competence is not only central to students' development, but also faculty, staff, and administrators that interact with constituents from diverse populations daily and hold decision-making power (Pope & Reynolds, 1997).

In order to fully integrate this type of intercultural understanding and competence, the tone should be set by upper administration. Our experience suggests that this level of commitment is dependent on how much intercultural learning and development they have engaged in themselves, which will impact their commitment to resourcing DEI units. Further, their understanding of the complexity of DEI organizational change efforts will

THE RIPPLE EFFECT OF BIAS, HATE, AND ACTIVISM **231**

determine the expectations they set for all members of the institution with regards to accountability for creating an inclusive academic community (see Williams, 2007).

PROMISING PRACTICES FOR CHANGE

When incidents occurred on campus, the Heritage administration typically used temporary strategies to address the situation such as listening forums, sending emails about respect, etc. However, once the sit-in occurred, the university administrators changed their approach by creating an action plan to address the students' demands and recommitting to an inclusive environment. Some of the major strategies implemented included sharing the complete history of Heritage, commitment to diversity education, improving communication when racialized incidents occur, and seeking collaborative change.

Proactively Address Negative History

With increased expectations to rename buildings and take down statues of controversial individuals, institutions are grappling with how to share the positive and negative aspects of their history. During the height of student activism, a professor started researching the untold history of Heritage and learned that enslaved people and convict laborers built the institution. The professor has been working with students, faculty, staff, alumni, and community members to research and share this history. One emergent strategy is to invest resources in telling the complete history of institutions. While the professor had some university support, it was an alumnus that actually gave the professor funding to move forward with the project, not the university. With the increased interest in the full history of Heritage, along with the demands from the student activists to rename the areas on campus that are named after White supremacists, the institution could no longer ignore the demands. After the sit-in, the Heritage administration committed to sharing the complete history of its campus. A history task-force was created to continue working on how the institution can share the complete history of Heritage. With the guidance of this professor, historical markers were placed throughout campus that not only include the positive history, but also the untold and challenging portions of the campus' history. While Heritage has a long way to go, this practice will shift the perspective that Heritage is hiding information. Institutions, in particular, PWIs that have a history of segregation, cannot change that past, but by acknowledging history and articulating a mission and vision that is inclusive, they signal their willingness to dispense with an exclusionary past (Hurtado et al., 1998).

232 CHERESE F. FINE ET AL.

Commit to Campus-Wide Diversity Education

Structural diversity, numeric representation, or representational diversity is a common strategy for institutions, including Heritage, that want to improve their racial climates. Institutions that commit to increasing the number of underrepresented populations must also understand that structural diversity alone will not result in an improved campus climate. Improving the campus racial climate requires addressing beliefs and attitudes towards diversity, the campus climate, and communities of color. Institutions can address this by implementing systematic and comprehensive educational programs that address prejudice and bias while creating opportunities for cross-racial interaction (Hurtado et al., 1998). Heritage has committed to understanding diversity by requiring employees to participate in diversity education and training programs. The institution has also mandated that the mandatory introductory student course focus more on understanding diversity. Consequently, a new director was recently hired in the diversity division to focus on diversity education for faculty and staff. Further, the multicultural center will offer programs and events that educate and celebrate diversity and promote cross-racial interactions among students.

Improve Communication When Incidents of Bias and Hate Crimes Occur

As racist incidents happen on campus, institutions also contend with how to respond, especially when it's related to freedom of speech. When an individual or group on campus participates in hate speech that impacts another person or group on campus, institutions are pressured to address or not address the situation. Heritage has committed to communicating effectively when incidents occur that negatively impact populations on campus. The university president has sent multiple emails over the past few years emphasizing a culture of respect following hate-speech incidents while emphasizing that hate speech is not aligned with the values of the university. The email strategy has not been working at Heritage because the language is vague and typically does not explicitly specify the incidents in question. As a result, it is perceived that the administration does not care. An alternative strategy to address hate speech and incidents is to explicitly denounce the actions of offending parties. Some great examples include: 1) University of Oklahoma President David Boren tweeting his disgust with Sigma Alpha Epsilon's racists chants (OU Daily, 2015, p. 2); 2), Elon University President Leo Lambert's response to the executive order on immigration (Anderson, 2017); and 3), most recently, Indiana University's Executive Vice President and Provost Lauren Robel's response to a professor who uses his social media pages to disseminate bigotry (Indiana

University, 2019). These examples were explicit and transparent. University administrators "must respect the boundaries of the First Amendment protections while refraining from judging all attempts to discuss bias and diversity on campus through a legal lens" (Miller et al., 2018, p. 6). However, institutions can take a firm stand on bigotry while promoting dialogue around bias and committing to continuous education and training on free speech (Miller et al., 2018).

Seek Collaborative Change

Student protests had a large impact on diversity-related departments and programs. Prior to the early years of activism, the diversity office consisted of a chief diversity officer and an administrative assistant. Following the years of activism, the office has expanded to a full division of staff and multiple units reporting to the new Vice President for Inclusion. However, the chief responsibility for change has fallen on the diversity division. This will not lead to campus-wide change that is necessary. Shifting a campus' racial climate must be everyone's responsibility, not just those who work in DEI. Administrators should seek out the expertise of those in diversity work, but implementation must be collaborative.

CONCLUSION

"A campus racial crisis does not emerge in thin air. Such crises are embedded within the social, cultural, and political context of a given campus" (Kezar et al., 2018, p. 8). Racist incidents that occur on college campuses may be perceived as isolated incidents, but they derive from the institutional culture and larger society. Whatever happens nationally, regionally, and locally will have a ripple effect on higher-education institutions. The murders of Trayvon Martin, Eric Garner, and Michael Brown and the Black Lives Matter movement started a wave of activism at Heritage that was uncommon at our institution. However, the Alt-Right movement also became prominent and started another wave of hate and White supremacy. The ideology behind this movement rippled down to students at Heritage, where individuals and organizations on campus, mainly White, conducted harmful acts against students of color.

Institutions seeking to address a negative campus climate first need to understand the complexities of their campus climate and the impact of larger community and national issues. Improving a campus' racial climate is not an easy feat, and some challenges will take longer than others to resolve; however, with a clear understanding of the organizational and

234 CHERESE F. FINE ET AL.

social dynamics that may lead to failed DEI moments, and a commitment to respond swiftly and comprehensively, institutions will be more prepared to address any DEI crises.

DISCUSSION QUESTIONS

1. In your opinion, what microsystem, mesosystem, and exosystem factors prompted student activism at Heritage University?
2. In this case, both student activists and some perpetrators of bias incidents were protected by free speech. How can we reconcile free speech, and the protections it offers, while creating a safe environment, free of bigotry, for all students?
3. Communication to the campus community about bias incidents can prove challenging at times.
   a. How can universities better negotiate these challenges? What key themes should be addressed in such messages?
   b. In your current role, how can you partner with university leaders to communicate positive messages of belonging to students that may feel marginalized and/or are targets of bias and bigotry?
4. As you reflect on the "Lessons Learned" section of this chapter, discuss how Bronfenbrenner's social–ecological model can be used by administrators to respond to:
   a. General campus unrest
   b. Regional and national issues that trigger campus unrest
5. What strategies can you use in your role to assist your campus community in increasing intercultural competence and reducing racist incidents?
6. How can your institution's diversity and inclusion strategies be enhanced to be more proactive, rather than reactive, to student activism?

REFERENCES

Alimo, C. J. (2012). From dialogue to action: The impact of cross-race intergroup dialogue on the development of white college students as racial allies. *Equity & Excellence in Education, 45*(1), 36–59.

Anderson, D. (2017, January 29). Statement regarding the executive order on immigration [Statement]. Retrieved from https://www.elon.edu/u/news/2017/01/29/statement-regarding-the-executive-order-on-immigration/

THE RIPPLE EFFECT OF BIAS, HATE, AND ACTIVISM 235

Bronfenbrenner, U. (1979). *The ecology of human development: Experiments by nature and design*. Cambridge, MA: Harvard University Press.

Carter, R. T. (2007). Racism and psychological and emotional injury: Recognizing and assessing race-based traumatic stress. *The Counseling Psychologist*, 35(1), 13–105.

Cross, W. & Fhagen-Smith, P. (2001). Patterns of African American identity development: A life span perspective. In C. L. Wijeyesinghe & B. W. L. Jackson (Eds.) *New perspectives on racial identity development* (pp. 243–270). New York: University Press.

Equal Justice Initiative. (2013, November 1). Convict leasing. Equal Justice Initiative. Retrieved from https://eji.org/news/history-racial-injustice-convict-leasing/

Gallaudet University. (2019). History behind DPN: What happened... The issues. Retrieved from https://www.gallaudet.edu/about/history-and-traditions/deaf-president-now/the-issues/history-behind-dpn

Garza, A., Cullors, P., & Tometi, O. (2019). Herstory. Black Lives Matter. Retrieved from https://blacklivesmatter.com/herstory/

Grier-Reed, T. L. (2010). The African American student network: Creating sanctuaries and counterspaces for coping with racial microaggressions in higher education settings. *Journal of Humanistic Counseling, Education and Development*, 49, 181–188.

Gurin, P., Dey, E. L., Hurtado, S., & Gurin, G. (2002). Diversity and higher education: Theory and impact on educational outcomes. *Harvard Educational Review*, 72(3), 330–366.

Gurin, P., Nagda, B. A., & Lopez, G. E. (2004). The benefits of diversity in education for democratic citizenship. *Journal of Social Issues*, 60(1), 17–34.

History. (2018). Just say no. History. Retrieved from https://www.history.com/topics/1980s/just-say-no

Hollis, C. P. & Govan, I. M. (2015). *Diversity, equity, and inclusion: Strategies for facilitating conversations on race*. Lanham, MD: Rowman & Littlefied.

Hope, E. C., Gugwor, R., Riddick, K. N., & Pender, K. N. (2019). Engaged against the machine: Institutional and cultural racial discrimination and racial identity as predictors of activism orientation among Black youth. *American Journal of Community Psychology*, 63(1–2), 61–72.

Hope, E. C., Velez, G., Offidani-Bertrand, C., Keels, M., & Durkee, M. I. (2018). Political activism and mental health among Black and Latinx college students. *Cultural Diversity and Ethnic Minority Psychology*, 24(1), 26–39.

Hurtado, S., Milem, J. F., Clayton-Pedersen, A. R., & Allen, W. R. (1998). Enhancing campus climates for racial/ethnic diversity: Educational policy and practice. *The Review of Higher Education*, 21(3), 279–302.

Indiana University. (2019). On the first amendment [Statement]. Retrieved from https://provost.indiana.edu/statements/index.html

Kezar, A., Fries-Britt, S, Kurban, E., McGuire, D., & Wheaton, M. (2018). Speaking truth and acting with integrity: Confronting challenges of campus racial climate. Washington, DC: American Council on Education. Retrieved from https://www.acenet.edu/news-room/Pages/Speaking-Truth-and-Acting-with-Integrity.aspx

Kindig, J. (2008). Vietnam war: Student activism. Antiwar and Radical History Project – Pacific Northwest. Retrieved from https://depts.washington.edu/antiwar/vietnam_student.shtml

Leath, S. & Chavous, T. (2017). "We really protested": The influence of sociopolitical beliefs, political self-efficacy, and campus racial climate on civic engagement among Black college students attending predominantly white institutions. *The Journal of Negro Education*, 86(3), 220–237. doi:10.7709/jnegroeducation.86.3.0220

236 CHERESE F. FINE ET AL.

Linder, C., Quaye, S. J., Stewart, T. J., Okello, W. K., & Roberts, R. E. (2019). "The whole weight of the world on my shoulders": Power, identity, and student activism. *Journal of College Student Development,* 60(5), 527–542.

Logue, J. (2016). A Broader protest agenda. Inside Higher Education. Retrieved from https://www.insidehighered.com/news/2016/04/19/student-protests-year-broaden-beyondssissues-race

McMahon, J. (2019, November 22). Inside 10 days that shook Syracuse University: Fear, power, confusion and 'not again'. Syracuse University News. Retrieved from https://www.syracuse.com/syracuse-university/2019/11/inside-10-days-that-shook-syracuse-university-fear-power-confusion-and-not-again.html

Miller, M. E. (2015, November 6). Black grad student on hunger strike in MO. After swastika drawn with human feces. The Washington Post. Retrieved from https://www.washingtonpost.com/news/morning-mix/wp/2015/11/06/black-grad-student-on-hunger-strike-in-mo-after-swastika-drawn-with-human-feces/

Miller, R. A., Guida, T., Smith, S., Ferguson, S. K., & Medina, E. (2018). Free speech tensions: Responding to bias on college and university campuses. *Journal of Student Affairs Research and Practice,* 55(1), 27–39.

Moore, K. M. (1976). Freedom and constraint in eighteenth century Harvard. *The Journal of Higher Education,* 47(6), 649–659.

Oliha-Donaldson, H. (2018). Let's talk: An exploration into student discourse about diversity and the implications for intercultural competence. *Howard Journal of Communications,* 29(2), 126–143.

OU Daily. (2015, March 19). President David Boren releases full statement on Sigma Alpha Epsilon incident. OU Daily. Retrieved from http://www.oudaily.com/news/president-david-boren-releases-full-statement-on-sigma-alpha-epsilon/article_02b02ee2-c667-11e4-903d-4fdd71bf61d2.html

Pope, R. L., & Reynolds, A. L. (1997). Student affairs core competencies: Integrating multicultural awareness, knowledge, and skills. *Journal of College Student Development,* 38, 266–277.

Rogers, I. H. (2012). *The Black campus movement: Black students and the racial reconstruction of higher education, 1965–1972.* New York: Palgrave Macmillan.

Rousmaniere, J. P. (1970). Cultural hybrid in the slums: The college woman and the settlement house, 1889–1894. *American Quarterly,* 22(1), 45–66.

Schoenfeld, H. A. (2012). The war on drugs, the politics of crime, and mass incarceration in the United States. *Journal of Gender, Race and Justice,* 15, 315–352.

Smith, W. A. (2008). Higher education: Racial battle fatigue. In R. T. Schaefer (Ed.), *Encyclopedia of race, ethnicity, and society* (pp. 615–618). Thousand Oaks, CA: Sage.

Solorzano, D., Ceja, M., & Yosso, T. (2000). Critical race theory, racial microaggressions, and campus racial climate: The experiences of African-American college students. *The Journal of Negro Education,* 69, 60–73.

Steil, Jr, G. & Gibbons-Carr, M. (2005). Large group scenario planning: Scenario planning with the whole system in the room. *The Journal of Applied Behavioral Science,* 41(1), 15–29.

Straus, V. (2011, September 16). Enrollments surge at historically black colleges amid rise in racial tensions. The Washington Post. Retrieved from https://www.washingtonpost.com/news/answer-sheet/wp/2016/09/11/enrollments-surge-at-historically-black-colleges-amid-rise-in-racial-tensions/

Szymanski, D. M. (2012). Racist events and individual coping styles as predictors of African American activism. *Journal of Black Psychology,* 38(3), 342–367. doi:10.1177/0095798411424744

Tugend, A. (2019, February 21). Seeking a haven in H.B.C.U.s and single-sex colleges. The New York Times. Retrieved from https://www.nytimes.com/2019/02/21/education/learning/hbcu-womens-colleges-haven.html

Turner, K. B., Giacopassi, D., & Vandiver, M. (2006). Ignoring the past: Coverage of slavery and slave patrols in criminal justice texts. *Journal of Criminal Justice Education, 17*(1), 181–195.

University of California, Berkeley. (2019). Visual history: Free speech movement, 1964. Free Speech Movement. Retrieved from https://fsm.berkeley.edu/free-speech-movement-timeline/

University of Michigan. (2019). Campus anti-apartheid movements intensify after Soweto. Divestment for humanity: The anti-apartheid movement at the University of Michigan. Retrieved from http://michiganintheworld.history.lsa.umich.edu/antiapartheid/exhibits/show/exhibit/origins/movement_on_college_campuses

Weinberg, J. (1990). Students and civil rights in the 1960s. *History of Education Quarterly, 30*(2), 212–224.

White-Johnson, R. L. (2012). Prosocial involvement among African American young adults: Considering racial discrimination and racial identity. *Journal of Black Psychology, 38*(3), 313–341. doi:10.1177/0095798411420429

Williams, D. (2007). Achieving inclusive excellence: Strategies for creating real and sustainable change in quality and diversity. *About Campus, 12*(1), 8–14.

Williams, J. (2018, June 27). Black students, college choice and HBCUs: Enrolling the next generation. Diverse Issues in Higher Education. Retrieved from https://diverseeducation.com/article/118831/

PART VII

CONCLUSION

IV   XVII

                                      CONCLUSION

Chapter 15

Dealing with the Past and Preparing for "Diversity's" Future: "Wicked" Problems and Multilevel Solutions for Higher Education

Hannah Oliha-Donaldson

There are questions for which a "yes" or "no" will do, and then there are questions that require a more intricate, well-reasoned, and thorough response. This text illustrates that the problems of diversity require an answer. In search of quick and actionable responses, many institutions have attempted to "solve" the "diversity problem" with agendas, programs, figureheads, conferences, and trainings, yet the problems remain. A quick review of institutional mission statements suggests that certain key words and ideas come up as institutions discursively define their identity (e.g., just, democratic, inclusive, multicultural, free of prejudice, committed to respecting the dignity and rights of others), yet it is clear that many institutions are falling short of their mission.

Reflective of this, many studies have been conducted illuminating the diverse ways that underrepresented and marginalized groups continue to struggle in higher education. There is research and data that speak to the disparities in educational attainment between majority students (e.g. race, gender, and class, for example) and their underrepresented counterparts (Bauman et al., 2005; "Indicators of Equity," 2015; Franklin, 2016; Snyder & Dillow, 2010; U.S. Census Bureau, 2010). Countless studies have been conducted on the effects of campus racial climate, stereotypes, racial microaggressions, and racial trauma on students (Fischer, 2010; Greer & Brown, 2011; Harris et al., 2019; Henry et al., 2011; Houshmand et al., 2014). Franklin (2016), for example, noted that "there is a cumulative effect of racial microaggressions that stress the psychological, physiological, and academic success of students of color" (p. 46). Over the last three decades,

242 HANNAH OLIHA-DONALDSON

innumerable studies and papers have addressed barriers to success for historically marginalized and underrepresented faculty (Oliha-Donaldson, 2018; Turner & Myers, 2000; Villalpando & Bernal, 2002; Shahjahan & Barker, 2009) and students (Anderson et al., 2013; Agnew et al., 2008; Cerezo et al., 2013; Farrell & Jones, 1988; Hernandez & Lopez, 2007; Jones, Castellanos, & Cole, 2002; Kim, 2009; Lunneborg & Lunneborg, 1985; Pyne & Means, 2013; Spaights et al., 1985). Also, studies and reports have addressed issues of belonging and alienation for historically marginalized and underrepresented persons (Loo & Rolison, 1986; Nora, 2004; Stebleton et al., 2014; Williams et al., 2005).

I could go on; indeed, if I wanted to, this chapter would be filled with citations of studies exploring the experiences of those historically underrepresented and marginalized in higher education. Unfortunately, many of the studies and reports reveal that we are failing in our mission. As discussed in the first chapter of this volume, decades ago President Truman realized that education was a human right and a critical tool for advancing democratic ideals and a free society, yet he acknowledged that segregation, prejudice, and discrimination were critical barriers to experiencing this most essential right. He asserted even then:

> If the ladder of educational opportunity rises high at the doors of some youth and scarcely rises at the doors of others, then education may become the means, not of eliminating race and class distinctions, but of deepening and solidifying them.
> (President Truman, as cited in Indicators of Equity, 2015, p. 7).

The same holds true for underrepresented faculty, staff, and administrators. If opportunity accrues to some and not others along identity lines, and if some bodies are more welcome than others (Ahmed, 2012), we remain far from our realization of a free and just society. The critical implication will be a fundamental fracture in our capacity to self-actualize as a community.

While it is clear that more work needs to be done in areas of social justice and equity in higher education, critics of diversity, which is the chief organizational framework chosen by U.S. institutions to address these issues, claim that valorizing group-based rights, social group identities, and cultural norms and practices "undermines national unity and stands in opposition to core American ideals of individual freedom and equality." (Bell & Hartman, 2007, p. 896). What is ironic is that the racial and gendered "center" (Bell & Hartmann, 2007; DiAngelo, 2011; Mohanty, 1984) that is spoken of so clearly in the literature, and that often articulates these "core" ideals, is built on a foundation of group rights, privileges, and identity.

So it is clear, as narratives in this volume illustrate, that we are in need of complex answers to the critical diversity, equity, and inclusion (DEI) challenges facing higher education today. Rittel and Webber (1973), while exploring the challenges of urban planning, presented the idea that social problems are "wicked" problems. In contrast to the natural sciences that deals with definable, bounded, and "tame" problems (Rittel & Webber, 1973), with solutions that can be easily apprehended, the world of social sciences deals with "malignant," tricky, vicious problems that resist definition, are difficult to grasp and nail down, are never truly solved, only "re-solved" (Rittel & Webber, 1973, p. 160), and are unpredictable and boundless. Further, one can never fully know the long-term effects of potential solutions. In fact, one should expect that solutions to a wicked problem may pose their own problems over an extended period of time. Wicked problems require an in-depth and thorough understanding of possible solutions, and to understand a wicked problem, one must understand its context. Every solution is "consequential" because it "leaves [a] 'trace' that cannot be undone" (Rittel & Webber, 1973, p. 163). Importantly, there are different types of wicked problems that vary in their degree of "wicked-ness" (Rittel & Webber, 1973; see also Alford & Head, 2017; Trickett, 2019), but the potential of a problem to grow increasingly complex, and to be understood and defined differently by different people, leading to multiple and possibly competing solutions, holds true.

DEI challenges in higher education are "wicked" problems. They are complex, difficult to grasp and nail down, resist easy solutions, and are tied to such complex processes (e.g., racism, sexism, classism) that they can never be truly solved, only ever re-solved. They can be addressed for a time, but may shape-shift, requiring new solutions. DEI problems require contextual knowledge to resolve them and a deep understanding of potential solutions and possible effects (for these effects will most likely need to be managed). Finally, they require engagement from multiple stakeholders to gain a deeper understanding of the problem, land on possible solutions, and see and prepare for unanticipated challenges that may arise as a result of solutions.

One example of this is the emerging practice of requiring faculty to provide a personal diversity statement at some institutions (Brown, 2019). The idea is that by requiring new potential hires to do so, one can begin to see how candidates can support the institutional mission with regards to diversity. While this is good in principle, there is fear that these statements may be used to penalize faculty in the long-run and may become permanent records in a faculty member's files that could have unforeseen consequences. So while dissenters claim it is a violation of academic freedom, supporters hail it as a "critical scholarly document" (Brown, 2019) centering diversity in educational practice.

As an example of a wicked DEI problem, I argue that a critical analysis of this practice should involve diverse stakeholders to both review and craft the

244 HANNAH OLIHA-DONALDSON

parameters of its use. Further, it should be expected that given the diversity of tenure and promotion requirements and the differences between research and teaching schools, parameters must differ across organizations, necessitating a localized, contextualized protocol. This elementary example illustrates but a few of the challenges of implementing DEI "solutions."

The framing of DEI problems as "wicked" promotes a collaborative, creative, and systematic approach to problem-solving. In short, it underscores the necessity of a multilevel understanding of contributing factors to the problem, "including how persistent structural contributions such as poverty, racism, sexism, and homophobia are reflected in and contribute to the "wickedness" of DEI issues in higher education" (Trickett, 2019, p. 205).

APPLICATION OF MULTILEVEL THINKING AS A PERSPECTIVAL LENS IN ADDRESSING DEI CHALLENGES

Popularized in the mid-1960s to early-1970s, the social ecological perspective was framed by Bronfenbrenner (1977; see also Rosa & Tudge, 2013) as a way to understand the complex processes between an individual and their environment. It was presented as a way to understand human development and the many social factors impacting growth (Bronfenbrenner, 1977, 1979; Stokols, 1996). By providing a richer understanding of the person–environment dynamic, it advanced the notion that humans do not merely exist in space and time, but are *shaped* by space and time. While Bronfenbrenner presented "it as a theory of human development, from the start the developing individual was consistently viewed as influencing, and being influenced by the environment" (Rosa & Tudge, 2013, p. 224; Oetzel & Ting-Toomey, 2013). At a foundational level, this framework calls for an examination of the contexts and settings that impact people as a necessary precursor for understanding lived experience (Flynn et al., 2011). Importantly, multilevel theorizing draws on principles of systems thinking through its focus on hierarchy and interdependence (Rousseau & House, 1994). It offers a window for grasping the interrelatedness of personal and social issues, and for developing a nuanced understanding of social phenomena (Rousseau, 2011).

As an interdisciplinary framework, it has been used by scholars in various disciplines, including, but not limited to, human development, social psychology, community health, and organizational behavior (Rosa & Tudge, 2013; Rousseau & House, 1994; Rousseau, 2011). In education, it has been used to offer an ecological analysis of research examining the experiences of graduate students of color (Flynn et al., 2011). Flynn et al. (2011) suggested that microsystemic analysis will offer a deeper understanding of this group.

WICKED PROBLEMS, MULTILEVEL SOLUTIONS **245**

It has been used in diverse ways in the communication discipline, but notably to advance the utility of systems thinking in constructing a complex understanding of intercultural conflict and culture-based ethical problems. It was mobilized by Oetzel et al. (2007) to advance a vision of intercultural conflict negotiation. They centered multilevel theorizing as a strategic tool necessary for constructing a complex and coherent picture of what is happening when conflict manifests across cultural differences.

Dorjee et al. (2013) used the social ecological framework to interrogate the critical issues embedded in the moral dimensions of an intercultural conflict. They addressed how a multilayered and context-sensitive analysis reveals the factors sanctioning cultural practices that may be deemed appropriate in some cultures and reprehensible in others. Finally, Ting-Toomey (2011) presented multilevel analysis as a useful strategy for understanding intercultural ethical dilemmas. The key claim made by these scholars is that conflict and intercultural ethical challenges do not just happen, but manifest within a rich web of co-creation that includes the individual and their personally held beliefs, immediate relationships impacting the individual, and organizational, community, and sociocultural factors.

Bronfenbrenner (1979) introduced four levels of analysis necessary for understanding the causal relationships between a person and their environment. The "macro-level" calls for an analysis of the overarching history, ideologies, beliefs, and values impacting organizations and organizational members (Bronfenbrenner, 1979). The "exo-level" reviews the impact of local institutions (Bronfenbrenner, 1979) and the effects of "their formal procedures or policies on individuals' reactions and actions" (Dorjee et al., 2013, p. 7). This level typically does not have direct impact on the individual, but may impact experience at micro and meso levels, and may have implications at macro levels.

The "meso-level" requires the analysis of immediate groups that directly impact us (e.g., informal community groups, friendship circles, and family) and organizations (workplace, etc.). The "micro-level" requires the exploration of intrapersonal (e.g., identity, personality, and personal sensemaking processes) and interpersonal factors (e.g. one-on-one interactions with others and their effects). Together, these levels represent a "nested arrangement of structures, each contained within the next" (Bronfenbrenner, 1979, p. 514), capturing again, the idea of multilevel effects and mutual impact.

Core Principles

The social ecological perspective, as theory and method, offers a perspective and roadmap for analyzing and seeking solutions to pressing DEI issues in higher education. Its application rests on a number of principles

246 HANNAH OLIHA-DONALDSON

advanced by Stokols (1996) in his paper, "Translating Social Ecological Theory into Guidelines for Community Health Promotion."

First, *a social ecological perspective calls for the examination of the collective impact of numerous environmental factors* implicated in an organizational diversity challenge, and that may be impacting the organizational context, and the emotional, physical, and social well-being (Stokols, 1996) of organizational members. These include: (1) macro considerations such as history, cultural values and beliefs, ideology, and worldview; (2) social factors; and (3) localized contextual factors in spaces of direct influence. In the narratives presented in this text, we see the impact of history and societal ruptures on student activism, for example.

Second, *personality and personal characteristics, choices, beliefs, and actions also matter and may impact personal outcomes* and the organization itself. Imagine an organization desiring its faculty to become representative of the larger community. This organization would most likely initiate a rash of faculty hires—probably without due consideration for organizational climate and its potential impact on new organizational members. It goes without saying that those "uncomfortable" with the operationalization of diversity as difference may not be so welcoming of the new hires. Believing that these new faculty will "water" down the curriculum with unnecessary content geared at making the "diverse" "feel included" (see "The Court," 1999, p. 19), and infiltrate the discipline with their "sub-standard" work that "nobody wants to read" (these sentiments were expressed in an article that shall remain nameless, so as not to legitimize these ideas or their holder), they will react accordingly. These resistant faculty members may create an uncomfortable atmosphere for colleagues deemed "diverse" and different from the "normal" and accepted colleague. If enough organizational members behave this way (avoiding new hires around the department, shutting them down at faculty meetings, or outright ignoring them) (see Williams, 2018), the atmosphere would become decidedly "chilly" (see Newkirk, 2019) for the new hires.

Third, a social ecological perspective employs principles of systems theory such as interdependence and negative feedback (Stokols, 1996): *social ecology requires a necessary emphasis on the interrelatedness of personal and contextual factors* (Stokols, 1996; see Oetzel & Ting-Toomey, 2013). Bronfenbrenner (1979) viewed the many layers of the model as Russian nesting dolls—each layer fits neatly into the other. Environment and context matter (effect of environment on individual), as do personal beliefs, choices, and actions (how we engage with our environment and those in it). Both of these factors are locked in a dynamic web of co-creation.

For example, one cannot only focus on personal behavior to understand the pressure points and hidden institutional roadblocks impacting women in higher education (although personal action and choices do matter!).

To tell a female assistant professor that is covertly left out of the informal social network in her department (Williams, 2018), feels as if tenure standards are unclear and at times shifting (typically in conversations about her chances of promotion), or perceives that some colleagues find her an unwelcome addition, that she must "try harder," is to reify the very conditions delimiting her success, with an implied claim that she must work harder (than her male counterparts, possibly) to succeed (Gallimore, 2019; Williams, 2018).

Fourth, *environmental factors are interconnected and interdependent* (Stokols, 1996; see also Oetzel & Ting-Toomey, 2013). Each layer is activated by the principle of reciprocal causation (see Oetzel & Ting-Toomey, 2013). What happens at the cultural level (macro) may very well impact what happens at the organizational level (meso), and vice versa (Stokols, 1996). We must account for "interdependencies that exist among immediate and more distant environments" (Stokols, 1996, p. 286) leading to "spill over" and "ripple effects." Certainly, a number of narratives in this volume illustrate the personal and organizational impact of these "ripple effects." Also, in 2015–2016, when news media were set ablaze with reports of student protests across the nation, the ripple effect was felt at the organizational level. It was as if the floodgates were opened to a new possibility. There was a bandwagon effect, as it were, and student groups, moved by news coverage of instances of microaggressions and inequality across the nation were activated into action and made lists of equality demands at various institutions (see Bakera & Blissett, 2018; "Embracing Campus," 2016).

Finally, *a multilevel framework is "inherently interdisciplinary"* (Stokols, 1996, p. 286). Functionally, this principle calls for creative problem-solving, cooperation among groups and individuals, and the understanding that one size does not fit all, and different departments within the same institution may need different protocols for success. The assumed one-size-fits-all model does not work when dealing with complex person and group organizational issues such as the inequities and lack of belonging experienced by organizational members that are minoritized because of gender, ability, LGBTQ status, national origin, race, religion, and social class (Trickett, 2019).

A multilevel perspective can be difficult to apply given the complex level of interrogation called for and the overwhelming amount of relevant information and concepts that may emerge (Oetzel et al., 2007). Also, nailing down the necessary scope of analysis may prove challenging, and the endeavor may be time-consuming or may uncover other unanticipated issues. Yet while a multilevel approach to organizational problem-solving can be complex, complex DEI challenges facing higher education institutions call for sophisticated solutions.

Application of Multilevel Thinking to Emerging Diversity, Equity, and Inclusion Challenges in Higher Education

Social ecology can be viewed as a set of principles, an overarching framework (Stokols, 1996), a perspective, or even a model (Adserias, 2017; Ahmed, 2012; Ahonen et al., 2014; Bell & Hartmann, 2007; Trickett, 2019; Newkirk, 2019). Further, it can provide "a cognitive map" or "way of thinking" about (Trickett, 2019, p. 207) an organization and its members. Therefore, in the context of this volume, multilevel thinking is mobilized as a worldview, a perspective, and a way of thinking about, analyzing, and addressing DEI issues. Organizational development scholars like Rousseau (2011) have asserted that we must think about organizational phenomena from a systems level by analyzing the impact of multiple levels. This allows us to develop a robust understanding of key issues, challenges, and possibilities. The goal is uncovering, as much as possible, the likely individual, interpersonal, organizational, community, historical, and ideological forces impacting organizational experience and organizational formations (e.g., climate, culture, policy, practice).

As higher education institutions are faced with increasingly complex DEI challenges, nuanced problem-solving strategies and solutions are necessary, and a social ecological perspective could help institutions understand the "interrelations among diverse personal and environmental factors" implicated in organizational "health and illness" (Stokols, 1996, p. 283). With this clearer picture of key issues and challenges, institutions can begin to proactively remedy, with detailed and contextual information, pressing DEI challenges. While Stokols made this statement with regard to human health and illness, it certainly applies to organizations that can sometimes feel like diseased bodies in need of strong medicine. I propose that a multilevel perspective applied to understanding and resolving DEI challenges is not only good, but necessary medicine for contemporary organizations dealing with the ebbs and flows of increased diversification and globalization (Smith, 2009).

A multilevel framework like social ecology is particularly useful for addressing DEI issues in higher education for a number of reasons:

- It reveals consistencies and inconsistencies of organizational problems (Oetzel & Ting-Toomey, 2013).
- It reveals the many factors that may be shaping personal worldview and organizational framing of key issues.
- Because of the different layers of analysis, a multilevel perspective creates "a rich tapestry of the phenomenon under study" (Ting-Toomey, 2011, p. 21).

- Multilevel problem-solving allows one to understand deeply held assumptions (Ting-Toomey, 2011) that may be hidden from view in everyday practice.
- A rich, nuanced interrogation of phenomena both one level up and down (Rousseau, 2011; Stokols, 1996) may potentially reveal the complicated organizational and personal ideological frameworks implicated in organizational challenges.
- It offers a layered, and hence, nuanced understanding of factors shaping organizational and individual outcomes: (1) personal values and beliefs; (2) interpersonal factors; (3) organizational practices; (4) community factors and issues; and (5) social, cultural, political, economic, and ideological factors.
- It offers a rich understanding of how "individual meaning, workplace meaning, community meaning, and socio-cultural meanings shape our expectations, intentions, viewpoints, and decisions" (Ting-Toomey, 2011, p. 29), shaping organizational behavior and outcomes.
- Multilevel analyses can help higher education professionals understand why some departments succeed and others struggle or fail.

Higher education spaces can no longer be seen as merely the background within which DEI issues manifest, but multilevel thinking invites us to frame these spaces as constituted by various levels of context (interpersonal, organizational, community, and sociocultural) that are bound in a matrix of cause and effects.

By highlighting the systemic and cooperative connection between individual and larger organizational policies and practices, this framework posits that DEI issues do not just happen, but manifest within an interlocking web of causation. As such, change must also be actualized through this interlocking web of causation, with clear understanding that it does not occur through one office and one person's actions (read diversity officer; see also Mangan, 2019; Newkirk, 2019), but rather through an ongoing personal and systemic commitment to diversity, equity, and inclusion (Adserias et al., 2017). Problematic institutional spaces do not merely exist or happen, they are socially constructed through instrumental action, maintained by organizational policies and practices, and influenced by sociocultural contexts. In the same way, transformational organizations (Adserias et al., 2017) do not just come about; they too require instrumental action and focused review and action that is process-centered and comprehensive.

PROMISING PRACTICES FOR CHANGE: BUILDING A BRIDGE OVER TROUBLED WATERS

The narratives in this volume illuminate a number of the pressing DEI issues facing higher education today. They illustrate why comprehensive solutions are needed for complex organizational spaces like higher education. Further, this text reveals that despite the many gains made since the Truman era Commission on Higher Education and the civil rights era, there is still unfinished social justice business, the problems of diversity remain, and answers are still elusive. In the upcoming section, I argue that change is possible, but to achieve this goal, there are foundational claims around which we must build: (1) second-order transformational changes are needed to shift problematically raced, classed, and gendered institutions; (2) to achieve second-order change, our efforts must be grounded in history and our solutions must seek to remedy and undo the effects of oppressive systems like racism and sexism; (3) we must move from an emphasis on "diversity talk" to "diversity work," which must center the destabilization of power, historical inequities, and oppressive institutional practices; (4) second-order change requires systems thinking; and (5) we must *all* be engaged in the "the work."

Second-Order Transformational Change

Complex DEI issues, which are "wicked" problems, warrant second-order transformational change (Trickett, 2019). First-order changes represent minor adjustments, shifts, and improvements (Adserias et al., 2017). They are superficial band-aid efforts that do not change an institution or its direction. First-order change does not touch an institution's core in any way, leaving the institution foundationally and functionally unchanged.

Conversely, second-order change functionally changes an institution, impacting its overarching mission, underlying values, daily processes, and organizational structure. Second-order change reflects transformational change, which requires the letting go of institutional norms, mores, processes, and practices that are problematic. Transformational change then, transforms an institution at its very core.

Complex DEI issues will not respond to first-order change. In fact, higher education is littered with such programs and practices, yet equity challenges remain. Institutions must commit to second-order change and must accept that such changes won't just happen. I posit that the work can be done using a multilevel approach to achieve second-order transformational change.

Reconnecting to History: Centering Social Justice and Resisting Inequity and Power

Ahonen et al. (2014) claim that practices constituting diversity research—and I am adding practice—do not sufficiently attend to the effects of context and power. Moreover, reflecting on power and context would "enable the taken-for-granted assumptions of diversity and its management to surface and allow diversity research [and practice] to break through its current impasse" (Ahonen et al., 2014, p. 2). Therefore, DEI's connection to issues of inequity and power must be central in policy-making and change-making in higher education. Decontextualizing diversity talk and work and disavowing its historical roots in social justice movements must be resisted if institutions will effectively respond to chronic disparities and inequities. This obfuscates the need to center historically marginalized groups. Until the playing field is truly level, calling back to history and reviewing its contemporary effects—on access, opportunity, and experience—must remain an essential part of DEI practice. Ongoing efforts to sanitize (Bell & Hartman, 2019) and "manage" diversity, while minimizing issues of power, privilege, and context must be challenged. As the contributors in this volume illustrate, DEI will not fix complex social justice problems, only solutions that destabilize and undo the effects of racism, sexism, xenophobia, and homophobia. Naming the problem is essential to finding solutions (Bernstein, 2016, p. 33).

Framing Diversity as More Than Representation

Similarly, efforts to reduce diversity to mere representation without centering the moral exigency of social justice, equity, and inclusion must be challenged. Diversity talk, and in particular, diversity practices, without the consideration of power, inequity, and institutional oppression are superficial at best and a profound waste of institutional resources at worst. Without an emphasis on equity and inclusion, problematic institutional cultures and climates go untouched. By default, historically marginalized groups will continue to cope with a problematic status quo.

A Multilevel Perspective Is Essential to Resolving Complex DEI Issues

Twenty-first century institutions must harness multilevel thinking to thrive in an increasingly complex globalized world. Further, complex problems require complex solutions. By implying "reciprocal causation between the individual and the environment," social ecology offers a sophisticated framework for understanding and addressing DEI issues (McLeroy et al.,

252 HANNAH OLIHA-DONALDSON

1988, p. 354). Understanding the context of an organization and the person–context causal relationship positions one to understand human behavior, policy, and practice in that context. Without this necessary knowledge, our understanding will be limited, superficial, and rudimentary, and our problem-solving capacity stunted (Flynn et al., 2011; Rousseau & House, 1994; Rousseau, 2011).

To address some of the challenges of utilizing a social ecological perspective (e.g., time-consuming and expensive), it is good practice to explore issues by going one level up and down. Specifically, consider what may be happening one level up and down when addressing DEI challenges. This ensures that at least two contexts are examined, offering a far richer view of an issue than a single level analysis (Rousseau, 2011; see also Oetzel et al., 2006; Oetzel et al., 2007; Rousseau & House, 1994).

Burying the Dead: DEI Issues Aren't Just "People of Color/Minority People Problems"

We must actively seek to depoliticize diversity efforts and make it "our" work, rather than "their" work (see Ahmed, 2012). A number of the narratives in this volume illustrate how people of color are disproportionately called on to be change agents and standard-bearers (often in name only and with no, or limited, institutional resources).

For decades, dominant thinking was that only "those most impacted" or "diversity workers" (see Ahmed, 2012) must labor for inclusion and equity in higher education. This thinking is reflected in the hours of unpaid and unseen labor expected of those considered "diverse," who are often called on to speak for and work towards DEI in their respective units, campus-wide, and even in their local communities when their bodies are seen as a (un)welcome interruption of racial, gender, and religious homogeneity, among others. Additionally, this dominant thinking is seen through the high turnover and burnout among diversity laborers, who are forced to carry the brunt of the weight of an institution's DEI efforts on their shoulders through programming, changing minds, and fostering a campus climate conducive to the recruitment and retention of underserved and historically marginalized populations.

CONCLUSION

Higher education spaces can no longer be seen as merely the background within which DEI issues manifest, but multilevel thinking invites us to frame these spaces as constituted by various levels of context (interpersonal, organizational, community, and sociocultural). As such, organizational context, cooperatively with interpersonal, community, and sociocultural factors, must become the focus of our understanding. Further, as DEI challenges

WICKED PROBLEMS, MULTILEVEL SOLUTIONS **253**

are social problems with a complex structure, problem-solving must engage a multilevel worldview and approach to strategic action. For example, as we seek to positively impact interpersonal dynamics among social groups, we must note that those dynamics do not occur in a vacuum; rather, they occur in a complex system of cooperative and interlocking dimensions. We must see that problematic interpersonal dynamics are symptomatic of the contexts in which they occur, even as they constitute those same contexts through a complex process of reproduction and reification (making intangible and abstract ideas like race and patriarchy material). An ecology of DEI theorizing and problem-solving in higher education is a necessary next step if we are to achieve the democratic ideals central to fulfilling the social justice and equity mandates of the civil rights movement.

Here is the question facing higher education institutions today: how do we become the institutions we profess to be? Obviously, this is not a "yes" or "no" question; however, it is also not a "representational," "diversity dean," "diversity hire," "diversity statement," "diversity council," or "quick diversity training" type of question either. The answer to this question will require intricate, well-reasoned, and thorough solutions.

DISCUSSION QUESTIONS

1. How can a multilevel perspective enhance DEI problem-solving at your institution? In your department/unit?
2. How can a multilevel perspective improve outcomes for historically marginalized groups at your institution?
3. In what ways could a "wicked problems" perspective shift dialogue about DEI challenges at your institution and shape problem-solving?
4. List three "wicked" DEI problems facing your unit/department. How can your unit/department use a multilevel perspective to address these problems?
5. Who is responsible for leading DEI change at your institution? In your unit/department? In your opinion, do they have the resources they need to implement second-order changes?
6. What might second-order DEI changes look like at your institution?

REFERENCES

Ahmed, S. (2012). *On being included: Racism and diversity in institutional life*. Durham, NC: Duke University Press.

Adserias, R. P., Charleston, L. J., & Jackson, J. F. L. (2017). What style of leadership is best suited to direct organizational change to fuel institutional diversity in higher education? *Race Ethnicity and Education*, 20(3), 315–331. DOI: 10.1080/13613324.2016.1260233

254 HANNAH OLIHA-DONALDSON

Ahonen, P., Tienari, J., Meriläinen, S., & Pullen, A. (2014). Hidden contexts and invisible power relations: A Foucauldian reading of diversity research. *Human Relations*, 67(3), 263–286. DOI: 10.1177/0018726713491772

Alford, J., & Head, B. W. (2017). Wicked and less wicked problems: A typology and a contingency framework. *Policy and Society*, 36(3), 397–413. DOI: 10.1080/14494035.2017.1361634

Anderson, K., Varghese, F. P., Trower, E., Sandlin, L., & Norwood, N. (2013). Perceptions of African American college applicants: The roles of race, criminal history, and qualifications. *Race and Social Problems*, 5(3), 157–172.

Agnew, M., Mertzman, T., Longwell-Grice, H., & Saffold, F. (2008). Who's in, who's out: Examining race, gender and the cohort community. *Journal of Diversity in Higher Education*, 1(1), 20–32.

Bakera, D. J., & Blissett, R. S. L. (2018). Beyond the incident: Institutional predictors of student collective action. *The Journal of Higher Education*, 89(2), 184–207. https://doi.org/10.1080/00221546.2017.1368815

Bauman, G. L., Bustillos, L. T., Bensimon, E. M., Brown II, M. C., & Bartee, R. D. (2005). *Achieving equitable education outcomes with all students: The institution's roles and responsibilities.* [Online]. Washington, DC: Association of American Colleges and Universities. https://www.aacu.org/sites/default/files/files/mei/bauman_et_al.pdf

Bell, J. M., & Hartmann, D. (2007). Diversity in everyday discourse: The cultural ambiguities and consequences of "happy talk". *American Sociological Review*, 72, 895–914.

Bernstein, A. R. (2016). Addressing diversity and inclusion on college campuses: Assessing a partnership between AAC&U and the Ford Foundation. *Liberal Education*, 102(2). https://www.aacu.org/liberaleducation/2016/spring/bernstein

Bronfenbrenner, U. (1977). Toward an experimental ecology of human development. *American Psychologist*, 32, 513–531.

Bronfenbrenner, U. (1979). *The ecology of human development.* Cambridge, MA: Harvard University Press.

Brown, S. (2019). UNC'S chancellor was criticized as a consensus builder. How she departed may have changed everything. *Chronicle of Higher Education*. https://www.chronicle.com/article/UNC-s-Chancellor-Was/245482

Cerezo, A., Lyda, J., Beristianos, M., Enriquez, A., & Connor, M. (2013). Latino men in college: Giving voice to their struggles and triumphs. *Psychology of Men & Masculinity*, 14(4), 352–362.

The Court of Public Opinion: The Ford Foundation campus diversity initiative survey of voters on diversity in education and an interview with Edgar Beckham (1999). *Equity & Excellence*, 32(2), 17–23. DOI: 10.1080/1066568990320204.

DiAngelo, R. (2011). White fragility. *International Journal of Critical Pedagogy*, 3(3), 54–70.

Dorjee, T., Baig, N., & Ting-Toomey, S. (2013). A social ecological perspective in understanding "honor killing": An intercultural moral dilemma. *Journal of Intercultural Communication Research*, 42(1), 1–21.

University Business. (2016). Embracing campus diversity and addressing racial unrest: How higher ed can take the lead in confronting this modern civil rights issue, *UniversityBusiness*.https://universitybusiness.com/embracing-campus-diversity-and-addressing-racial-unrest/

Farrell, W. C., & Jones, C. K. (1988). Recent racial incidents in higher education: A preliminary perspective. *The Urban Review*, 20(3), 211–226.

WICKED PROBLEMS, MULTILEVEL SOLUTIONS 255

Fischer, M. J. (2010). *A longitudinal examination of the role of stereotype threat and racial climate on college outcomes for minorities at elite institutions.* Germany: Springer.

Franklin, J. D. (2016). Racial microaggressions, racial battle fatigue, and racism-related stress in higher education. *Journal of Student Affairs - NYU,* 12(1), 44–55.

Flynn, A. M., Sanchez, B., & Harper, G. W. (2011). An ecological analysis of research examining the experiences of students of color in graduate school. *Journal of Diversity in Higher Education,* 4(1), 1–11.

Gallimore, A. D. (2019). An engineering school with half of its leadership female? How did that happen? *The Chronicle of Higher Education.* https://www.chronicle.com/article/An-Engineering-School-With/246214

Greer, T. M., & Brown, P. (2011). Minority status stress and coping processes among African American college students. *Journal of Diversity in Higher Education,* 4(1), 26–38.

Harris, T. M., Janovec, A., Murray, S., Gubbala, S., & Robinson, A. (2019). Communicating racism: A study of racial microaggressions in a southern university and the local community. *Southern Communication Journal,* 84(2), 72–84. https://doi.org/10.1080/1041794X.2018.1492008

Henry, W. J., Butler, D. M., & West, N. M. (2011). Things are not as rosy as they seem: Psychosocial issues of contemporary black college women. *Journal of College Student Retention: Research, Theory and Practice,* 13(2), 137–153.

Hernandez, J. C., & Lopez, M. A. (2007). Leaking pipeline: Issues impacting Latino/a college student retention. In A. Seidman (Ed.), *Minority student retention* (pp. 99–122). Amityville, New York, NY: Baywood.

Houshmand, S., Spanierman, L. B., & Tafarodi, R. W. (2014). Excluded and avoided: Racial microaggressions targeting Asian international students in Canada. *Cultural Diversity and Ethnic Minority Psychology,* 20(3), 377–388.

Indicators of Equity (2015). The Pell Institute. http://pellinstitute.org/downloads/publications-Indicators_of_Higher_Education_Equity_in_the_US_2019_Historical_Trend_Report.pdf

Jones, L., Castellanos, J., & Cole, D. (2002). Examining the ethnic minority student experience at predominantly white institutions: A case study. *Journal of Hispanic Higher Education,* 1(1), 19–39.

Kelly, D. G. (2009). *Diversity's promise for higher education: Making it work.* Baltimore, MD: The Johns Hopkins University Press.

Kim, E. (2009). Navigating college life: The role of student networks in first year adaptation college adaptation experience of minority immigrant students. *Journal of the First Year Experience and Students in Transition,* 21(2), 9–34.

Loo, C. M., & Rolison, G. (1986). Alienation of ethnic minority students at a predominantly white university. *Journal of Higher Education,* 57(1), 58–77.

Lunneborg, P. W., & Lunneborg, C. E. (1985). Student-centered versus university-centered Solutions to problems of minority students. *Journal of College Student Personnel,* 26(3), 224–228.

Mangan, K. (2019). The University of Iowa keeps losing diversity officers. The turnover has raised alarms. *Chronicle of Higher Education.* https://www.chronicle.com/article/The-U-of-Iowa-Keeps-Losing/247438

Mohanty, C. T. (1984). Under western eyes: Feminist scholarship and colonial discourses. *Boundary,* 2(12), 333–358. http://links.jstor.org/sici?sici=0190-3659%28198421%2F23%2912%3A3%3C333%3AUWEFSA%3E2.0.CO%3B2-Y

McLeroy, K. R., Bibeau, D., Steckler, A., & Glanz, K. (1988). An ecological perspective on health promotion programs. *Health Education Quarterly,* 15, 351–377.

Newkirk, P. (2019, November 6). Why diversity initiatives fail. *The Chronicle of Higher Education.* https://www.chronicle.com/interactives/20191106-Newkirk

Nora, A. (2004). The role of habitus and cultural capital in choosing a college, transitioning from High school to higher education, and persisting in college among minority and nonminority students. *Journal of Hispanic Higher Education,* 3(2), 180–208.

Oetzel, J. G., Dhar, S., & Kirschbaum, K. (2007). Intercultural conflict from a multilevel perspective: Trends, possibilities and future directions. *Journal of Intercultural Communication Research,* 36(3), 183–204.

Oetzel, J. G., Ting-Toomey, S., & Rinderle, S. (2006). Conflict communication in contexts: A social ecological perspective. In J. G. Oetzel & S. Ting-Toomey (Eds.), *The Sage handbook of conflict communication: Integrating theory, research, and practice* (pp. 727–740). Thousand Oak, CA: Sage.

Oetzel, J. G., & Ting-Toomey, S. (2013). Culture-based situational conflict model: An update and expansion. In J. G. Oetzel & S. Ting-Toomey (Eds.), *The Sage handbook of conflict communication* (2nd ed., pp. 763–789). Thousand Oaks, CA: Sage.

Oliha-Donaldson, H. (2018). Journeying "home": Reflections on pedagogy, resistance, and possibility. *Women, Gender, and Families of Color,* 6(1), 3–11.

Pyne, K. B., & Means, D. R. (2013). Underrepresented and in/visible: A Hispanic first-generation student's narratives of college. *Journal of Diversity in Higher Education,* 6(3), 186–198.

Rittel, H. W. J., & Webber, M. M. (1973). Dilemmas in a general theory of planning. *Policy Sciences,* 4, 155–169.

Rosa, E. M., & Tudge, J. (2013). Urie Bronfenbrenner's theory of human development: Its evolution from ecology to bioecology. *Journal of Family Theory & Review,* 5, 243–258.

Rousseau, D. M. (2011). Reinforcing the micro/macro bridge: Organizational thinking and pluralistic vehicles. *Journal of Management,* 37(2), 429–442. DOI: 10.1177/0149206310372414

Rousseau, D. M., & House, R. J. (1994). Meso organizational behavior: Avoiding three fundamental biases. In C. L. Cooper & D. M. Rousseau (Eds.), *Trends in organizational behavior* (1st ed., pp. 13–30). New York, NY: John Wiley.

Shahjahan, R. A., & Barker, L. (2009). Negotiating academic learning and research: The spiritual praxis of graduate students of color. *Equity & Excellence in Education,* 42(4), 456–472.

Smith, D. G. (2009). *Diversity's promise for higher education: Making it work.* Baltimore, MD: The Johns Hopkins University Press.

Snyder, T. D., & Dillow, S. A. (2010). *Digest of education statistics 2009* (NCES Report No. 2010–013). Washington, DC: National Center for Education Statistics, Institute of Education Sciences, U.S. Department of Education. Retrieved from http://nces.Ed.gov/pubs2010/2010013.pdf

Spaights, E., Dixon, H. E., & Nickolai, S. (1985). Racism in higher education. *College Student Journal,* 19(1), 17–22.

Stebleton, M. J., Soria, K. M., & Huesman, R. L. J. (2014). Recent immigrant students at research universities: The relationship between campus climate and sense of belonging. *Journal of College Student Development,* 55(2), 196–202.

Stokols, D. (1996). Translating social ecological theory into guidelines for community health promotion. *American Journal of Health Promotion,* 10, 282–298.

Ting-Toomey, S. (2011). Intercultural communication ethics: Multiple layered issues. In G. Cheney, S. May, & D. Munshi (Eds.), *The ICA handbook of communication ethics* (pp. 335–352). Mahwah, NJ: Lawrence Erlbaum Publishers.

Trickett, E. J. (2019). Ecology, wicked problems, and the context of community interventions. *Health Education & Behavior*, 46(2), 204–212.

Turner, C. S. V., & Myers, S. L., Jr. (2000). *Faculty of color in academe: Bittersweet success*. Boston: Allyn and Bacon.

U.S. Census Bureau. (2010). State and county quick-facts. Retrieved from http://quickfacts.census.gov/qfd/states/00000.html

Williams, D. A., Berger, J. B., & McClendon, S. A. (2005). Toward a model of inclusive excellence and change in postsecondary institutions [Online]. Washington, DC: Association of American Colleges and Universities. https://www.aacu.org/sites/default/files/files/mei/williams_et_al.pdf

Williams, A. (2018). What factors hold back the careers of women and faculty of color? Columbia U. went looking for answers. *Chronicle of Higher Education*. https://www.chronicle.com/article/What-Factors-Hold-Back-the/244841

Villalpando, O., & Bernal, D. D. (2002). A critical race theory analysis of barriers that impede the success of faculty of color. In W. A. Smith, P. G. Altbach, & K. Lomotey (Eds.), *The racial crisis in American higher education* (pp. 243–269). Albany: State University of New York Press.

Editor

Hannah Oliha-Donaldson, Ph.D.
University of Kansas
Oliha-Donaldson is an Assistant Teaching Professor in the Department of Communication Studies. She publishes in the area of critical intercultural communication, and diversity and higher education. She engages in research and advances pedagogical practices that center social justice, equity, and inclusion and that expose the barriers to community-building in U.S. higher education and beyond. Her work has been published in the *Howard Journal of Communications* and *International Communication Gazette*.

Contributors

Cécile Accilien, Ph.D.
Kennesaw State University
Accilien is a Professor and Chair of the Interdisciplinary Studies Department. Her primary areas of interest include Haitian Studies, Gender Studies, and Film Studies. She is the author of *Rethinking Marriage in Francophone African and Caribbean Literatures* (Lexington Books, 2008). She has also co-edited and contributed to other volumes and journals.

Felicia Black, Ph.D.
San Diego State University
Black is an Assistant Professor in the Department of Child and Family Development.

Black's research interests include teacher professionalism and professional development, practitioner inquiry methodologies, and applications of critical perspectives in early care and education research.

Anjuli Brekke, Ph.D.
University of Wisconsin-Parkside
Brekke is an Assistant Professor in the Department of Communication. Her research interweaves cultural studies, rhetorical studies and sound studies to explore the potential and limitations of digital oral storytelling to foster spaces for listening across difference.

260 CONTRIBUTORS

DeOnte T. Brown
Clemson University
Brown is an administrator in student affairs who has worked in the areas of college access programming, college life coaching, and more recently, orientation, transition, and retention.

He primarily serves underrepresented students, including students of color and first-generation college students.

Audra Buck-Coleman, MFA, Ph.D.
University of Maryland, College Park
Buck-Coleman is a former Associate Professor of Design and Graphic Design Program Director in the Department of Art. She has designed, authored, and directed design projects, including Sticks + Stones, an international multi-university collaborative graphic design project that investigates how words and images perpetuate oppression, prejudice, and discrimination and how design can disrupt these cultural systems.

Yea-Wen Chen, Ph.D.
San Diego State University
Chen is an Associate Professor in the School of Communication, researching critical approaches to better understand uneven, if not unequal, communication patterns between, across, or in-between cultural groups. She continues to lead and develop research projects and teaching practices that honor voices and experiences on cultural margins inside and outside of U.S. academia.

Crystal U. Davis, Ph.D.
University of Maryland
Davis is an Assistant Professor of Dance, Head of the Master of Fine Arts in Dance Program in the School of Theatre, Dance, and Performance Studies, and author in the *Palgrave Handbook on Race and the Arts in Education.*

Andrea Delgado, Ph.D.
Humboldt State University
An Assistant Professor in the Department of English, Delgado's research draws upon critical ethnic studies, rhetoric, and media studies to explore the generative relationship between personal narrative and history embedded in the cultural production of Los Angeles communities.

Thierry Devos, Ph.D.
San Diego State University
Devos is a Professor in the Department of Psychology. Devos' research interests are primarily in the area of intergroup relations. The goal of his

CONTRIBUTORS **261**

current work is to understand how implicit intergroup biases are embedded in social and cultural contexts.

Anne C. Dotter, Ph.D.
Johnson County Community College
Dotter is the Director of the Honors Program and Community Based Learning at Johnson County Community College.

Brian J. Evans, M.F.A.
Bates College
Evans is an Assistant Professor of Dance at Bates college. His research interests include embodying atrocity, touch literacy programming on college campuses, and using the embodied arts for understanding our world.

Cherese F. Fine, Ph.D.
Clemson University
Fine is a scholar-practitioner with experience in areas of academic affairs, student affairs, and diversity and inclusion. She conducts research and coordinates programs centered on college access and readiness, and student retention for underrepresented student populations.

Leah N. Fulton
University of Minnesota-Twin Cities
Fulton is a graduate student in the Department of Organizational Leadership, Policy, and Development (OLPD).

Angela N. Gist-Mackey, Ph.D.
University of Kansas
Gist-Mackey is an Assistant Professor in the Department of Communication Studies with an expertise in organizational communication. She is an interpretive critical scholar that largely researches issues of social mobility and power. Her research has been published in outlets including the *Journal of Applied Communication Research, Communication Monographs,* and *Organization Studies,* among others.

Jerad E. Green, M.A.
Clemson University
Green is a diversity educator and practitioner in higher education and a PhD student studying Educational Leadership. His career in higher education has focused on advancing equity and justice programmatically and structurally, particularly within multicultural centers and offices for diversity and inclusion.

262 CONTRIBUTORS

Tina M. Harris, Ph.D.
Louisiana State University
Harris holds the Douglas L. Manship Sr. Dori Maynard Race, Media, and Cultural Literacy Endowed Chair at the Manship School of Mass Communication. She is an internationally renowned interracial communication scholar with particular interests in race, media representations, and racial social justice.

Roberto Hernandez, Ph.D.
San Diego State University
Hernandez is an Associate Professor of Chicana and Chicano Studies. Hernández is a community-based scholar and writer whose research, publications, and teaching focus on the intersections of colonial and border violence, the geopolitics of knowledge and cultural production, decolonial political theory, social movements, and comparative ethnic studies.

Jade C. Huell, Ph.D.
California State University Northridge
Huell is an Assistant Professor of Communication Studies and Director of CSUN Performance Ensemble: Creatives for Social Change in the College of Arts, Media and Communication.

Sureshi Jayawardene, Ph.D.
San Diego State University
Jayawardene is an Africana social scientist in the Department of Africana Studies. Jayawardene's research raises questions about Black geographies, race, coloniality, Africanity, and self-definition in the lives of Afrodiasporic communities in South Asia.

Lisa S. Kaler
University of Minnesota-Twin Cities
Kaler is a graduate student and research assistant in the Department of Organizational Leadership, Policy, and Development (OLPD).

Erin Lee, M.P.H.
University of Washington, Seattle
Lee received her Master of Public Health degree from the University of Washington, Seattle. Her current research explores the motivations of community-based doulas providing low-income women perinatal health services in King County, WA.

CONTRIBUTORS **263**

Meggie Mapes, Ph.D.
University of Kansas
Mapes is a faculty member and Director of the Basic Course Program in the Department of Communication Studies. She publishes widely in the areas of pedagogy and gender.

Saugher Nojan
University of California, Santa Cruz
Nojan is a Ph.D. Candidate in Sociology. Her research focuses on social inequalities, anti-Muslim racism, immigrant/refugee integration, civic/ political engagement, and education. She is a fellow for the UC National Center for Free Speech and Civic Engagement.

Rashawn Ray, Ph.D.
University of Maryland, College Park
Ray is a Professor of Sociology and Executive Director of the Lab for Applied Social Science Research. He is also one of the co-editors of *Contexts Magazine: Sociology for the Public.* Ray is currently a David M. Rubenstein Fellow in Governance Studies at The Brookings Institution in Washington, D.C. He is a former Robert Wood Johnson Foundation Health Policy Research Scholar at the University of California, Berkeley.

Daniel L. Reinholz, Ph.D.
San Diego State University
Reinholz is an Assistant Professor in the Department of Mathematics and Statistics. Reinholz's research focuses on creating tools for educational transformation to improve equity and mitigate systemic oppression. He is a co-founder of the Access Network, a national network of programs in the United States that aim to increase equity in the physical sciences.

Michael J. Stebleton, Ph.D.
University of Minnesota-Twin Cities
Stebleton is an Associate Professor and Coordinator of Graduate Programs in Higher Education in the Department of Organizational Leadership, Policy, and Development (OLPD). Stebleton's current research focuses on understanding the experiences of first-generation and immigrant college students. His publications appear in a variety of academic journals, including the *Career Development Quarterly,* the *Journal of College Student Development,* the *Journal of Employment Counseling,* and the *Journal of College and Character.*

264 CONTRIBUTORS

Kendra D. Stewart-Tillman, Ph.D.
Clemson University
Stewart-Tillman is a social justice educator and practitioner whose work and research focuses on targeted support of underrepresented students in higher education and building intercultural capacity for all students. She is currently the Executive Director of the Harvey and Lucinda Gantt Multicultural Center.

Meshell Sturgis, M.A.
University of Washington, Seattle
Sturgis is a doctoral candidate and instructor in the Department of Communication where she critically studies the visual culture of self-representation in alternative media such as comic books and artist books.

Zer Vang
University of Minnesota-Twin Cities
Vang is a graduate student in the Department of Organizational Leadership, Policy, and Development (OLPD).

Feion Villodas, Ph.D.
Department of Psychology, San Diego State University
Villodas is a faculty member in the Department of Psychology. Villodas' research focuses on adapting evidence-based intervention strategies for diverse populations to promote the physical, mental, and psychosocial well-being of ethnic/racial minority populations.

Dianna N. Watkins-Dickerson
University of Memphis
Watkins-Dickerson is a doctoral candidate in the Department of Film and Communication. She is a military veteran, Air Force chaplain, wife, and mother whose research questions coalesce at the intersections of rhetoric, race, religion, and gender.

Index

Page numbers in **bold** font refer to content in **tables**.

Abetz, J. S. 72–73
academic freedom 6–7
accented identities *see* foreign-national educators
accented speech 191
accountable practices 213–215
Adichie, C. N. 153
Adserias, R. P. 24
Adventures of a Black Woman in Academia 83–84
affirmative action 19, 20, 143
Agarwal, N. 133
Ahmed, S. 82, 129, 160, 168, 188, 191, 194–196, 198
Ahonen, P. 15, 24, 26, 28, 251
Akomolafe, S. 189
Al-Amin, J. 128
Allport, G. W. 114
Andersen, M. 21
Angry Black Woman Scholar, The 82
Annie E. Casey Foundation 40, 47
antifeminism 17
Anzaldúa, G. 3, 145
apathy 8
Armstrong, A. 83–84, 89
artistic activities 109–112; differential impact of diversity coursework 112–114; implications and lessons learned 114–119, **115–117**; promising practices for change 119–120

Asian-American students 65, 147–148; *see also* racial discrimination
assimilation 44
Association for Asian American Studies (AAAS) 19
assumed centers 7–9, 26–27, 99, 242, 251
Augustine, J. M. 72
authority 83, 85–87

Baez, B. 180
Bailey, M. 81
Baldwin, J. 6
Barnett, R. C. 62
Bazemore, S. D. 189
Bell, D. 81
Bell, J. M. 25–27
Bendapudi, N. 5
Benhabib, S. 153
biases: Heritage University case study 223, 224, 229, 232–233; San Diego State University (SDSU) seminars 161–168
black female instructors 79–81, 212–213; foreign nationals 191–193; implications and lessons learned 88–91; literature review 81–84; low recruitment 164; respect and authority 85–88; service-loads 180; tokenism 178–179; University of Memphis 84–85
Black History Month 173, 175, 176
Black Lives Matter 4, 6, 207, 220, 221

266 INDEX

black students 17, 38; protests 6, 219–222; University of Maryland, College Park (UMD) 114–119; University of Washington (UW) 146–147, 149–150; *see also* Heritage University case study; racial discrimination
blackface 119; *see also* women's college blackface incident
Bonilla-Silva, E. 89–90
Borden, V. M. 180
Boren, D. 232
Braveman, P. 42
Bronfenbrenner, U. 10, 73, 144, 152, 225, 244–246
Brown, M. 222
Brown v. Board of Education (1954) 18, 84
Burke, M. C. 74
Burris, M. A. 132
Butler, J. 219
Buzzanell, P. M. 182

Campus Pride Index 161
categorical diversity 22
Cauce, A. M. 143
causation 10, 245, 247, 249, 251–252
centeredness 7–9, 26–27, 99, 242, 251
Chakravartty, P. 104
Charland, M. 103
Charlottesville, Virginia 6
Chewning, L. V. 183
Chronicle of Higher Education, The 188–189
Civil Rights Act (1964) 17–18, 220
civil rights movement (1960s) 17–19
Civil War (1861–1865) 204
Claremont McKenna College, Los Angeles 5–6
class discrimination 80
Cleckley, B. J. 20
climate 7, 24, 38, 46, 131, 133, 142; organizational 10, 161, 178, 196, 209, 222, 232–233; political 120; racial 213, 232; surveys and reports 119, 130
Coast Salish 142
co-facilitation 165–166
collectivist culture 45, 65
College of Ethnic Studies (San Francisco State University) 18
Collins, P. H. 81
Collins III, R. 120

colonialist narratives 100–102, 104–105
color-blind racism 89–90
Commission on Higher Education (1947) 16–18, 23, 250
Communication Education 38
communication studies 98–104
community-focused pedagogy 103–105
Concerned Student 1950, 5, 9, 177, 219
constitutive communication 103–104
consumerism 97–98
contact theory 114
Copeland, R. 84–85
cotton balls symbolism 173–176
co-witnessing 154–155
Crenshaw, K. W. 141, 190
critical race theory (CRT) 80–81
Cross, W. 226
cross-group interactions 228, 232
cultural autonomy 18
cultural disadvantages 39
culture of resistance 39
curricular failings 102

Daily Helmsman, The 84
data gathering 49
De la Torre, A. 161
Deaf President Now (DPN, 1988) 219
Deloitte 46, 52
democratic ideals 23
developmental networks 183
differences, respect for 20, 25
differential labor 163–165, 213, 252
disconsciousness 8
dismissal 195–196
diversity agendas 24
diversity definitions 25–26, 40–41
diversity education 120, 230–232
diversity for equity 23
diversity talk/discourse 10, 16, 21–29, 251
diversity workers 129; differential labor 163–165, 252; San Diego State University (SDSU) 159–160, 168–169
documentation 82
Dorjee, T. 245

Elon University 232
Embodied Anti-Racism Workshop 214
embodied practices 213–214

empowerment education models 98–99, 101
enrollment 4, 16, 84, 227
environmental factors 10, 247
equal opportunity specialists 90
equity definition 41–44
ethnic studies programs 20
Evans, T. M. 84
expectations, personal 73
external assessments 50–51

failures, pedagogical *see* pedagogical failures
fairness *see* equity definition
families 227–228
Feltey, K. 73
feminism 18–19
Fernandez, J. S. 132
financial crisis of 2008 213
financial sustainability 215
Fire Next Time, The 6
Flynn, A. M. 244
Ford Foundation 25
foreign-national educators 188–191; implications of discrimination 195–196; personal discrimination narratives 191–195; promising practices for change 196–198
Forum Theatre 214
forums 229–230
Fothergill, A. 73
framing diversity 46, 251
Frangopol, D. M. 183
Franklin, J. 43
free expression 86, 143, 223, 226, 232–233
Freire, P. 214

Gallaudet University 219
Garmezy, N. 182
gender discrimination 4, 7, 17, 180; foreign nationals 191–195; women's liberation movement (WLM) 18– 19; *see also* black female instructors; scholar-mothers
gender elites 26–27
genealogy, of diversity *see* historical background
George Washington University (GW) 119
Giroux, H. 97–98, 102–103, 106

global citizenship 16
Going Down Jericho Road 87
Goins, M. N. 205
Goldstein Hode, M. 175–177
Graduate and Professional Student Senate Academic Conference (2019) 142, 145–151; implications and lessons learned 151–152; promising practices for change 152–155
Gray, F. 115
Grenier, R. S. 74
Grey-Little, B. 178
Guarino, C. M. 180
Gurin, P. 228

Hamer, Fannie Lou 83
Harley, D. A. 79, 80, 83, 91
Hartmann, D. 25–27
Harvard Butter Rebellion (1766) 219
hate crimes 119, 127, 161, 176, 232–233
health equity 41–42
Hendrix, K. G. 80, 84
Heritage University case study 222–224; meso level implications 227–231; micro level implications 225–227; promising practices for change 231–233
Hester Williams, K. D. 144
Hispanic-Serving Institutions (HSI) 161
historical background 15–16; 1st wave, 1940s-1970s 16–19; 2nd wave, 1970s-1990s 19–21; 3rd wave, late 1990s 21–22; 4th wave, 21st century 22–23; diversity talk 21–29
Historically Black Colleges and Universities (HBCUs) 180, 227
historically marginalized groups (HMGs) 5, 7, 9, 18, 36, 52, 129, 242, 251, 252; *see also* black female instructors; black students; foreign-national educators; Muslim students
homophobia 4
Honey, M. K. 87
hooks, bell 81, 97, 160, 197
hope 155
How We Fight White Supremacy 216
Hung, M. 43
hunger strikes 6, 177, 219
Hyde, J. S. 62

268 INDEX

Ibarra, H. 183
identity 28, 45, 167, 181, 242; black
 females 82, 85, 88, 178;
 development 109, 226; identity-
 based incidents 7, 23, 29, 64, 115,
 119; organizational 37, 241; politics
 of 141–142; privilege 211; religious
 128, 130; scholar-mothers 67, 69, 70,
 72, 74
immigrants *see* foreign-national
 educators
implicit biases *see* biases
imposter syndrome 39, 64
in-between place 4
inclusion definition 44, 46
Indiana University 232
Indigenous communities 104, 142, 162
in/out duality 4–5, 9
institutional change 10, 38, 51, 168
institutional history 25, 231
institutional idealism 150
institutional inertia 127–129
institutional landmarks 4
integration, of DEI 45–46
intercultural competence 222, 223
intercultural conflict 45, 245
intersectional identities 190, 196
interviews 114, 148
Invisible Minority, The 189
Islamophobia 128 130
Iverson, S. V. 28

Jewish students 17
Johnson, Lyndon B. 17–18
Johnson, S. 84–85
Jones, J. 209
Jonestown massacre (1978) 206, 208–209
Joseph, R. L. 154

Kaepernick, C. 115
Kawewe, S. M. 79
Kelderman, E. 9
Keleher, T. 47
Kelley, R. D. G. 147, 155
Kennedy, John F. 17–18
Kezar, A 233
King, D. 81
King Jr., Martin Luther 3, 84
Krizek, R. 99
Ku Klux Klan (KKK) 118
Kumeyaay people 162

labor: differential 163–165, 213, 252;
 invisible 79, 88, 152; unpaid 142,
 213, 221
Lambert, L. 232
land acknowledgement 162
Lanhgout, R. D. 132
Latham, W. 9
latino/a students 150–151
learning disabilities 44
Lee, F. 154
LeMaster, M. 98
linguistic violence 177–179
listening 75, 130, 135, 148, 153
local examples, utilizing
 166–167
Loh, W. 119
Lynch, K. D. 62

Mac Donald, H. 6
maid syndrome 79
mainstreaming 44
majority identities 8
Maneater, The 177
Martin, J. M. 178
Martin, T. 221
maternal microaggressions 63–64,
 66–70, 72, 75
McIntosh, P. 8
McKay, N. 79
McNair, J. 118
Meisenbach, R. 175–176
Memphis State Eight 84–85
#MeToo 4
microaggressions 39, 43, 63, 80, 141,
 180, 241; maternal 63–64,
 66–70, 72, 75; San Diego State
 University (SDSU) seminars
 161–168
Mills, C. W. 210
Mohanty, C. T. 7–8
Moraga, C. 145
motherhood *see* scholar-mothers
multiculturalism 20–21
multilevel frameworks 10, 244–245;
 application to emerging DEI
 challenges 248–249, 251–252; core
 principles 245–247
multiple jeopardy 81
multiple roles 62, 64, 65
Muslim Student Association (MSA)
 130, 131, 134–135

INDEX **269**

Muslim students 127–128; at California institutions 128–131, 161; implications of photovoice project 136–137; photovoice project process 131–134; promising practices for change 138; reflections on photovoice project 134–136
Myers, V. 90

Nader, L. 152
Nakayama, T. 99
Nasir, N. S. 128
National Association for Chicana and Chicano Studies (NACCS) 19
National Association for the Advancement of Colored People (NAACP) 174
National Center for Education Statistics (NCES) 82
National Council for Black Studies (NCBS) 19
neoliberal culture 97–99, 101
Nigrescence 226
Nishime, L. 144
normalization 7, 27, 73–74
#NotAgainSU 222
N-word 176, 178

Obama, Barack 108
Oetzel, J. G. 245
Oliha-Donaldson, H. 154
online surveys 114–119, **115–117**, 189
Orbe, M. 47
organizational culture: disconnect between DEI 37–45; and foreign-national educators 188–198; future DEI steps 47–51; integration of DEI 45–46; and linguistic violence 177–179; and symbolic violence 173–177
organizational DEI: disconnect between DEI 37–45; future steps 47–51; integration of DEI 45–46
Owen, D. S. 26

parenthood normalization 73–74; *see also* scholar-mothers
participatory-action research (PAC) 127–128, 131–132; *see also* photovoice project
Pasztor, S. K. 46

pay inequity 50
pedagogical failures 97–99; case study 99–100; implications and lessons learned 100–103; promising practices for change 103–105
peer-to-peer interaction 111, 228
People's Institute for Survival and Beyond (PISAB) 214
Pettigrew, T. F. 114
Phenomenology of Whiteness, A 82
photovoice project 131–134; implications and lessons learned 136–137; promising practices for change 138; reflections on impact 134–136
police brutality 220–222
polyvocal narratives 153–154
Pomona College, Los Angeles 6
post-racial ideology 29
Powell, L. 19–20
power 21, 91, 168
Prater, R. 85
praxis, pedagogical 214
prayer space 128–131
Predominantly White Institutions (PWIs) 79, 80, 83, 102, 142, 173, 190, 227
privilege 8, 167–168; *see also* white privilege
Privilege Walk 110–111
professional development 75
professional learning seminars *see* San Diego State University (SDSU) seminars
Professors of Equity (SDSU) 159–162, 165, 168–169
projected images 7
proportional representation 181
protests 6, 29, 121, 143, 155, 219–222; *see also* Heritage University case study
public denouncements 232–233
public speaking 98–104
Putnam-Walkerly, K. 40, 44

questionnaires 112–113

Race and Equity Initiative (University of Washington) 143–144
Race Equity and Inclusion Action Guide (REIAG) 40, 41, 44, 47–51

270 INDEX

race fatigue 80, 226–227
Race Forward: The Center for Racial
Justice Innovations 47
racial discrimination 119, 127, 161, 176,
232–233; anti-Muslim 128, 130; civil
rights movement (1960s) 18–19;
color-blind racism 89–90;
Commission on Higher Education
(1947) 17; defining 47; in diversity
work 164; health toll of 149;
linguistic violence 177–179;
microaggressions 39, 43, 63, 80, 141,
180, 241; police brutality 220–222;
public testimonials 147; rising
tensions 5–7; scholar-mothers 65, 69,
71; segregated South 34; stereotypes
70, 110, 111, 128, 196, 208, 223;
symbolic violence 173–177; and Tina
Harris' background 34–37; white
privilege 8, 27, 68, 102, 104, 211–
212; *see also* black female instructors;
Heritage University case study; white
supremacy; women's college
blackface incident
Racial Ecologies 144
racial elites 26–27
Racism Without Racists 89–90
radical transparency 215–216
Rankin, K. 216
reflexivity 38, 42, 45, 46, 51, 103–105,
111, 166–167
*Regents of the University of California v.
Bakke* (1978) 19, 128–129
religious discrimination 17
religious expression 86
representational diversity 22, 232
resilience 59, 76, 134, 138, 173,
182–183
resources 136–137
respect 85–87
reverse discrimination 19
rhetorical practices 102–103
Richardson, B. 173–174
Richardson, G. E. 182
Riddell, S. 44
Rios, F. 90
ripple effects 247
Rittel, H. W. J. 243
Robel, L. 232
Roberson, Q. M. 41
Robertson, W. 174

Rock Chalk Invisible Hawk 178
role conflicts 62, 64, 69
Root, C. P. 101
root causes 49–50
Rousseau, D. M. 248
Russell, E. 40, 44

safe spaces 128–131, 182, 190, 207, 223,
230
San Diego State University (SDSU)
seminars: contextual background
161–163; diversity worker profiles
159–160; implications and lessons
learned 163–165; promising
practices for change 165–168
San Francisco State University (SFSU)
18, 220
Santas, A. 214
scholar-mothers 59–61; history of
tension 62–63; implications and
lessons learned 72–73; Leah's story
69–71; Lisa's story 66–69; maternal
microaggressions 63–64, 66–70, 72,
75; promising practices for change
73–76; Zer's story 64–66
Schreiber, E. J. 38, 51
second-order transformational change
250
segregated institutions 17
segregated South 34
self-care 182
self-determination 18
self-identification 110–112
self-reflexivity 38, 42, 45, 46, 51, 111,
166–167
Settlement Movement (1889) 219
shared language 48
silence 72, 73, 80, 83, 212
Simmons, J. 38
Sison, M. D. 45–46
slavery history 50, 177, 220
Smith, B. 104
Smith, D. G. 28
Smith, R. A. 83, 86–87
Smith, W. 43
social ecological perspectives 10–11,
144, 225, 244–245; application to
emerging DEI challenges 248–249,
251–252; core principles 245–247
social justice 16, 17, 19, 21, 22, 24, 44,
251

INDEX **271**

Soliman, M. 183
Solomon, A. 216
Southern Poverty Law Center (SPLC) 118
spectral engagement 154
Spellman, M. 6
Spitzer, L. 190
stakeholders 48–49, 76, 243–244
Starks, H. L. 87
stereotypes 70, 110, 111, 128, 196, 208, 223
Sticks + Stones project 109–112; differential impact of diversity coursework 112–114; implications and lessons learned 114–119, **115–117**; promising practices for change 119–120
Stokols, D. 246–248
structural diversity *see* representational diversity
structural inequity 24
structural obstacles 212–213
Struggle of Being a Racial Minority in the Academy, The 205
student activism 219–222; *see also* Heritage University case study; protests
student support 120, 137
studying up method 152
Sue, D. W. 63
support systems 182, 197–198
sustainability 214–215
symbolic violence 173–177
Syracuse University 222
systemic oppression 38, 42, 43, 48
systems theory 10, 246–247

Taylor, C. 211
Teaching to Transgress 198
Third World Liberation Front (TWLF) 18
This Bridge Called My Back 145
Ting-Toomey, S. 245
tokenism 52, 141, 179, 181
tolerance 20
transformational change 10, 38, 250
Translating Social Ecological Theory into Guidelines for Community Health Promotion 246
Tropp, L. R. 114
Troup, C. L. 98

Trudy (Gradient Lair) 81
Truman, Harry S. 16, 18, 242
Trump, Donald J. 102–103, 118

Undoing Racism Workshop (PISAB) 214
Union Methodist Church (UMC) 204
University of California, Berkeley 6
University of California, Davis 19, 128–131
University of Kansas (KU) 5 173; lessons learned from linguistic violence 179–181; linguistic violence 177– 179
University of Maryland, College Park (UMD) 108–109; *see also* Sticks + Stones project
University of Memphis (U of M) 84
University of Minnesota, Twin Cities 60
University of Missouri (Mizzou) 5, 173–177, 219
University of Oklahoma (OU) 232
University of South Carolina 7
University of Virginia (UVA) 6
University of Washington (UW) 6, 141–143; Graduate and Professional Student Senate Academic Conference (2019) 145–151; implications of 2019 GPSS conference 151–152; promising practices for change 152–155; resisting ecologies of constraint 143–145
UW Bothell 142
UW Tacoma 142

Van Stee, S. K. 178
violence 115; linguistic violence 177–179; symbolic violence 173–177

Wade, R. 40
Wahl, S. T. 38
Wallace, M. 21
Walley-Jean, J. C. 196
Wang, C 132
Wanzer-Serrano, D. 105
Ward, K. 62, 72, 73
Webber, M. M. 243
Wellin, C. 37, 44–45
West, C. 155
western feminism 7–8

272 INDEX

white privilege 8, 27, 68, 102, 104, 211–212
white supremacy 29, 44, 81–82, 87, 115, 167, 212, 214, 216; recentering history 100–102, 104–105
wholeness 72–73
wicked problems 243–244, 250
Wilder, J. 82–83
willful ignorance 211–212
Williams, C. 82
Williams, L. 205
Wolfe, T. 5, 9
Wolf-Wendel, L. 62, 72–73
women's college blackface incident 203, 206–208; college in context 204–205; implications and lessons learned 208–213; promising practices for change 213–216

women's liberation movement (WLM) 18–19
women's studies courses 19
workplaces *see* organizational DEI

xenophobia 4

Yant, K. M. 18
Yiannopoulos, M. 6, 143

Zamudio, M. M. 90
Zhou, J. 190
Zimmerman, G. 221